HYT
3/00

Frank Allen Bullock

ALAN BULLOCK

Building Jerusalem

A PORTRAIT OF
MY FATHER

ALLEN LANE
THE PENGUIN PRESS

ALLEN LANE
THE PENGUIN PRESS

Published by the Penguin Group
Penguin Books Ltd, 27 Wrights Lane, London w8 5tz, England
Penguin Putnam Inc., 375 Hudson Street, New York, New York 10014, USA
Penguin Books Australia Ltd, Ringwood, Victoria, Australia
Penguin Books Canada Ltd, 10 Alcorn Avenue, Toronto, Ontario, Canada m4v 3b2
Penguin Books (NZ) Ltd, Private Bag 102902, NSMC, Auckland, New Zealand

Penguin Books Ltd, Registered Offices: Harmondsworth, Middlesex, England

First published by Allen Lane The Penguin Press, 2000
1 3 5 7 9 10 8 6 4 2

Set in 11/14 pt PostScript Monotype Sabon
Typeset by Rowland Phototypesetting Ltd, Bury St Edmunds, Suffolk
Printed in England by The Bath Press, Bath

A CIP catalogue record for this book is available from the British Library

ISBN 0-713-99362-6

Contents

Illustrations

Author's Note

For the translation of the Bible into English, my father relied largely upon the Revised Version (New Testament 1881; Old Testament 1885). Occasionally he would return to the 1611 King James (Authorized) Version for the splendour of its language, and towards the end of his life he would choose from time to time to use the New English Bible, though only those parts of the New Testament (1961) which had been published before his death in 1964. The reader will find, therefore, that biblical quotations in the text are taken variously from these three versions.

Sometimes, for immediacy of communication, my father paraphrased passages from the Bible in his talks and sermons. Where this involved an element of interpretation or a synthesis of different translations, his paraphrase has been retained and the biblical wording has been indicated in a footnote; otherwise the biblical text has been restored.

Acknowledgements

This book could never have been put together without the help of six friends.

My wife, Nibby Bullock, was as devoted to my father as I was and as committed to the book at every stage.

Andrew Best has acted as my literary agent for many years and took a particular interest in the book; not least by providing it with its title, *Building Jerusalem*.

Stuart Proffitt also worked with me on an earlier book. When he moved to Penguin Books he did not lose his interest, but took on *Building Jerusalem* and showed how sharp-eyed and committed he could be as an editor.

Ralph Waller, Principal of Harris Manchester College, Oxford, read the book from cover to cover and urged me to make no cuts in it.

As a copy-editor with the real instincts of a scholar, Bob Davenport showed how many were the questions still left to be answered.

Last but decidedly not least is Patricia Ayling, who has typed innumerable drafts and never allowed herself to be ruffled by crises.

I am also grateful to the following for permission to reproduce copyright material:
Faber and Faber Ltd for an extract from *The Dog Beneath the Skin* from *Plays and Other Dramatic Writings, 1928–1938* by W. H. Auden (Faber, 1989); Faber and Faber Ltd and Harcourt, Inc. for an extract from *The Hollow Men* from *Collected Poems, 1909–1962* by T. S. Eliot (Faber, 1974), copyright 1936 by Harcourt,

ACKNOWLEDGEMENTS

Inc., copyright © 1964, 1963 by T. S. Eliot; the Reece Halsey Agency
for an extract from the Introduction to *The Perennial Philosophy*
by Aldous Huxley (Chatto & Windus, 1946).

Alan Bullock

I will not cease from mental fight,
    Nor shall my sword sleep in my hand,
Till we have built Jerusalem
    In England's green and pleasant land.

William Blake, 'Jerusalem'

PART I

BACKGROUND

I

Beginnings

By 1887, when my father was born, what we commonly think of as the Victorian Age was over, although Queen Victoria (who celebrated her Golden Jubilee in the year of my father's birth) was to remain on the throne until 1901. Of the great writers of that age, Dickens, Thackeray, George Eliot, Darwin, Carlyle, Mill, Emerson, Cobden and Bagehot were already dead; Matthew Arnold, Browning and Cardinal Newman were to follow them before the decade ended. The period during which my father grew to manhood, 1887–1914, was a fascinating transitional period in which, behind the outward structure of Victorian thought and morality, revolutionary forces and ideas were taking shape.

My grandfather, Allen Bullock, was a signalman at Box Tunnel on the Great Western Railway, the famous line which Isambard Kingdom Brunel had laid between London and Bristol. Frank Allen Bullock was the only child of Allen Bullock's marriage to Jane Porter, and appeared so weak and delicate that he was not expected to live. It was his mother, however, who died within ten days of his birth – a loss which her son was to feel keenly. But the immediate question was whether he would survive her. His Aunt Lydia carried him off in a clothes-basket to her home in Batheaston, a village on the outskirts of Bath, where she lived with her parents and two brothers.

From Vale View Terrace, Batheaston, where the Porters lived, there was a fine view over the meadows running down to the Avon and up to the Downs beyond. This was my father's home for the rest of his childhood – a real home in which he would never be starved of affection, and to which he always looked back with gratitude for the kindness with which he was brought up by his grandmother and his Aunt Lydia. Lydia's two brothers, William and Arthur, were both skilled gardeners, the craft to which Frank was later apprenticed. 'My people, the Porter family', as he referred to them, were strongly religious and deeply attached to the Congregational chapel at Batheaston. Both his uncles were local preachers, and he himself began to preach in nearby villages from the age of seventeen. Theirs was a very orthodox form of Christianity, from which my father later broke away, but its practice had a powerful influence on him in his youth. 'Family prayer, preceded by Bible reading, was an unbroken custom in our home and I was never put to bed until after it.' One result of this was the deep acquaintance with the Bible my father acquired, as he listened night after night to the magnificent language of the Authorized Version.

Reading the Bible and family prayers had been the heart of Protestantism since the Reformation. Frank's generation was the last in which this was still a widespread practice; by my time it had already died out, bringing the loss of that general familiarity with the biblical stories and figures which had been central to European civilization – Catholic and Byzantine as well as Protestant – at all levels, from the palace to the peasant, for fifteen hundred years.

In the late nineteenth century the division between Chapel and Church powerfully reinforced the lines of English class distinction, with the clergy of the established Church of England firmly on the side of the gentry. The Congregationalists were descendants of the earlier Independents to whom Oliver Cromwell had belonged, the most important of the Puritan sects in the religious conflicts and civil war of the seventeenth century. Their original quarrel with the national Church established under Elizabeth was the same as that of the Presbyterians: a rejection of episcopacy and an insistence on the independence and autonomy of each local congregation. After the persecution which followed the Restoration in 1660, the Toleration Act of 1689 gave them the right to practise their religion, but, in common with other Nonconformists, they were subject to a number of penalties which marked them out as second-class citizens. These did not prevent them from playing a disproportionate part in the commercial and industrial development of Britain, but excluded them from the responsibilities (and patronage) of government and local government, as well as from the two universities, Oxford and Cambridge.

The fight for the removal of these disabilities, in the face of Anglican and Tory opposition, sharply revived old social antagonisms. By the end of the nineteenth century, most of them had been got rid of, but strong feelings on both sides were still alive and were a potent force in politics.

In 1832 the Congregationalists combined in the Congregationalist Union of England and Wales; but each congregation continued to control its own chapel and services, which accounts for the strong attachment the Porters felt for the community to which they belonged in Batheaston and which was the centre of their lives. Like most Nonconformists, they valued respectability, and were conservative in their religious beliefs. But, also like good Nonconformists, they valued personal independence as much as that of their chapel. The 'Nonconformist conscience' and the Nonconformist vote represented a political force, the continued support of which Gladstone, John Bright, Joseph Chamberlain, Campbell-Bannerman and Lloyd George in turn regarded as crucial to the success of the Liberal Party.

When my father broke away from the religious beliefs of his family, he did not cease to be a Nonconformist. His attitude towards the established institutions of both Church and State remained strongly coloured by his Nonconformist inheritance, and he regarded the claims of authority in either sphere with scepticism. With as strong a feeling for personal independence as any of his forebears, he turned to a Nonconformist tradition – the Unitarian – which imposed no doctrinal test and left him free to work out his own religious position. And during the period when he was active in politics he was naturally attracted to the radical wing of the Liberal Party.

Frank left school in 1900 at the age of thirteen, having learned reading and writing and arithmetic, if nothing else. He might have gone to work in a shop, a factory or an office with few prospects for advancement. Instead he had the good fortune to be trained as a gardener.

Climate and soil made Bath a city in which it was easy to grow almost anything; the leisured and professional families of Edwardian Bath, and the big houses in the surrounding countryside, had the means and the taste to keep up their gardens in style and to provide a market for the fruit, flowers and vegetables produced by market gardeners such as Frank's two uncles. There were long hours of back-breaking work involved in gardening in the days before motor-mowers and other mechanical aids, but, for a boy who was eager and quick to learn, there was a great deal to be mastered which stimulated instead of deadening the intelligence. His uncle Arthur taught him, and long after he had ceased to be a gardener it was a pleasure to see the experienced touch with which he would take a fork in his hands and transform a flower or vegetable bed. In addition to the practical knowledge Frank picked up, he also learned about the scientific side of gardening, the propagation and cross-fertilization of species, from a head gardener at one of the houses where he worked who had been trained at Kew and who took a liking to him.

II

These were times when men and women who earned their living with their hands, as the great majority did, worked long hours – sixty hours a week was common – and walked (or at most cycled) to and from their place of work. But Frank developed the habit of reading, and always found a quiet spot and read a chapter during the dinner hour. Among books with which he became familiar in this way as he grew up were Macaulay's *Essays*, Carlyle's *Sartor Resartus*, *The French Revolution* and *Past and Present*, and Froude's *Short Studies in Great Subjects*. Such books were not easily come by. There were few, if any, books in his home besides the Bible and *The Pilgrim's Progress*. But he managed to save up enough to make an occasional second-hand purchase, and borrowed others from the Bath public library. At this stage there was no one to guide him, and he made his own way into the world of books – an experience which gave him a sense of intellectual adventure which he never lost.

In October 1905 Cassell's started to publish a new edition, in thirty-two weekly parts, of their *Popular Educator*, designed to provide a continuation course for the great majority whose education had gone no further than the elementary school. Each number ran to ninety-six pages and provided straightforward instruction, complete with exercises, in a comprehensive range of subjects from languages (French, German, Latin, Greek, Italian and Spanish) through mathematics and the sciences (physics, chemistry, physiology) to such practical subjects as bookkeeping, commercial correspondence (in three languages), drawing and elocution. My father bought the parts at sixpence a time as they came out in their bright orange colours, and at the end he had an encyclopedia of three thousand pages, from which he remembered acquiring (among other things) the rudiments of Greek and a better understanding of English. He rapidly developed his own taste in literature. Among the English poets, Wordsworth and Coleridge (including the *Biographia Literaria*) became lifelong companions; Tennyson's *Idylls of the King* led him to Malory; Cary's translation introduced him to the world of Dante, and Bayard's of *Faust* and the *Conversations with Eckermann* to that of Goethe. But no poet gave him more delight than Browning. He read aloud to me when I was a child 'The Bishop orders his Tomb at St Praxed's' Church, 'A Toccata of Galluppi's' and many passages from *The Ring and the Book*. My father used to say, 'How I came to know these books, and to read and love them, I cannot remember except for that "hand on my shoulder" of which Browning speaks.'

Besides the expansion of his mental horizons through reading, the other influence which he recalled from these early years was 'a passionate and romantic love of nature. From my attic window I had a magnificent view of the meadows running beside the river Avon and beyond where hills and downs presented a wide prospect of ever-changing landscape and skyscape.'

He came across a book, *The Story of My Heart*, first published in 1883, which seemed in almost uncanny fashion to put his feelings about nature into words. Its author was Richard Jefferies, the son of a small Wiltshire farmer and largely self-educated, who was writing about the same part of the world that Frank lived in and who combined a rapturous expression of delight in life with a naturalist's precise observation of the countryside. Jefferies had died in poverty from a wasting disease while still under the age of forty, in the year my father was born. His over-intense style is out of keeping with contemporary taste and makes him hard to read today, but both the extravagances of his prose poem and the vague pantheism which it expressed spoke directly to a young man emerging from adolescence. 'I was not more than eighteen', writes Jefferies, 'when an inner and esoteric meaning began to come to me from all the visible universe, and indefinable aspirations filled me.'*

The inner experience with which Jefferies began his story, at the age of eighteen, was set on the top of a Wiltshire hill which he used to climb when he wanted to escape from 'the petty circumstances and annoyances of existence'. The coincidence did not escape my father when he wrote many years later:

There was a hill called Brown's folly and this I climbed many times alone, and once after dark to the great danger of neck and limb. As I grew older and more independent, I escaped from morning chapel services and wandered out into the country to seek some self-awareness and new relationship with the mystery of religion and life – much to the bewilderment and anxious concern of my relatives. These long walks and communings had a deep effect upon my inner life.

This sounds very much like the crises of faith described in much nineteenth-century writing. In Frank's case, however, it was not a loss of faith but the search for a more satisfactory way of expressing it.

---

* *The Story of my Heart* (pocket edition, Longmans, London, 1917), p. 199. The fact that by then the book had been reprinted fourteen times shows how much it appealed to my father's generation.

The demand made by the religious communities I had frequented was that of belief: only believe the scheme of salvation presented by orthodoxy and all was well. Refuse to believe and you were in danger of damnation. But nothing was ever said about the reality of a spiritual life. I found I could not believe, especially in the terrible doctrine of eternal punishment, and said so frankly. I became suspect. Then one day I was reading the novel *John Inglesant* by Joseph Shorthouse and came upon the passage where John Inglesant goes to various clergymen asking if they can tell him anything about the spiritual life. I suddenly knew that that was what I also was seeking. That was the birth of my awareness of an inner life and the way of ascent to the Beatific Vision.

Frank never forgot the moment of illumination which marked its beginning, ascribing to *John Inglesant*, with which it was associated, an interest which I could never discover in the book myself. But that was natural. Shorthouse (like Richard Jefferies) had asked the question explicitly at the right moment for Frank, and this more than made up for the fact that he never came near giving an answer. My father would eventually be ready to fashion an answer for himself. But this development in Frank's inner beliefs took place over a period of several years and did not reach a turning point until his decision to enter the Unitarian ministry in 1913. Before that there were to be several changes in his circumstances.

With the death of Frank's grandmother, the home in Batheaston was broken up. Frank found a new home with his Aunt Lydia, who had already moved away on her marriage to Fred Butt. The three Butt brothers owned and worked a quarry just over the Wiltshire border at Kingsdown. The entrance to it was a dark passage cut into the hillside from which they brought out blocks of the Bath stone of which the city had been built. Fred Butt's house, a small farm, stood on the same southern slope of the broad valley formed by the By-Brook flowing down to join the Avon at Bathford. With its woods and hedgerows, it is as attractive and characteristically English a stretch of country as one could find anywhere in the southern counties.

Frank took with him to his Aunt Lydia's house his grandmother's sister, Great-Aunt Shepherd, an old lady to whom he was deeply attached and of whom he would tell many tales. The early death of her husband had prostrated her and left her inconsolable until one day he appeared to her in spirit and told her that her fretting had compelled him to come and assure her that all was well with him. Whatever may have been the nature of this experience, which was brief and never repeated, it released her from her obsession with her sorrow. Great-Aunt Shepherd had a number of psychic experiences, but took them as part of the natural and normal course of events. Her psychic gifts did not make her nervous. After her husband's death, Squire Fuller, for whom Frank's grandfather Jack Porter had worked and who knew the family well, put her in charge of one of the lodge gates of his estate of Neston Park on the outskirts of Atworth. This provided her with a cottage, in which she lived on her own. One night after dark, when she heard someone trying to get in through the gates, she ran out, grappled with the intruder, and threw him headlong into the bushes, only to discover that it was the squire himself. He was delighted with her courage, and sent her a brace of pheasants.

There was a strong affinity between Frank and his great-aunt. One reason may have been the fact that she did not share the religious sentiments of her sister and her family. She was never critical of their beliefs, but she had her own inner life and expressed its quality in the uncomplaining devotion with which she nursed her sister. After the move to Kingsdown she became bedridden herself, and Frank helped his Aunt Lydia to look after her with much affection until she died. Shortly after her death he married, on 30 March 1912, and set up house with his wife in the neighbouring village of Box.

My mother, then twenty-four, was the eldest of a family of eight (five sons and three daughters) brought up in the Somerset village of Paulton, ten miles from Bath, by my maternal grandparents, Charles and Eliza Brand. It was not easy to provide for the growing number of children in the small house in Jubilee Terrace, and at the earliest possible moment, when she was ten, my mother was sent out to earn her own living.

Her first job, as a parlourmaid, was in the house of a dentist in Seymour Street, Bath, where she was paid five shillings a month besides her keep. Homesick and lonely, when she was sent to bed she used to sit in the cold at the top of the attic stairs to catch the sound of voices below. Despite her initial unhappiness, however, my mother proved herself a willing and capable worker, managing, like my father, to turn her years in service into an apprenticeship which was later to stand her in good stead. She not only acquired high standards in the everyday tasks of keeping a home, but learned much from mistresses who took an interest in her, developing a natural taste which found expression in the art of embroidery, her love of flowers, and an eye for colours and well-cut clothes. One mistress whom she remembered with gratitude was Miss Barlow, who lived in Titan Barrow, at Bathford, a handsome villa with four large Corinthian columns built in 1748 by John Wood the Elder, the architect who created eighteenth-century Bath. Miss Barlow employed not only my mother as a parlourmaid but my father too, as a gardener; it was not long before they began to spend their time off together, cycling into Bath or singing in a concert party which visited nearby villages.

It was an attraction of opposites. My mother was tall, a handsome young woman who carried herself well; my father was short, but more than made up for his lack of height by a personality which at once attracted attention, and the sense of excitement in living conveyed by his lively blue eyes. If my mother was more reserved and lacked my father's growing confidence, she was able to match it with an energy and loyalty that never flagged. How long they took before deciding they wanted to marry I do not know; the difficult question was how they could afford to set up home together.

At the age of twenty-five Frank was a capable and by now experienced gardener, and he had also begun to discover his powers and acquire a local reputation as a speaker. He took every opportunity he could to go and speak in village chapels and chapel societies (where he talked about the books he had been reading), and in the course of 1911 he had found a way to use his talents in a political context as well.

Surprisingly, Bath and the surrounding county constituencies were not solid Tory country. In the 1906 election, not only both the Bath seats, but the four divisions of Wiltshire, and the Wells as well as the Frome divisions of Somerset, were all carried by the Liberals. There was a swing back in the two 1910 elections, but two of the Wiltshire and one of the Somerset divisions were held by the Liberals, while in Bath the Tories regained the two seats by only narrow majorities in polls of over 92 per cent. All three elections were fiercely contested.

The year 1911 was marked by the passage not only of the Parliament Act, curbing the powers of the House of Lords, but of Lloyd George's National Insurance Act, later to be seen as the first big step towards the creation of the British welfare state. This undertook to finance, by compulsory contributions from employers, employees and the State, the insurance of the whole working population against sickness, and of certain sections of it against unemployment. The scheme aroused strong opposition from a variety of interests, including the trade unions, friendly societies and doctors.

The Liberals organized a nationwide campaign to counter the distorted versions of what was planned. After talking over their prospects with my mother, Frank decided to strike out on his own, give up his job as a gardener, and get himself taken on as a speaker who would visit all the villages in West Wiltshire to explain the proposals. After being coached in the Act by a barrister in Bristol, he was sent out night after night from Chippenham to collect whatever audience he could, even when it was hostile (as it frequently was), and find a way of holding its attention under all sorts of conditions – sometimes in village schoolrooms or, when these were barred against him, in the open air. It was a rough experience with meagre pay: he was still poor, and later recalled arranging the cloth over the chairman's table in such a way as to conceal the holes in his boots. But once he found he could hold his own he enjoyed it, and after the campaign was over he went on to spend several evenings a week explaining the Liberals' plans for land reform and the development of smallholdings.

III

By this time my mother and father had married and set up their home together in Box. Their future remained uncertain, however, until Frank received an unexpected offer from Squire Fuller. George Pargiter Fuller, educated at Winchester and Christ Church, Oxford, was not only the owner of a fine estate at Neston Park but had been the Liberal MP for West Wiltshire at the time when Joseph Chamberlain's 'Unauthorized Programme', with its proposals for land reform, had won much support in the Liberal Party. He was succeeded in the House of Commons by his son Sir John, who won the Westbury division for the Liberals in 1900, 1906 and both the elections of 1910. The old squire was still keenly interested in the land question, and when his attention was attracted by Frank's proselytizing activities he offered him the chance to put some of his ideas into practice by creating a fruit garden.

Fuller's offer came as a godsend. My father was to receive a wage of sixteen shillings a week, rent-free accommodation, and the profit from any produce sold from the garden. A bungalow was to be built for the young couple, and in the meantime they went to live in an old cottage at Hobbs Bottom near Atworth. Their day began at six o'clock in the morning, when the workmen arrived from Neston Park to get the garden into shape under Frank's direction. Walls had to be repaired, greenhouses as well as the bungalow built, and heated pits dug. At the same time he himself had to clear and prepare the ground as well as plant fruit trees. When the day's work was done, he was still engaged several evenings a week in addressing village audiences on land reform and smallholdings. This meant a cycle ride to Chippenham, ten miles away, where he was picked up by car and taken to outlying villages, with another cycle ride back home when he had finished. This was a hard life for my mother as well, as she had to spend many hours by herself in a lonely cottage with no neighbours to talk to. But for both of them the great thing was that they were independent and were working for their own future.

Their course soon took another unexpected turn. On Sundays

the two of them cycled to a village chapel where Frank preached. On one such Sunday, he was invited to take the services at Conigre Chapel in the Wiltshire town of Trowbridge. Founded in 1655, the Conigre congregation belonged to the General Baptist connection, which rejected the Calvinist view of predestination. In the second half of the eighteenth century many General Baptist churches – including Conigre Chapel – moved towards Unitarian views. At the time when Frank first preached there, the Trowbridge congregation were without a minister. His liberal religious views made a strong appeal to them, and after several more visits he received an invitation to become their minister.

Before he could make up his mind, he needed to know more about what Unitarians stood for. There was a Unitarian chapel at Trim Street in the centre of Bath, established at the end of the eighteenth century by a congregation which, like that at Trowbridge, traced its origins back to the seventeenth century. Frank's attention had been caught by the announcement of a special series of sermons at Trim Street on the history of Greek religion. Any mention of the Greeks always excited his interest, and he did not need to read Matthew Arnold's *Culture and Anarchy* to recognize that this was a subject which would have been unthinkable in the orthodox Nonconformist tradition in which he had been brought up. John MacDowell, the resident minister, was president of the Bath Literary and Debating Society, another eighteenth-century foundation, and when Frank sought MacDowell's advice he was deeply attracted by the liberal attitude in religion as well as the interest in ideas and books which he encountered. He discovered that no theological tests would be demanded of him and that he would be free to preach as liberal a gospel as he wished. So, after several talks with MacDowell, my father made up his mind to accept the invitation from Trowbridge and my mother loyally agreed to share in this new and, as it must have seemed, startling departure.

To begin with, he was to act as a lay preacher while he studied under John MacDowell to pass the qualifying examinations set by the British and Foreign Unitarian Association and so become a recognized minister. He gave up his political commitments, but insisted that he must keep his promise to George Fuller to leave the fruit farm as a going concern. It took uncommon determination to keep up with the schedule he had set himself. After a week spent in hard physical work out of doors, he cycled into Trowbridge each Saturday, preached morning and evening on Sunday, taking a young people's class in the afternoon, and stayed over on Monday to do pastoral work and spend the evening at the institute associated with the chapel before cycling back late on Monday night to Atworth and another week of work. Study had to be fitted in early in the morning and at night; his weekly tutorial with MacDowell meant another cycle ride into Bath and back, with a couple of sermons and any talks prepared somehow in any spare moments. No wonder that my mother frequently found him fallen asleep over his books after midnight and had to rouse him to get him into bed.

But the farm was ready for occupation by a new tenant in eighteen months – half the time Frank had been given – and Squire Fuller generously released him from his undertaking to develop the fruit farm, so allowing him to move in 1914 to a house in Rock Road, Trowbridge, where I was born before the year-end, on 13 December 1914, four months after the beginning of the First World War.

It has become a commonplace, looking back, to take the outbreak of war in 1914 as the date which marks the end of the old Europe and the onset of a violent epoch in which the continent, twice ravaged by war and left divided after 1945, lost its position as the political and economic centre of the world to new concentrations of power established in the USA, Soviet Russia and eventually the Far East.

In 1914, however, my father had no more idea than the rest of the nation, or the British government, that Britain had reached and passed the peak of her power and prosperity; nor did he or they foresee that the war which Britain had just entered would be different from any previous war in the number of lives it would cost and the disruption it would cause. On the other hand, he understood naturally, without the effort which its rediscovery long afterwards cost my generation of historians and critics, the continuity between the world before 1914 and the world after 1918.

The twentieth century was very different from the nineteenth, but the origins of much which we took to be the result of the war are to be found in the period between the late 1880s and 1914, in which my father grew up. One test is to take the names of those who are most closely associated with the radical new departures of the twentieth century – in politics, in literature and the arts, in science, philosophy and the social sciences – who were alive and active before 1914, from Lenin and Gandhi, Proust, Joyce and Yeats, Picasso, Matisse, Stravinsky to Einstein, Niels Bohr, Bertrand Russell and Max Weber. Freud was fifty-eight in 1914; Ibsen, Strindberg and Cézanne already dead. Most of these names did not become part of the common intellectual currency until the 1920s. I doubt if my father had ever heard of more than one or two – Ibsen, perhaps – before 1914. But when he died he saw them as his contemporaries and understood that their ideas were formed before 1914, even if it took the impact of the 1914–18 war to provide a receptive audience for them.

At a more everyday level there were changes widely recognized at the time as evidence of a very different temper in Edwardian England, and suggesting greater changes to come: in the radical politics of Lloyd George and Churchill; in the suffragette movement; in the labour unrest and the trade-union movement; in the rise of the popular press; in manners, morals and social relations. Looking back from 1924, Virginia Woolf summed it up in the striking remark:

In or about December 1910 human character changed. All human relations have shifted – those between masters and servants, husbands and wives, parents and children. And when human relations change, there is at some time a change in religion, conduct, politics and literature. Let us agree to place one of these changes about the year 1910.*

The years 1913–15, during which my father was in charge of Conigre Chapel, first part- then full-time, were the beginning of a

---

* *Collected Essays* (Hogarth Press, London, 4 vols., 1966–7), vol. 1, pp. 320–21.

new life devoted, to begin with, to intense study. He came to this not as a university student does today, as the next stage in a continuous educational process in which he is carried along, often involuntarily, but after thirteen years of hard manual work during which he had had to find both the time and the motivation for study on his own.

The disadvantages of his lack of formal education were compensated for by the excitement of finding himself free to follow his intellectual and spiritual interests. The Christmas after I was born, for instance, he read A. C. Bradley's *Shakespearean Tragedy*, and he never forgot the revelation which it provided of what interpretative criticism could add to the understanding of literature. His main interest, however, was in biblical criticism:

It was evident [he wrote later] that, in dealing with the Old Testament, orthodox scholars were not afraid to write plainly about the elements of myth and legend, but when they came to the Gospels and the New Testament they confined themselves to textual questions and had little to say about historical criticism. There was a general acceptance of the Gospels as possessing historical validity, even including the myth of the Nativity and the legend of a physical resurrection.

True, there was Schweitzer's revolutionary book *The Quest of the Historical Jesus* (1906, English translation 1910), but while this dealt fully with the eschatological elements in the Gospels, it had nothing to say on the mythical. We had to wait for Carl Jung before we had any means of assessing the great value of the mythical elements in all so-called historical religions. The Christians were very ready to acknowledge the mythical nature of Hindu and Buddhist traditions, but always affirmed the historical nature of the Gospels, failing to recognize that all ancient scriptures draw heavily upon myth and symbol as well as ritual.

Indeed it was a period of great uncertainty and confusion. While many attempts were made to rationalize religious beliefs and tradition, the value of the imagination as a mode of apprehending reality was as yet unrecognized.

Frank had no difficulty in passing his examinations with the highest possible marks, but he ran into trouble when he tried to incorporate in his sermons some of what he had learned. As long as he gave a broad poetical interpretation of the Bible there was little difficulty, but once he began to discuss the radical issues raised by the so-called higher criticism these were of so revolutionary and unsettling a character that he alarmed and offended the older members of the congregation.

No doubt, as he recognized later, he lacked skill and experience in presenting such material, but the real difficulty lay deeper: in the failure of every denomination to bridge the gap between ministers and students, who were aware of the findings of modern scholarship, and the laity, who were left in ignorance of them:

Hence among Unitarians arose a deep neglect of biblical sermons, to be replaced by sermons about topical subjects; and in the orthodox churches a literal and fundamentalist attitude to the Bible on the part of the laity and the neglect of the radical discipline of biblical scholarship on the part of ministers and clergy.

They all forgot to treat the Bible as great literature, with all those values that belong to great literature. Later we were to learn to use this material as possessing great imaginative power and beauty quite different from a dead rationalism. Indeed an escape from barren historicism and literalism was the great emancipation into what we shall later discuss as the birth of a new spiritual consciousness.

Nonetheless, the frustration which he felt in his preaching determined him to seek an early change of ministry, and so it was that in 1915 he followed the example of his tutor in Bath, the Reverend John MacDowell, in accepting an invitation to become the minister of a Unitarian chapel in Lancashire.

2

The Move to the North

I

The move to Lancashire took my father and mother into a new
world, as far removed from Wiltshire as if it had been a foreign
country:

When we stepped out of the train on Leigh station [my father recalled],
we were immediately aware that we had arrived in the industrial North.
The mill girls still wore shawls and clogs and poured through the cobble-
stone streets with much noise from clacking feet and chattering tongues.
The houses looked dwarf and mean. You could see that the women
maintained a brave fight with soot and smoke: doorsteps and window
ledges were whitened every Saturday with rubbing stone.

The streets were poorly lighted and the trams rocked on the main
road between Lowton St Mary's and Bolton in an alarming manner because
of the subsidence caused by coal mining. The miners, still in their pit
clothes and dirt, had to ride on the open-top trams in rain and sleet; they
were not allowed inside the downstairs compartment in order to preserve
clean seats for the better-clad passengers. At least this allowed them to
smoke after the complete prohibition underground because of the ever-
present danger of a pit explosion from firedamp, the miners' word for
methane.

All the buildings were built of red brick, which soon became coated with
grime. Such trees as survived were stunted, with meagre foliage. The
Unitarian church in Twist Lane seemed small and ugly after the spaciousness
of the Conigre Chapel we had left.

From his very first encounter with the North, however, my father
fell in love with its people, first in Lancashire, then more slowly in

the West Riding of Yorkshire, those two famous names so closely bound up with the history of industrial Britain.

The warm-hearted welcome we received from everyone we met made up for everything. There was a frank directness in their approach and warm hospitality. There was a democratic spirit of freedom, a zest and energy of living, a kind of excitement about life that was exhilarating and refreshing. John McDowell had come to live in Pendleton, on the outskirts of Manchester, and I went to visit him soon after coming to Leigh. As I was leaving his house, he bade me stand in the road with him and feel the mental electricity in the very air of the place as the hum of the city reached us.

For the first three years after his move to Leigh, however, everything else was overshadowed by the war. As a minister of religion, my father was not required to take part in the fighting, but, while maintaining the church services for his Leigh congregation, he volunteered for non-combatant work as a postman, and then, early in 1918, for service with the YMCA in France.

Frank's arrival at the front coincided, in both time and place, with events which were to prove the turning point of the war. The Eastern Front had collapsed and, at Lenin's insistence, the revolutionary government which had seized power in October 1917 finally accepted Russia's defeat by signing the Treaty of Brest-Litovsk on 3 March 1918. Concentrating its forces for an equally decisive operation in the West, the German High Command opened a series of major attacks, the first of which – meticulously prepared throughout the winter – was launched on 21 March 1918.

Frank had been posted to take charge of a YMCA centre at Doullens, and told to make his way there via Amiens. When he got to Amiens, where he had to change trains, he found himself engulfed in the chaos of the British Fifth Army in retreat and of reinforcements being moved up to close the gap. He completed his journey in a railway carriage from which the windows, doors and floorboards had long since disappeared, leaving those who could find a foothold to watch the wheels turning on the rails below.

Frank reached Doullens in time to see the French premier, Clemenceau, and the British War Minister, Milner, leaving the historic conference in the Town Hall at which it had at last been agreed to establish unity of command and put the British, French and American troops on the Western Front under the direction of Foch as generalissimo.

Violent fighting continued until the end of April, with the British forces stretched to the limit of endurance, but Amiens was held; and when the Germans renewed their offensive at the end of May, and again in July, it was against the French sectors of the front further east.

With the July offensive the Germans had exhausted their power of attack. On 8 August the British Army launched a counter-offensive to remove the threat to Amiens and the railway lines to Paris. Doullens was at the base of the triangle Arras–Albert–Doullens in which the attack was mounted. Troops were switched by bus from one sector of the front to another, passing through Doullens en route, where the YMCA maintained a twenty-four-hour service of food, hot drinks, and cigarettes. By nightfall on the first day – later described by Ludendorff as 'the black day of the German Army' – Canadian and Australian troops had advanced from seven to nine miles, and started a tide which carried the British Fourth Army by the end of September through the Hindenburg Line, the last completed system of German defences. The same day, 29 September, Ludendorff's nerve broke and he and Hindenburg demanded that a peace offer coupled with a request for an armistice should be made immediately. This was the beginning of the end, leading within the next few weeks to revolution in Germany, the abdication of the Kaiser, the proclamation of a republic, and finally, on 11 November, to the end of the war.

This is the way the historian sees these months in retrospect; but their impact on Frank, both at the time and later, was in human terms – the experience of how human beings behave when caught up in such overpowering events. From March until September Doullens was close to the front line, subject to bombardment and the constant movement of troops in and out of the battle. In a devastated land, the YMCA hut in the Lace Hall was an oasis where exhausted men could relax and, however briefly, recover their individuality.

Apart from their material needs, many men were anxious to talk and unburden their minds. On Sunday evenings the hall was cleared and a service was held, after which there was an open discussion of the sermon – an unusual feature for those days, which was very popular and attracted a crowded congregation. Throughout his life my father had a great gift for drawing out and speaking to the religious and personal difficulties of men and women with little education who did not find it easy to put their feelings into words. In France, in 1918, this was an invaluable asset in helping men who were living under conditions of abnormal stress and with the constant threat of death or mutilation.

The greatest gain from his nine months in France was confirmation of his belief that in most men and women, however 'ordinary' their lives might appear, there were latent depths of feeling and untapped reserves of energy, faith and courage on which they failed to draw except in moments of crisis. He returned home with an increased confidence that his vocation was to find ways of persuading people not to spend their time blaming or railing against external circumstances, but to recognize and make use of the resources they already possessed within themselves to make their lives more satisfying.

II

In the early months of 1919 Frank returned to Leigh and settled down to the life of a Unitarian minister in the industrial North. Despite appearances to the contrary, Leigh had a long history. From the beginning of the thirteenth century the daily life of the generations who inhabited Leigh can be followed in a series of legal documents recording wills, lawsuits, leases, inventories, marriage settlements, assaults and affrays.

Linen weaving and the cloth trade were staples from the Middle Ages; coal was mined in West Leigh from at least the sixteenth century. Until the end of the eighteenth century change in Leigh was as slow as in the rest of England; but between 1801 and 1841 the Industrial Revolution, of which South Lancashire was one of the original centres, was to double the town's population from five to eleven thousand. More than that, it produced in the textile factories and coal mines the first industrial working class, the conditions of whose lives in cities like Manchester and towns like Leigh made an unforgettable impression on contemporaries as different as Engels and Dickens, Carlyle and Mrs Gaskell.

Cotton and coal were the foundations of Lancashire's and Leigh's prosperity. While the women worked in the cotton or silk mills (over two-thirds of working women were occupied in textiles) the men worked in the mines, which employed over a third of the male labour force.

By 1851 there were seventeen pits in Leigh. More were sunk in the latter part of the century, and by the 1900s, when the British coal industry reached its peak, with a labour force of 1,100,000 (800,000 of them working underground), the South Lancashire coalfield ranked as one of the biggest in the United Kingdom, after South Wales, Durham, Scotland and Yorkshire.

The peak period of Leigh's development was in the final quarter of the nineteenth century; by the time my father moved there, the rapid growth of the nineteenth century had ended. Boundary changes brought the population to 40,000 in 1901, but fifty years later, in 1951, it was no more than 46,000. At the same time the cotton and coal industries on which the town's prosperity depended went into a permanent decline after the short-lived boom of 1919–20. The years 1920–26, the period when I was a boy in Leigh, were a time of rising unemployment and more or less continuous industrial conflict, culminating in the General Strike of 1926. Labour unrest had first found forceful expression in the days of Chartism, and August 1839 was long remembered for Leighth Feight (Leigh Fight), when a crowd of a thousand armed with sticks, and demanding the right to vote, threatened to burn down a number of mills if they did not stop work. The next time the Riot Act was read in Leigh was in 1881, when 15,000 striking miners marched down Church Street, and the 12th Hussars were moved into the neighbourhood.

Trouble in the 1920s was on a different scale. The first national coal strike had taken place in 1912, and plans for a triple alliance of miners, railwaymen and transport workers, delayed by the war, were put into operation after the armistice.

The miners were in the forefront of the fight, provoked by lack of work, drastic cuts in wages, and the refusal of the Government to carry out the nationalization of coal recommended by the Sankey Commission in 1919. In the 1920s, however, there were none of the social services which mitigated suffering in the 1980s; it was literally hunger which drove the miners back in 1926, and even then their famous solidarity kept them out for more than six months after the General Strike in their support had been called off.

As a Liberal, my father was on the opposite side politically to the miners and critical of their leaders. But his admiration for the men's endurance and loyalty was unstinted. He never forgot going to the scene of a mine explosion and seeing the miners being forcibly restrained from going back down the mine to rescue their mates, even though this might cost them their own lives.

They worked hard and they played hard. Their great sport was pigeon flying, and on a Sunday afternoon if you walked down the Avenue, one of the better residential parts of the town, you had to stand with everybody else against the walls, out of the way, while miners tossed their birds in the air. Large sums changed hands in bets between them on a pigeon race . . .

There were no pit baths in those days, and when I went to visit a miner's family I would often find the father sitting in a tin bath before the fire as naked as the day he was born, while his wife or eldest daughter washed his back, and we discussed affairs as naturally as if he had been sitting fully clothed in an armchair.

It did not take long for both my father and my mother to become active in politics, for Leigh was a town with a strong Liberal tradition. With the extensions of the franchise in 1867 and 1885, however, the North-West became a stronghold of Tory democracy. It was a commonplace of Edwardian politics that if the Liberals were to recover power they had to win back the North-West. This was precisely what they did under the radical leadership of Lloyd George and Churchill. In the election of 1906 they captured 54 out of the 71 seats, and, although they had lost 7 of these in January 1910 and 16 in December, they still retained the majority. The key to the Liberal revival had been their success in creating an alliance with Labour on a progressive programme of social democracy, defined by Churchill as 'the cause of the left-out millions' and given expression in the radical legislation which formed the basis of the later welfare state. After the war, however, the progressive alliance with Labour had broken down, the Liberal Party was split, and the Labour Party, refounded as a national party in 1918, was bidding to replace it by appealing to an enlarged electorate on a socialist ticket. The election of 1918 – which Lloyd George, once the great hope of radical progressivism, fought and won as the leader of a coalition with the Tories – threw the whole future of the Liberal Party into question. Leigh still returned a Liberal, but, by the time my father became chairman of the Leigh Liberal Club and my mother president of the Liberal Women's Association, the Liberal cause was threatened by a strong challenge from Labour.

After a confused period in which the wartime coalition broke up (October 1922), Lloyd George made a determined effort in December 1923 to recapture the Liberal ascendancy. So did my father, locally, succeeding in getting Lloyd George to speak in Leigh, where the Liberal candidate was a progressive mine owner, Robert Burrows (one of the first to install pithead baths). The campaign was vigorously fought and the Theatre Royal was packed to the rafters to hear Lloyd George, then at the height of his powers as an orator. My father was in the thick of the fight, and there was great excitement when the votes were counted (on 6 December), with the square outside the Town Hall filled with a noisy crowd of several thousands. Labour had won, but the Labour supporters had not forgiven some of my father's barbed remarks in the campaign. As Frank came out, a great shout went up, 'There's the little bugger!', and the crowd surged forward. Frank, undismayed, waved cheerfully, but my mother, who was held tight for her own protection between two large policemen, was furious – particularly with the policemen.*

The ill-feeling did not last. The miners admired a fighter, and my father was well liked for the rest of his time in Leigh. But the hopes of a Liberal revival were dashed and Leigh became a safe seat for Labour, which has held it ever since without a break.

Looking back on the social conditions of the 1920s and 1930s in industrial towns like Leigh, my father wrote in the 1960s that he could not waste any regrets over the Liberal defeat. A number of local Liberals said he would have won more votes than the official candidate, and urged him to think of a political career for himself. Lloyd George on his visit to Leigh spoke to him to the same effect, and my father certainly considered the possibility. If he had any doubts, however, they were settled by the Liberal defeat and, without abandoning his Liberal views, Frank turned his back for good on any further active involvement in politics.

III

One of the greatest pleasures of Frank's life in Leigh was his membership of the Leigh Literary Society. The Society had been founded in 1878 by nine young men with the object of 'cultivating a taste for the study of Literature, Science and Art'. Its history illustrates well the powers of self-help which could be mobilized in a provincial town like Leigh before the rise of the mass media. The central purpose of the Society was to organize a series of weekly meetings from October to March, and it did this with such success that by the time Frank became its president, in 1920–2, it had a membership of over a thousand, rising to a peak of 1,200 in its jubilee year of 1928. A drama section presented plays at the Theatre Royal, staging several by Shaw, Wilde and Barrie as well as Euripides' *Medea* and Molière's *Le Misanthrope*. In most

---

* I was allowed to stay up late for the occasion and was waiting excitedly for my parents in a friend's house, from which the sound of the shouting and booing was clearly audible. I heard the story at first hand the same night in the Liberal Club.

sessions a visiting lecturer was engaged: such lecturers included two eminent historians from Manchester University, S. R. Gardiner and T. F. Tout, as well as, later, the drama critic and playwright St John Ervine, the music critic Percy Scholes, and J. Cumming Walters, the editor of the local Manchester paper, the *City News*, which for decades subsidized its famous stable companion, the *Manchester Guardian*. Cumming Walters soon became a friend of my father's, and regularly sent him books to review – a form of journalism which Frank extended by writing articles on town planning for another well-known paper, the *Bolton Evening News*. But the Society still drew on its own members for lectures, and Frank regularly gave two in each session, on subjects as diverse as Conrad, Samuel Butler, H. G. Wells's fortnightly *Outline of History* (which I myself read eagerly as a boy), Dante, Blake, Shaw, Yeats, Rabindranath Tagore and Walter Pater.

Through the Literary Society, Frank became a member of the group which made Leigh a lively town to live in, and formed a wealth of friendships, particularly with men, which he was never to find when he eventually moved to the much larger city of Bradford. Of those he remembered with most gratitude, Tommy Collins, treasurer of his chapel and secretary of the Literary Society, was a printer from Evesham in Worcestershire whose brisk and businesslike manner belied his great love of reading. Tommy Mack, a paper merchant and born humorist whose dreamy eyes and drooping moustache gave him a close resemblance to a benevolent walrus, shared the same passion for books, but no one could ever accuse him of being either brisk or businesslike. What he most enjoyed was to sit in the office at his warehouse and talk with my father about writers and ideas, when he should have been out getting business. Among his favourite authors, on whom he lectured to the Society, were Charles Lamb, Thoreau, Emerson, Samuel Butler and G. K. Chesterton. He bought books recklessly and then enlisted my father to help him smuggle them into his house, under the suspicious eyes of his wife, as a *loan* from Frank, which was never returned. Besides Tommy Collins and Tommy Mack, Fred Bowen also served as president of the Literary Society: he was manager of the town gasworks, with an M.Sc. degree (degrees were far less common in those days), but was widely read in philosophy, especially Hegel's, and lectured to the Society on early astronomers, on the relation of science to literature – and on George Meredith.

Dick Greenough was involved in the Literary Society as he was in everything else that went on in Leigh. His father had been chairman of the Leigh Local Board before the town was incorporated as a borough; his brother was one of its first mayors, and he himself was an alderman. He had built and owned the Courts Hotel, the best place for good food and drink in the district, and had established a successful brass foundry. He was a huge man, with a pointed beard, a red bandanna handkerchief and an uninhibited manner – he more than once sat down by a brazier to mind a hole in the road and sent the corporation workmen off to get a drink. The many stories about him, his enjoyment of life and his generosity combined to make him a legendary Lancashire 'character' in his lifetime.

Dick was a good Liberal as well as a Unitarian – when he moved into a new house he called the builders back to widen the lavatory so that he could read his *Manchester Guardian* there without having to fold it. When he was dying he asked my father, 'What are my chances in the next world?' Frank reassured him by asking in return, 'How many people have you helped in this one, Dick?' The old man thought for a few minutes, and then said, 'I reckon a few hundred have called at my door, Frank, and I don't know of any man or woman who asked who has ever been sent away without help of some sort.' There was no one in Leigh who could doubt that this was true.

As I look back, industrial Lancashire in the 1920s appears an ugly and depressing place in which to grow up. Leigh was a town of raw red-brick terrace houses, begrimed with soot. There was still farmland and open country to be enjoyed in South Lancashire, even a cornfield immediately outside the back gate of our terrace house. But industry spread a blight around the towns: the desolate slag heaps which provided the characteristic landscape of the mining districts; the 100-foot-high brick chimneys of the cotton mills – one, Carrington Mill, was opposite where we lived – belching out clouds of smoke and soots the size of tenpenny pieces. Pollution, however, was a word never heard until long afterwards. A damp climate was considered an advantage for cotton-spinning, and this combined with the smoke in winter to produce an impenetrable yellow fog; most of the time the sky was overcast.

At the time, however, as any child will who knows nothing different with which to compare it, I took the industrial environment I grew up in as the norm, and by using a child's imagination I turned it into a magic world of my own. Whenever he could, my father took me with him to see people, relying on a book to keep me quiet while he talked to them. This gave me far more of the company of my father than most sons enjoy, and established a strong bond between us which never weakened. My father's salary was modest, perhaps as much as a solicitor's clerk, not a professional man like a solicitor himself, might earn; but my mother was a good manager, and though she had no servant girl to help her this hardly worried her. We lived plainly, but lacked nothing that mattered.

The Unitarian chapel itself was built of the usual ugly red brick, but this did not matter in a town where, with the exception of the parish church, there was no building of the slightest distinction. What mattered was the people. The 1920s were still a time in England, outside the larger cities, when churches and chapels continued to form natural centres of social life.

The services at Twist Lane were reasonably well attended, and on special occasions such as the Harvest Festival the chapel would be packed with a congregation of two or three hundred people. There was a thriving Sunday school held twice on Sundays, and Frank introduced the custom of telling a story to the children in the morning service, after which they could leave. Saturday-night 'socials' and dances, hotpot suppers, whist drives, amateur dramatics, Sunday-school treats, chapel outings, chapel bazaars, bring-and-buy sales – all once familiar features of urban England's, especially Northern and Nonconformist England's, social life – drew in families and young people from all over the town. Since nobody owned a car, we caught a tram or bus and walked the rest of the way, on Sundays the whole of the way, wet or fine. My mother was in her element in this bustle of activity, an invaluable partner for my father, whose interests remained centred on his role as preacher and teacher.

The Unitarian was always one of the smaller denominations, but it was well established in Lancashire, where there were few towns which did not have a Unitarian chapel. Some, like the neighbouring town of Bolton, had more than one, and in Manchester and Liverpool, where there were several congregations, Unitarians still played a prominent part in civic life. The Unitarian connection in Leigh dated from 1859, and the chapel and hall in Twist Lane had been built in 1897. The foundation stone had been laid by the Eckersleys, a wealthy Unitarian family from nearby Tyldesley, who later gave nearly £2,000 to augment the minister's stipend fund.

The congregation represented a cross-section of society. Besides a handful of businessmen, there were a small number who held administrative posts. They included John Morley, the secretary of the South Lancashire Tramways Company, who acted as chapel secretary, and Florence Darlington, who rose to a senior position in the Manchester City Treasurer's office. The other members of the congregation worked in shops, offices and cotton factories, or belonged to miners' families.

My father soon established a reputation as a preacher, but he did not leave behind anything comparable with the mass of sermons and lectures preserved for the years after he moved to Bradford in 1926. In Leigh he was still serving his apprenticeship; he was not yet forty when he left, and the maturing of his ideas with which this book is concerned came later. At this stage we must establish the character of the religious tradition with which he identified himself.

3

The Unitarian Heresy

I

The origins of Unitarianism are to be found in the ancient world, where, proclaimed by Arius, a fourth-century priest of Alexandria, it took the form of a denial of the Trinity and the divinity of Christ. Arius taught that there is only one God, without equal, and that Christ was not divine but an instrument created by God, who became incarnate in Jesus and took a human body, but in so doing did not become a man. Known as the Arian heresy and condemned at the Council of Nicaea in AD 325, this doctrine attracted widespread support and was not stamped out in the Eastern Roman Empire until it was proscribed at the Council of Constantinople in 381.

Anti-Trinitarian views reappeared at the time of the Reformation and encountered persecution from both Catholics and Protestants. In France, Michael Servetus, the physician to the Archbishop of Vienne, expounded them in his *Christianismi Restitutio*, published anonymously, and was denounced to the Inquisition and imprisoned by the Catholics; when he escaped and fled to Protestant Geneva, he was arrested on Calvin's orders and burned at the stake in 1553.

Some Italian Arians, fearing the same fate, found refuge in Poland, then a land of toleration, where the Minor Reformed Church (Polish Brethren) was founded in 1565. Inspired by Faustus Socinus, an Italian exile who arrived at Cracow in 1579, this flourished for half a century, with as many as 300 congregations accepting Jesus as God's revelation, but considering him as divine by office rather than by nature and rejecting the Trinity. Suppressed in Poland by the Counter-Reformation in 1638, Socinian ideas survived in Transylvania, the eastern half of the old Kingdom of Hungary. There King John Sigismund (died 1571) granted wide religious toleration and encouraged Ferenc David, bishop of the Reformed Church, to found the world's oldest group of Unitarian churches, which have survived the vicissitudes of Hungarian history and have maintained contact with English and American Unitarians to the present day.

In Shakespeare's England, heretics holding anti-Trinitarian views were burned at the stake. In Cromwell's, the Civil War was as much about religion as about government, and England was described as 'an island of a hundred religions'. The Puritans, however, were as hostile to Socinian views as were Anglicans and Catholics; John Biddle, who denied the Trinity and other orthodox views as well, was put in prison and later banished to the Isles of Scilly – but escaped burning.

The restoration of the monarchy was followed by the restoration of the Established Church and its revenge on the Puritans. The Act of Uniformity of 1662 required all ministers of religion to give their unqualified consent to everything contained in the restored Anglican Prayer Book. It was followed by the Conventicle Act of 1664, making prison or transportation the penalty for those attending Nonconformist worship, and by the Five Mile Act of 1665, which forbade ministers who had been ejected from their office from residing within five miles of any incorporated town.

Rather than accept the Act of Uniformity, some 1,700 ministers – one-fifth of the number in the Church of England – suffered ejection from their office and their livings without compensation. Few, if any, of them were Arians, Socinians, or anything other than orthodox in their beliefs; their stumbling block was Parliament's insistence on their express repudiation of all the changes made in the past twenty years and on the restoration of the bishops. Nonetheless it was out of congregations founded by ministers from among those ejected and their descendants that some 160 English Unitarian churches developed later – just over half the total there were in my father's time, including two of the three (Trowbridge and Bradford) of which he became minister.

In seventeenth-century England the 1689 Act of Toleration and

Locke's *Letters on Toleration* (published in 1689, 1690 and 1692) heralded a marked change in the religious climate. The revolutionary settlement of 1689, the evaporation of the religious zeal and fever of the century, the advance of science and the spread of theism combined to produce a new mood more congenial to Unitarian beliefs.

Religious tests were fully maintained until the nineteenth century, and persons, whether Protestant or Catholic, who refused to take communion according to the rites of the Church of England were still debarred from holding office either under the Crown or in the municipalities. Catholics were excluded from Parliament, and Dissenters of every kind from the two universities. In this way, the Church of England kept a firm hand on its privileges but at the same time abandoned persecution. The Toleration Act granted the right of public worship to Protestant Nonconformists. It still made exceptions of Catholics and the growing number of Nonconformists who denied the Trinity. In practice, however, these exceptions were largely ignored.

The generation between 1690 and 1720 saw the beginning of the continuous history of many Dissenter congregations and the building of many characteristic meeting houses. The number in 1715 is put at 1,843, with a total membership of 338,000. This amounted to 6 per cent of the population of England and Wales – the great majority of them holding orthodox beliefs, but with a growing number prepared to accept Arian views. These rejected the doctrine of the Trinity, and ranked Christ as below the Father in divine status, but still distinct and higher in nature than all other created beings – in effect, a belief halfway to later eighteenth-century Unitarianism.

As the century progressed, the gap widened between the orthodox Dissenters and the more open-minded 'Rational Dissenters' as they called themselves. The moral enthusiasm of the evangelical revival, led by Whitefield and Wesley, attracted the former but repelled the latter. These were drawn to the moral rationalism of Locke and Newton, which was more compatible with a Unitarian view of God as the Author of Nature. The Dissenting academies, providing an alternative to the public schools and the two universities from which Nonconformists were excluded, fostered an inquiring spirit. The most famous of them, the Warrington Academy, founded in 1757, numbered Josiah Wedgwood as one of its founders, Joseph Priestley as one of its tutors, and Malthus as one of its students.

Priestley was the dominant figure of English Unitarianism in the second half of the eighteenth century and well into the nineteenth. A man of abounding intellectual energy and a born controversialist, he was an experienced scientist, philosopher and radical political theorist as well as a theologian and Unitarian divine at Leeds and Birmingham. One of the founders of modern chemistry, he was elected a fellow of the Royal Society in 1766 and the next year published his *History of Electricity*. In 1777 he was awarded the Society's Copley Medal for his investigation of the properties of gases. He discovered ten new gases – among them ammonia, sulphur dioxide and carbon monoxide – although he failed to grasp the importance of his most famous discovery, that of oxygen. Between 1772 and 1780, he published no less than six major treatises, beginning with *Institutes of Natural and Revealed Religion* and ending with *A Free Discussion of the Doctrines of Materialism and Philosophical Necessity* and *Letters to a Philosophical Unbeliever*, directed at David Hume.

Priestley rejected the Trinity of the orthodox in favour of the unity of God, and at the same time removed the Arians' ambiguity about the status of Christ in favour of an unqualified belief in Jesus as a man. Insistence on Jesus' full humanity, far from depreciating his role, enhanced it. 'A man who had learned to be perfect was far more telling as a teacher and as example, than a god who had temporarily taken on human form for a morally loathsome sacrifice.'*

Priestley's determinism – or 'necessarianism', as he called it – was based on his belief in God's plan to bring all mankind to perfection in this or another life. 'All evil', he wrote, 'is ultimately subservient to good, and it is the intention of Providence finally to

---

* R. K. Webb, 'The Unitarian Background', in *Truth, Liberty, Religion*, ed. Barbara Smith (Manchester College, Oxford, 1986), p. 12. I am much indebted to this essay.

exterminate it.' Priestley argued that, far from being a fatalistic view, this required man to cooperate in carrying out God's plan. As one of his disciples, Thomas Belsham, put it, 'The farmer who believes that God knows and has ordained that the next harvest shall be plentiful, or otherwise, does not for that reason neglect to cultivate and to sow the ground.'

Priestley described himself as a Unitarian Christian, claiming that his view represented the original teaching of Christ, which had been perverted and suppressed by the Church. So did his friend the Reverend Theophilus Lindsey, a former fellow of St John's College, Cambridge, vicar of Catterick in Yorkshire. Lindsey was the leader of a group of Church of England clergymen, graduates of Cambridge, who sought unsuccessfully to secure relief for Anglican clergy from having to subscribe to the Thirty-nine Articles. The same year a parallel move to abolish subscription on the part of candidates for a degree at Cambridge was defeated by only a narrow vote in the university senate. (The Chancellor of the University, the Duke of Grafton, belonged to the reform party and wrote a pamphlet criticizing the Book of Common Prayer on Unitarian grounds.)

In 1774 a number of the Cambridge reformers joined Lindsey in founding the first avowedly Unitarian chapel, Essex Street Chapel in London, later to become the headquarters of the Unitarian denomination. At the opening service both Joseph Priestley and another of Lindsey's friends, the American Benjamin Franklin, were present, as well as two Whig noblemen, the Earl of Shelburne and Earl Spencer.

The Whig connection was important, but did not save Unitarians from unpopularity and the threat of worse when the French Revolution produced a strong reaction in England against all forms of radicalism. Priestley, who was a staunch supporter of the American as well as the French Revolution, saw his chapel and house in Birmingham burned down by a patriotic mob in 1791, and three years later emigrated to America.

II

It was only after the wars with France were over that a cautious revival of the Unitarian cause in Britain was possible. A preliminary step was the success in 1813 of a Unitarian MP, William Smith, in persuading Parliament to abolish penalties on those who impugned the doctrine of the Trinity. But Unitarians still had to be married, and often buried, according to the rites of the Church of England. Their main energies went into proselytizing, and in 1825 a number of missionary societies formed themselves into the British and Foreign Unitarian Association. Their success was modest. By the time of the religious census of June 1851, the number of Unitarian chapels had reached 250 in England, around 30 in Wales and a handful in Scotland. The English congregations recorded an attendance of 50,000 at the three Sunday services, making them one of the smallest denominations, even among the Free Churches, which also included Methodists, Baptists and Congregationalists. The other Dissenters frequently regarded them with the same aversion as did orthodox Anglicans, seeing them as indistinguishable from atheists or at least deists. 'It is a capital hit in the country to abuse anyone as a Unitarian,' Sydney Smith said; 'the squires think it is something to do with poaching.'*

Nonetheless, despite the prejudice against them for their heterodox views, which continued well into the twentieth century, most historians have recognized the disproportionately large role in relation to their insignificant numbers which Unitarians (like the Quakers) played in the economic, political and intellectual life of nineteenth-century England.

Among the names of Unitarian families who took a leading part in the economic development of the world's first industrial society are Wedgwood, Courtauld, Fielden (of Todmorden), Strutt (of Belper), Ashton (of Hyde) and Brunner (of Liverpool). Unitarians such as William Smith, an MP since 1784, were prominent in the

---

* A quotation from Crabb Robinson's diary, 6 February 1836, which I owe to Professor R. K. Webb of the University of Maryland.

campaigns to abolish the slave trade, to emancipate the Catholics, to found University College, London – without religious tests, 'the godless place in Gower Street' – and to pass the 1832 Reform Act. Of fourteen Dissenters in the reformed Parliament elected after the Act, thirteen were reported to be Unitarians. The *Manchester Guardian* was founded in 1830 by a Unitarian, John Edward Taylor, and its greatest editor, C. P. Scott, belonged to Cross Street Chapel, where the Victorian novelist Mrs Gaskell's husband had been minister, and where the congregation in 1829 contained five future mayors of Manchester and a dozen future MPs. Between 1841 and 1887 Birmingham could count twenty Unitarian mayors, among them the greatest municipal leader of the century, Joseph Chamberlain, whose restless energies, transferred to the national stage, split first the Liberal and then the Conservative Party.

Much of the vitality of early- and mid-nineteenth-century England was still to be found in its provincial cities, not yet concentrated in London. To Manchester and Birmingham – both Unitarian strongholds – can be added Liverpool, where a group of leading Unitarian families (such names as Rathbone, Holt, Booth, Roscoe) played a unique role, and also Norwich, Nottingham, Bristol and Leicester, in the last of which the first five mayors after the Municipal Reform Act of 1835 all belonged to the same denomination.

From Carlyle and Dickens, John Stuart Mill, George Eliot and the *Westminster Review* to Browning and Darwin, most of the literary and intellectual figures of mid-Victorian England had connections with this Unitarian elite in one way or another. It was her Unitarian friends in Coventry, the Brays, and Charles and Sara Hennell, who introduced George Eliot (then still Marian Evans) to the German higher criticism of the Bible and persuaded her to translate David Friedrich Strauss's *Life of Jesus*. In 1869 James Martineau, the outstanding Unitarian intellectual of the century, was elected to the Metaphysical Society, whose other members included Gladstone, Tennyson, Browning, Ruskin, T. H. Huxley and Cardinal Manning. In the next generation, Philip Henry Wicksteed, son of one of Martineau's closest associates, achieved an international reputation for his contribution to economic theory and to Dante scholarship, and J. Estlin Carpenter became a pioneer scholar in comparative religion, which he taught at the Unitarian Manchester College, which moved to Oxford in 1889.

By the time my father entered the Unitarian ministry, the denomination had suffered a decline from the position it held in the nineteenth century. Many of the leading Unitarian families of Victorian times had acquired respectability by joining the Church of England or were no longer so active; at the same time, the provincial cities, in which Unitarian strength had lain, had lost much of their independence and confidence to London. But it was a tradition to be proud of, and Unitarianism still retained some of the prestige it had enjoyed as the most liberal and intellectually progressive of the Nonconformist Churches. Moreover, the century and more which separated my father from the Rational Dissent of Joseph Priestley's day (Priestley died in 1804) had seen changes in Unitarianism which were of great importance to a young man seeking greater freedom of religious belief.

Rejection of the doctrine of the Trinity was compatible with very different religious attitudes. Priestley's Rational Dissent rather surprisingly combined a philosophical radicalism with a literal acceptance of the historical truth of the Bible. His theology postulated a progressive corruption of Christ's original teaching, which had now to be recovered, but still assumed that, when this was achieved, the unique authority of the Christian revelation would remain guaranteed by Christ's miracles and resurrection.

III

Such views were dominant among Unitarians in the early part of the nineteenth century, and continued to be represented throughout it. But in the 1830s and 1840s they were challenged by a quite different attitude, which was as responsive to nineteenth-century romanticism as Priestley's had been to eighteenth-century rationalism. The leaders of this new movement in the late 1830s were James Martineau, John Hamilton Thom and Charles Wicksteed, all three ministers of Unitarian chapels in Liverpool, and J. J.

Tayler, whose chapel was in Manchester. For several years they met every month. Inspired by the preaching of William Ellery Channing, the leader of New England Unitarianism, 'the Quaternion', as they were known, drew many English Unitarians to a faith which was instinctive rather than logical, devotional rather than polemical, and found its authority in the inner promptings of emotion and conscience rather than in the external existence of Scripture. Rejecting Priestley's necessarian doctrine, they asserted the free will and personal responsibility of the individual. Priestley's version of Unitarianism was criticized on the one hand as too intellectualized, too lacking in sensibility; on the other for its scripturalism, its reliance on the biblical record of miraculous intervention, now undermined by German scholarship's questioning of the credibility of the Gospels.

By contrast, Martineau's faith was undisturbed by the higher criticism, which he devoted much time to mastering. In a sermon of July 1848 he declared:

If I think the *records*, which are the vehicle of Christianity, less perfect than I once supposed; if they leave some things uncertain, on which I should be grateful to be assured; if the element of Hellenistic theory and Jewish misconception seems larger than I had thought; yet all this does but disengage the inspired Author in greatness more solitary and signal; and by substituting for the vague gaze of reverence, a real, human view of that amazing time fills me with a *far* deeper interest in the men and a profounder trust in the religion.*

Martineau found the essence of the Christian religion in Jesus' personal ministry among the Galilean peasants. This contained no trace of the claim that Jesus was the millennial Messiah (the 'Jewish misconception') or of the doctrines of the Trinity, the Incarnation or the Atonement by the blood of Christ, all of which were later additions after his death. It was consistent with this view that Martineau should place the Seat of Authority in Religion – the title

* James Drummond and C. B. Upton, *The Life and Letters of James Martineau* (Nisbet, London, 2 vols., 1902), vol. I, pp. 159–60.

of his best-known work* – not in anything external, such as the Church (as Catholics did) or the Bible (as Protestants had done), but in the direct intuition of God in the human conscience.

It was this combination, of 'a severe critic but also a profound mystic', that gave Martineau and his closest associates, such as John Hamilton Thom and J. J. Tayler, their influence. In their sermons and prayers, their choice of hymns – reflecting a preference for poetry over theology, comparable with their preference for the Gothic style in church building† over that of the older Dissenters' meeting houses – they sought to foster imaginative and affective elements in religion. These had become separated from the intellectual to the impoverishment of both, one finding expression in the exaggerated emotionalism of the evangelical revival, the other in a system of abstract beliefs divorced from religious experience.

Martineau and the other members of the Quaternion focused their faith upon the personality of Jesus, seeing him as the human image of God, the fully developed Christ, an image which exists, potentially, in the moral nature of all men and women – 'Christ in you'.

Those who followed the Priestleyan tradition were eager to organize on a denominational basis of commitment to clearly defined beliefs, flourished the Unitarian name, and devoted themselves to recruiting new members, often from the working class. Martineau, on the other hand, and those who followed him, were concerned not to compromise the future by forming a Unitarian denomination and insisting on a dogmatic formulation which would 'check the spontaneous course of gradual change'. Their desire to keep the door open for a comprehensive Church attracted a few liberal-minded clergymen in the Church of England, such as Frederick Robertson of Brighton (1816–53), whose sermons,

* Although the book was not published until 1890, when Martineau was eighty-five, it was the fruit of sixty years' study and teaching in which he had elaborated these views.
† J. J. Tayler and his Manchester congregation engaged Sir Charles Barry, the architect of the new Houses of Parliament, to design a new chapel in the Gothic style. Others followed at Hyde, Cheshire (1848), Mill Hill, Leeds (1848), Hope Street, Liverpool (1849), and Banbury (1850).

published after his early death, became classics of Christian teaching much admired by my father. But their attempt to create a Free Christian Union, in which Martineau took a leading part, lasted only a couple of years (1868–70).

Both parties – Martineau and his friends, along with all other Unitarians – were still denied the name of Christian and denounced by the ignorant as infidels and blasphemers: grave charges in nineteenth-century Britain. Barred from a fellowship at Oxford or Cambridge, because he did not assent to the Thirty-nine Articles, Martineau was turned down for the professorship of the philosophy of mind at University College, London, because one party objected to his being a minister of religion at all and the other to his being an unorthodox minister. The only scope open to this gifted man as a teacher, other than in his pulpit or in the reviews to which he contributed, was in Manchester College, the descendant of the original Warrington Academy, with hardly more than a dozen students preparing for the Unitarian ministry. Not until his eighties was his distinction given public recognition, when an address was presented to him expressing 'the feelings of reverence and affection entertained towards you . . . by those acquainted with your charac-ter and writings'. It was signed by 650 eminent Victorians, led by Tennyson, Browning, Benjamin Jowett, W. E. H. Lecky, Max Müller and J. R. Seeley and followed by representative figures from the world's leading universities.

Martineau has been compared to Friedrich Schleiermacher, the leading figure in German nineteenth-century Protestantism, in his eagerness 'to commend Christianity to the cultured through tra-ditional systems apprehended psychologically rather than argumen-tatively'.* His ideal of a comprehensive Church made a strong appeal to the older Unitarian chapels in the larger provincial cities such as Liverpool, Birmingham, Manchester, Nottingham and

---

* I have borrowed the phrase from H. L. Short's two chapters in the book which he wrote with C. G. Bolam, Jeremy Goring and Roger Thomas, *The English Presby-terians, from Elizabethan Puritanism to Modern Unitarianism* (Allen & Unwin, London, 1968), p. 272.

Norwich, with active, educated, well-to-do congregations largely drawn from the liberal middle class. Martineau's views, however, continued to be regarded with suspicion or rejected by those Unitarian congregations more recently founded – often as a result of missionary preaching in opposition to orthodoxy – who were attracted by a Priestleyan combination of Scripture, reason and radicalism, with a predominantly lower-middle- and working-class membership.

The 'Liberal landslide' of 1906, which brought a large number of radicals to the House of Commons, powerfully stimulated this alternative version of Unitarianism, and was followed by an almost immediate influx of young men from Methodism and other denominations into the Unitarian ministry. For the most part, they sought their training not at Manchester College – by now, against Martineau's wishes, moved to Oxford – but from the Unitarian Home Missionary College, originally founded over a stable in 1854 by John Relly Beard, a Hampshire carpenter's son who was a minister in Manchester, to train working men of poor education to become Unitarian ministers. In 1905 the College moved into larger premises and sponsored the Van Mission which toured the market places of the North of England.

My father's sympathies were divided. Since Unitarians were Englishmen, class differences had a lot to do with their divisions, and, as a poor boy whose formal education was limited, he might have been expected to have more in common socially with the second group. This was strongest in the North, especially in the cotton and mining towns of Lancashire like Leigh. On the other hand, as we shall see in the next chapter, the most important influence on him during his years in Leigh – his friendship with F. P. Sturm – encouraged a natural interest in a mystical rather than a rationalist approach to religion, an interest more compatible with Martineau's views than with Priestley's. It was from this starting point that he began to work out his own distinctive vision.

4

Frank Pearce Sturm

I have left until now the most interesting of my father's friendships in Leigh, which was different from all the others.

It happened in this way [Frank later wrote]. When I first came to Lancashire, I heard many stories of a Dr Frank Pearce Sturm. Sturm was known to be a brilliant aural surgeon but also a reputed poet and a recluse with an unapproachable, indeed outrageous, manner.

I was determined to meet him and so one morning I called at his home, Brunswick House. His dispenser, Prescott, answered the door; then retreated to Sturm's consulting room, where I heard him say, 'Doctor, there's a bloody parson wants to see you.'

A moment later, Sturm came to the door and said, 'What the devil do you want?' I told him who I was and that, as president of the Literary Society, I had called to ask if he would give the Society a lecture or paper. I was immediately invited to go upstairs to his study. We had a fascinating talk about books, and I was invited to return in the evening.

When he did so, Frank found, besides Sturm, his wife, Lotte, who was also a doctor. He never succeeded in getting Sturm to speak to the Literary Society, but the three soon became close friends, meeting regularly on Tuesday evenings for five or six years until Frank's move to Bradford in November 1926. He was the only man in Leigh who ever succeeded in penetrating the barriers Sturm deliberately created between the everyday world and his inner life, and one of the few men anywhere who was admitted to his confidence. In return, my father wrote, 'he opened for me a new world of beauty and imagination'.

Sturm delighted to wrap himself in mystery, and neither Frank nor Sturm's few other friends, including the poet W. B. Yeats, ever succeeded in discovering anything of his background. When Yeats included a poem by Sturm in his *Oxford Book of Modern Verse* (1936), enquiries about the date of his birth failed to produce an answer and the book was published without one. It was not until a young American scholar, Richard Taylor, started to gather material for a study of Sturm in the 1960s that the essential facts of his life were uncovered.*

His origins were prosaic enough. He was born in 1879, in Longsight, Manchester, the eldest of the three children of a shipping merchant who lost everything at the time of the Boer War, when Sturm was preparing to go to university. Both his father and his mother came from Scottish families who had connections with Aberdeen, where Sturm entered the university at the age of twenty-two. At the end of May 1904 Sturm married a fellow student, Charlotte Augusta Fanny Schultze (known always as Lotte), born in Stettin twenty years before. After a succession of locum jobs, in 1909 they moved to Leigh, where Sturm secured the degree of Master of Surgery at Manchester University and in 1915 was elected a fellow of the Royal Society of Medicine. Husband and wife shared the practice which they bought, Lotte accompanying Sturm on all his calls in an old-fashioned taxicab in which he was driven round the town. He rapidly acquired a reputation as a general practitioner, even though he terrified patients with his brusqueness, and was much in demand for his skill as a surgeon.

The war took Sturm into the Army Medical Corps. He was gassed in 1917 and returned to London to convalesce. He did not, however, resume his practice in Leigh until 1919. During the intervening years he not only wrote poetry but also pursued the

---

* *Frank Pearce Sturm: His Life, Letters and Collected Work*, edited with an introduction by Richard Taylor (University of Illinois Press, Urbana, 1969). At the time of publication Dr Taylor, who acknowledges in the preface his debt to my father 'for sharing his invaluable knowledge of Sturm's character and pursuits', was assistant professor of English at Dartmouth College, New Hampshire. In my turn I acknowledge my own debt to Dr Taylor.

study of mysticism. Both interests brought him close to Yeats, with whom he established a lifelong friendship.

My father and Sturm were both short and square in build, with large heads and, in Sturm's case, piercing eyes which (my father noted) always seemed to be staring at something above the head of the person he was talking to. Temperamentally, they shared an irreverent hostility to the orthodox and conventional, coupled with a taste for bold and heretical speculation. They were drawn together, however, from very different intellectual and spiritual traditions, and it was this which made my father's friendship with Sturm – eight years older and a much better-educated man – so fruitful for his own development. Sturm, one could say, was Frank's university.

Once past the waiting room and the consulting room in Brunswick House, then up the stairs, one entered a different world, filled to overflowing with books. There were medical textbooks and rows of medical journals, for the doctor kept up with and contributed to the field in which he was a specialist. But these were kept separately in the consulting room. The several thousand volumes upstairs were either works of literature, in several languages, or Sturm's extraordinary collection of books devoted to the mystical-religious speculations and art of a score of different cultures, ranging from ancient Egypt and medieval Europe to modern Japan. His sitting room, lined with books from floor to ceiling, was decorated with a fine collection of oriental embroideries and at least three figures of the Buddha. It was here that the members of 'the Lodge' – Sturm, Lotte and Frank – met on Tuesday evenings. Once the candles on the mantelpiece had been lit, only discussion of the sacred mysteries and religious topics was allowed; afterwards there followed drink, gossip and any sort of nonsense Sturm might take it into his head to pursue.

Sturm was a good Latinist and well acquainted with French as well as classical literature. Frank thought that his only equal as a reader of poetry was Dylan Thomas. He would read aloud not only from English poets, but from Virgil, for example, or from Baudelaire and the French symbolists, Verlaine and Mallarmé, translating as he went. He introduced my father to Yeats, whom Frank came to prize as the greatest of modern poets, and to William Blake, another lasting passion of Frank's.

During the years when Frank saw him regularly, Sturm was already moving from poetry to mysticism as the central preoccupation of his life. It was in fact Sturm's knowledge of mystical literature and Yeats's preoccupation with the revision of his own mystical prose work, *A Vision*, which formed the substance of Sturm and Yeats's correspondence.*

Sturm's part in it is relevant to my story because his letters convey better than anything else the mixture of learning, fantasy and teasing which Frank found so attractive in his conversation. Two short quotations give the flavour. The first is a letter dated 23 February 1926:

Dear Yeats,

However dog the Latin, you can't keep '*hominorum*' because it isn't Latin.

And you can't pretend Giraldus wrote dog Latin, for he was the most learned of the 12th century translators from the Arabic . . .

There are two ways in which you can deal with '*hominorum*':

(1) Admit the error and correct it in the next edition.

(2) Assert it to have been a misprint for '*homunculorum*', which is quite good Latin and would give a satyric twist to Giraldus for it would make the title of his book: *The Mirror of Angels and Manikins* or *Angels and Dolls*. And *homunculus* is a word that would have come readily to the pen of Giraldus, for it was the name given to the artificial men that the alchemists of his day were for ever trying to concoct in their stew pans.

Of course the proper title: *Speculum Angelorum et Hominum* is the more dignified.

Perhaps Giraldus himself created such an *homunculus* and trained it as a body servant, and perhaps he was strangled by it in a deserted burial

---

* This has been printed in full by Richard Taylor in his book about Sturm. In a letter of 4 March 1926, Yeats refers to Sturm as 'a very learned doctor in the North of England who sends me profound and curious extracts from ancient philosophies on the subject of gyres' (p. 59).

ground outside Fez, where he had arranged to meet Christian Rosycross, then on his eastern travels. That they met, or arranged to meet, I am convinced.

F. P. Sturm

The second letter was dated 26 August 1929, and written at the Royal Hotel, Southport:

My dear Yeats,

This place only remotely resembles the Tavern of the Screaming Seraph at Byzantium . . .

I have been reading your new introduction to the Great Wheel, which I suppose is to be a re-moulded *Vision*.

Do get some friend who knows Latin to read the proofs this time. I know that I am a pedant, but pedants read you. We cough in the ink till the world's end, as you cruelly said, but the least of us would save you from the errors which spoil *Vision* as it is now.

Personally, I think your philosophy smells of the fagot.

Some dead and damned Chaldaean *mathematikoi* have got hold of your wife and are trying to revive a dead system.

All these gyres and cones and wheels are parts of a machine that was thrown on the scrap heap when Ptolemy died. It won't go. There is no petrol for such.

The ghosts of the *mathematikoi* are weeping over their broken toy universe: the *Primum Mobile* no longer moves, the seven planetary spheres of crystal are dull as a steamy cookshop window – so they are trying to speak through your wife and are using much that she has read in the past.

However, all that you write is letters. No doubt many an Inquisitor has sighed as he condemned some author to the flames. You would not have escaped . . .

My new book, when I write it, is to be in seven parts, and is to be called Seven Fagots for the Burning of the Great Heretic Yeats – or The Wheel Dismantled – printed for the author by Michael Paleologus, and is to be purchased at the Sign of the Seraph, in Byzantium.

Yours,

F. P. Sturm

No wonder that Frank, with such talk ringing in his ears, had some difficulty in recognizing where he was as he made his way home through the deserted streets of Leigh.

Both Frank and Lotte Sturm had at one time been on the point of becoming Roman Catholics. They had been prevented only by Sturm's unshakeable belief, which dated from childhood, in his own previous existence and reincarnation. Despite his exclusion from its communion on this account, he remained drawn to the Roman tradition by his love of its ritual and its antiquity. Protestantism was of no interest to Sturm; he was indeed hostile to any form of orthodox Christianity other than Roman Catholicism, but continually read the Gospels (especially the mystical Gospel of St John) with great attention. With the background of a wide reading in the Gnostics and other heterodox Christian teachers, he had arrived at his own original view of Christ's teaching, always related to the ancient wisdoms of Egypt and the East.

The belief in pre-existence and reincarnation, which proved the stumbling block to Sturm's reconciliation with the Roman Catholic Church, opened the way to his other principal religious interest, in Eastern religions. Buddhism attracted him more than any other, and in the mid-1930s he wrote to my father of his 'convinced, hard-won, ineradicable, and never-to-be-shaken knowledge that the Buddha's teaching is the only doctrine of reality the mind of man can rest upon'. But he was also drawn to Vedanta (Hindu mysticism), founded on the Upanishads and the *Bhagavadgita*, and was able to quote widely from Sufi writings, the Kabbalists, and the Arab philosophers and alchemists. (Sturm had a complete set of the *Theatrum Chemicum* in his library.)

The reason for the persistence with which Sturm explored other religious traditions besides the orthodox Christian was his desire to collect evidence of a universal mystical tradition of which the Christian revelation was a part. One of the keys to this was the *Corpus Hermeticum*, the scriptures of a mystic sect in Egypt which at various dates between AD 100 and 300 brought together wisdom from Egypt, Greece and Asia. Another was the Neoplatonist teaching of Plotinus (*c.* AD 205–70), and of 'Dionysius the Areopagite' (*fl. c.* AD 500). This reached back to the *Timaeus* of Plato and forward to the Italian Renaissance, when Marsilio Ficino was commissioned by Cosimo de' Medici to provide translations into Latin of all three – Plato, Plotinus and Dionysius – as well as the *Corpus Hermeticum* and his own reconciliation of Neoplatonism and Christianity. Yet a third was the *Fama Fraternitatis* of the Brotherhood of the Rosy Cross, first published in 1614 and drawing on earlier alchemical thought.

Frances Yates has since made clear the widespread influence of these ideas, loosely known as the hermetic tradition, on European thought (including scientific thought) of the fifteenth, sixteenth and early seventeenth centuries.* But, at the time when Sturm and my father were discovering the tradition for themselves, knowledge of it was confined to a handful of scholars. I still recall my father's excitement when, returning home from a Christmas-morning service at Twist Lane, he found Sturm and Lotte just about to depart in a taxi after leaving on his snow-covered doorstep as a Christmas present Stephen McKenna's translation of Plotinus, beautifully printed in five handsome volumes, the first of which bears (in coloured inks) the inscription:

To F.A.B.

From the Hermetic Lodge: Congregation of the Outer RC†

25.xii.25. F.P.S. C.A.F.S.

Optimi Consultores Mortui.‡

Only years later did it occur to me that there was anything surprising in this taking place in a coal and cotton town in industrial Lancashire, sixteen hundred years after Plotinus' death.

On another occasion Sturm returned from London with two copies (one for himself, the other for F.A.B.) of the sermons of Meister Eckhart (*c.* 1260–1327), the medieval German mystic who drew heavily on Neoplatonist ideas and whose thought has in

---

* See Frances A. Yates, *Giordano Bruno and the Hermetic Tradition* (Routledge & Kegan Paul, London, 1964 – the year of Frank's death).

† This was appropriately decorated with red roses, the Rosicrucian symbol.

‡ 'The best advisers are the dead.'

modern times been compared (by Rudolf Otto) with that of the Hindu mystic Sankara (AD ?700–?750) and (by the Japanese scholar Suzuki) with Zen Buddhism. With Eckhart, Frank bracketed another German mystic, Jakob Böhme (1575–1624), whose writings became one of the main sources of his own religious thought.*

II

It was of course obvious to both Frank and Sturm that no form of human experience has attracted so many charlatans as religion. This did not put them off. There were many examples of men and women who were among the greatest of spiritual teachers (to name only four, St Francis, St Teresa, John Bunyan, William Blake) but whose accounts of how they came to be inspired by visitations, visions and moments of illumination were difficult to believe if taken literally.

For both my father and Sturm, mysticism was the object of a lifetime's serious and absorbing study. But this was compatible – especially in their younger days – with a lively, often irreverent, curiosity about all forms of psychic phenomena (Sturm called them 'cosmic curiosities'), from ghosts, hauntings and visions to cases of possession, precognition and extrasensory perception. Their expectations were sceptical – in most cases with good reason. For neither man was belief in the reality of the spiritual dimension of life dependent on the 'evidence' of such phenomena, which, even when fraud or self-deception could not be established, were too trivial and materialistic to compare with the insights of the great religious teachers or of the masters of literature and art. But both enjoyed a good mystery, as they enjoyed a good ghost story, without worrying overmuch whether it was explicable or not.

The Society for Psychical Research had been founded in 1882 (by Henry Sidgwick, the Cambridge philosopher, among others) scientifically to investigate psychical phenomena – in particular the claims of mediums to transmit messages from those who had died.

---

* See below, pp. 186–9.

Among the earliest frauds which it exposed was the claim of
Madame Blavatsky, one of the most colourful figures of the late
nineteenth century, to have derived the philosophical-religious
doctrines which she made the basis of Theosophy from masters
under whom she had studied in Tibet and who (she claimed)
continued to communicate with her after she had left Tibet and
after some of them had died. Madame Blavatsky was entirely
unabashed by the exposure, which she made no attempt to counter,
and which made no difference to her followers in the Theosophical
Society (which she had founded in 1875).*

Madame Blavatsky died in 1891, too early for Frank to meet
her. By the 1920s, her place as president of the Theosophical Society
had been taken by a hardly less remarkable woman, Annie Besant.
She spent much of her life in India, where she founded the Indian
Home Rule League in 1916 and promoted the Star of the East
movement, a cult associated with Krishnamurti, a protégé of Mrs
Besant whom she regarded as a Messiah. Frank took the chair for
her when she addressed a crowded meeting in Bolton Town Hall,
and had no doubt of her powers as an orator. He remained sceptical,
however, of her claims on behalf of Krishnamurti, and was justified
by the latter's own later repudiation of them – an event which very
nearly proved fatal to the Theosophical Society.

One of the most interesting figures Frank met through Sturm
was the Austrian Rudolf Steiner (1861–1925), who had broken
away from the Theosophists and founded his own Anthroposoph-
ical Society. Steiner believed that man had once participated more
fully in the spiritual world through a dreamlike consciousness but
had since become restricted by his attachment to material things.
His object was to recapture this perception of spiritual things
(which, he believed, was innate in everyone) by training the human
consciousness to rise above preoccupation with the material world.
His lasting success was to be achieved in education, and by the
time of my father's death in 1964 some eighty Steiner schools,

* See Ruth Brandon, *The Spiritualists*, subtitled, *The Passion for the Occult in
the Nineteenth and Twentieth Centuries* (Weidenfeld & Nicolson, London, 1983),
pp. 236–9.

attended by more than 25,000 children, had been established in Europe and the USA, as well as schools for backward children and schools of drama, speech and painting.

Sturm told with relish the story of how he met Steiner in London and put the Master to the test by asking him if he knew anything about the Greek system of notation. He would re-enact vividly the scene as 'the old fraud' threw himself back in his chair and, staring blankly into the distance, claimed that he was reading the Akasic Record, from which he was able to explain to Sturm in detail the intricacies of the notation.* But twenty years later Sturm wrote of Steiner in his journal, 'Who or what he was, or where he came from no man knows, but he brought the only complete and satisfying philosophy the West has known ... Twenty years ago I thought him a cleverer charlatan than Blavatsky, but now I know him for the forerunner of the Second Coming.'† My father was never given to such extravagant flights, but reading Steiner's lectures added to the accumulation of ideas and experience from many sources which marked this period of Frank's life.

The interest in Theosophy and Anthroposophy which could bring together groups in such unlikely places as Leigh and Bolton seemed to my father part of 'an intense psychic, mental and spiritual restlessness' which marked the period of the First World War and the post-war years. This was even more marked in the much wider interest in spiritualism.

Around Leigh, and in the North generally, there were many groups of working people who met in cottages and small halls to hold seances, which were widely attended in the hope and faith of communication with the many who had died in the war. In many ways there was an uprush of psychic manifestations which demanded attention from those like myself who tried to keep an open mind in relation to anything related to the human psyche.

* Taylor, *Frank Pearce Sturm*, p. 3, a story confirmed by my father.
† Entry for 13 June 1936, in Taylor, *Frank Pearce Sturm*, p. 123.

Although several of his friends were convinced of the validity of the messages from 'the spirit world', Frank was not. 'The conclusion I arrived at', he wrote later, 'was that although these were presented in good faith, and there was no doubt about many of the phenomena, we did not then know enough about the mysterious working of the unconscious mind to make convincing interpretations of such communications.'

Sturm's own restless exploration of psychic phenomena led to a minor stroke. He was ordered to take a month's complete rest and to read nothing. Later Lotte Sturm and Frank persuaded him to accompany my father on a visit to Paris. Whatever good it did to Sturm, for my father this was a revelation – the only journey he ever made outside the British Isles apart from his war service, with a guide who knew Paris well, who could speak French fluently, and who went out of his way to make sure that Frank saw the Louvre, Notre-Dame, Sacre Cœur, and all the other famous sights as well as such curiosities as the museum devoted to Gustave Moreau (1826–98), the symbolist painter known for his erotic depictions of mythological and religious subjects. When the curator, who had been Moreau's personal servant, asked if they loved the Master, Sturm answered 'yes' without hesitation, and so secured entry to the private rooms, which were kept exactly as they had been at Moreau's death, including his uniform as a member of the Académie Française laid out on the bed on which he had died. The old man said sadly that few Europeans or Americans visited the collection – only Japanese, who found the symbolism of Moreau's work irresistible; but he was delighted with Sturm's parting epigram: 'This is not Art, it's Literature.'

Once he had recovered, Sturm swore henceforward to make no further experiments with the occult powers and to confine his speculations to reading and discussion.

Despite their close friendship and their common interests, my father's approach to religion and the spiritual life was very different from Sturm's. He did not, for example, share Sturm's obsession with reincarnation and the doctrine of karma. Even more important was the difference in their views of this life and the external world in which it is lived. By the time Frank knew him, Sturm had already abandoned literature for mysticism. In 1936, recalling in his journal that he had written nothing for fifteen years, Sturm added that he no longer had any desire to write: 'Meditation is the death of art. It is rightly called by the Chinese the philosophy of the Empty Gate. Meditation drains the illusory objective world of all colour and enchantment, and without these what is the poet?'* For the same reason, in the mid-1930s, although by then he had acquired a reputation as an ear, nose and throat specialist, Sturm abandoned the practice of surgery as another illusion.

As Sturm turned in upon himself and withdrew from anything more than superficial contact with human beings other than his wife, my father turned outward, following his vocation as a preacher, a man who took delight in the external world and in the extraordinary variety of human life. He told me later that at about the age of forty he was liberated from the introspective habits of his earlier years and the bondage of self, and came to marvel, as if with eyes opened for the first time, at both the natural and the human world in which he found himself.

This change of outlook must have taken place about the time he left Leigh (that was in his fortieth year), and may well have contributed to the decision to move. By then he had learned all he could from Sturm, and, although they continued to exchange occasional letters, he was evidently ready to enter a new phase.

There were also, of course, other reasons for leaving Leigh. Chief among them was his decision, after ten years, to take on a bigger church which would offer him more scope as well as a better salary. He would have loved to have been appointed as minister of one of the historic Unitarian congregations in the North – Cross Street, Manchester, or Joseph Priestley's church at Mill Hill, Leeds, or Martineau's in Liverpool. Without a university degree, however, or at least a period of study at a theological college, he had to recognize that that was beyond his reach. Wise enough not to let this worry him, when offered instead a choice between Bury in Lancashire and Bradford in Yorkshire he chose the latter, and remained there for the rest of his life, from 1926 to 1964.

* Taylor, *Frank Pearce Sturm*, p. 63.

5

Bradford

I

As had happened in the case of Leigh, Bradford was thrust into history by the Industrial Revolution, but on a different scale. Up to the middle of the eighteenth century, it had slowly developed into a small market town isolated by the moors which surrounded it except for the side valley of Airedale. What transformed Bradford was the invention of the steam engine and its application to spinning and weaving, not of cotton as in Lancashire, but of wool – in particular the production of worsted cloth. There had been one mill in Bradford in 1801; in 1841 there were 67. As a result, the population had grown from under 5,000 in 1751 to 103,778 in 1851, making Bradford the seventh largest urban centre in England. There had of course been a massive general rise in the population of England and Wales at this time – from 9 million in 1801 to 21 million in 1851, an increase of over 130 per cent. Bradford's growth, however, was still greater. In no decade between 1811 and 1851 did the growth of its population fall below 50 per cent.

This growth overwhelmed a town wholly unprepared for it, and there was no previous experience elsewhere on which to draw. In 1851 less than half its inhabitants had been born within the borough. The Irish made up 10 per cent of the total.

The bitterly resisted substitution of power-looms for the domestic industry of hand-loom weaving meant not just unemployment but the replacement of male labour by that of women and children, who had to adapt to the unfamiliar discipline of a twelve-hour working day spent within the world of the factory. Worst of all were the conditions in which the working population had to live. Even the Commissioners appointed by Parliament in 1844 'to inquire into the Sanitary Conditions of Populous Towns', and familiar with the human misery which accompanied industrialization, thought Bradford exceptional. 'The dirtiest, filthiest and worst regulated town in the Kingdom' was one Commissioner's view; 'simply unfit for human habitation' was another's.

Nonetheless, the great quarter-century of Victorian success and self-confidence (1848–73), reflected in the Great Exhibition of 1851, had its effect in Bradford as well as in the other industrial cities. In 1846 the railway finally reached Bradford; in 1847 the town was given the authority to elect a mayor and council, and by 1881 its population had reached 183,000, largely due to the incorporation of surrounding districts.

The entrepreneurs who made Bradford 'Worstedopolis, the worsted capital of the world' showed remarkable ability, both in technological innovation and in planning, funding and managing the business empires they built up. An example essential to the woollen industry was the dyeing industry, developed by the Ripley family, which created a near-monopoly in the Bowling Dyeworks, claimed to be the biggest dyeworks in the world. The prosperity such men created not only made their fortunes but generated employment and a rising standard of living for the fast-growing population.

As so often in the merchant communities of the past, the pride and self-confidence of Bradford's leading citizens was given visible expression in the town's architecture. The biggest of its mills – Titus Salt's Saltaire and Samuel Lister's Manningham Mills, both still standing – are masterpieces of Victorian architecture. The offices and warehouses of its leading firms, although smaller, were equally impressive, built of stone and finely proportioned, especially those in Little Germany. The greater part of Bradford's textile exports was destined for Germany, and most of the shipping houses until the First World War were of German origin.

The planning of the city centre was complete with the Italianate Town Hall, the Gothic Wool Exchange, the Mechanics' Institute and St George's Hall, built by public subscription in 1851–3. The last named provided seats for over 3,000 people to hear the Bradford

Festival Choral Society singing Handel's *Messiah* or to listen to a speech by W. E. Forster, a Quaker businessman with radical ideas who became a Liberal MP for Bradford and carried through Parliament the first national Education Act of 1870 as a member of Gladstone's government. To match the rebuilding of central Bradford, no less than five much-used public parks were created, beginning with Peel Park in 1863 and Lister Park ten years later, the latter housing the city's art gallery in the Cartwright Hall.

II

The 1851 religious census showed that Bradford was one of the strongest Nonconformist towns in England. As everywhere else in the country, the majority of the population did not go to church, but, in Bradford, of those who did 64.5 per cent were Protestant Dissenters and only 22.3 per cent were Anglicans. This statistic for Dissenters did not, however, include the Unitarians, whose numbers, like those of the Quakers, remained far below those of the Wesleyan Methodists and the Baptists. Nor did they compensate for this with the influence and leadership which Unitarians exercised in Leeds, Liverpool, Manchester and Birmingham. In Bradford that role was played by the Congregationalists – notably Horton Lane Chapel.

The prejudice against Unitarianism was still strong, and their numbers were limited to the two or three hundred members of Chapel Lane Chapel, compared with the thousands attracted to the 168 chapels of the mainstream Nonconformists. The Bradford Unitarians traced their origins back to the Act of Uniformity of 1662 and the ejections which followed it. The Reverend Jonas Waterhouse, the vicar of Bradford, was one of those ejected. For ten years he and his people are said 'to have met secretly for worship in solitary places'. When the law was relaxed, the Reverend Thomas Sharpe, another who had suffered the loss of his living, secured a licence to turn a part of his library at Horton Hall into a room for worship. The same Sharpe family again took the lead in establishing in 1688 a separate meeting house at Chapel Fold, Little Horton Green.

Another move followed thirty years later, in 1719, when the congregation took advantage of the gift of a piece of land by Robert and Elizabeth Stansfield to build a new meeting house. This was the first Nonconformist place of worship in the centre of Bradford, on a site where, 250 years later, I was to preach the final sermon before the congregation carried out yet another move, to a new building close to the chapel's original home in Little Horton. Old prints show the eighteenth-century meeting house to have been square-built with galleries and box-pews on the ground floor.

It is misleading, however, to use the name 'Unitarian' at this stage. A better description is 'English Presbyterian', indicating the type of Church government (no bishops) over which the original split in the Restoration Church of England had taken place. The eighteenth-century founders did not openly question any of the central Christian doctrines, but deliberately left the trusts under which Chapel Lane Chapel and many other Dissenting chapels were founded as 'open' trusts. These did not require either minister or members of the congregation to subscribe to any particular doctrinal formulation, and left them free to move towards the Unitarian position and adopt that name when opinion moved in favour of greater toleration.

In the case of Chapel Lane Chapel the change was made during the forty-five-year ministry (1768–1813) of the Reverend John Dean, who was also a founder and the first treasurer of the Bradford Library and Literary Society, formed in 1774. Despite their modest numbers, the congregation's standard of education was high and their commitment to progressive ideas strong. Among their ministers were Dr Vance Smith, later a member of the national Committee of Biblical Scholars which produced the Revised Version of the Bible in the 1880s, and the Reverend John Henry Ryland, who founded the Bradford Mechanics' Institute.

Nor had the Unitarians any difficulty in building and paying for a new chapel – 'in a modified Gothic style' – which was erected in 1867–9 with a hall and accommodation for a Sunday school and other activities in an adjoining building, Channing Hall, at a total cost of £7,000. The Dawson family of Royds Hall contributed a gift of £1,000, and the whole cost was met by 1871. The site was a good one, on the other side of the road from the new Town Hall built in 1873, and a line of carriages stood around the front of the chapel during services.

By the time my father moved to Bradford, in 1926, the heroic period of its history was over. Although not recognized at the time, the 1870s had seen the end of the expansion of Bradford. At the same time, in the mid-1870s, the Bradford textile industry underwent a number of setbacks from which it never recovered. With the growth of textile industries elsewhere in Europe and the USA and the erection of protectionist tariffs, in the twenty-five years before the First World War irregular working became more common, with two bad periods of unemployment in 1893–4 and 1903–4.

Equally striking was the change among the entrepreneurial class. An increasing number were adopting respectability by joining the Established Church, purchasing large landed estates far from the West Riding (Samuel Lister's cost him close on three-quarters of a million pounds to match his title of Baron Masham) and educating their sons at public schools. The next generation distanced themselves from involvement in the industry on which their wealth depended, putting pressure on the workers to accept cuts in wages in order to maintain or increase profits. This put an end to paternalistic ideals, leading to the growth of trade unions and (following a five-month strike at Lister's Manningham Mills in 1891) to the foundation of the Independent Labour Party and eventually to the Labour Party.

Change also affected the Churches. The ethos of Bradford remained religious, particularly Nonconformist, until 1914. But there was deep uneasiness about the future – especially among Nonconformists. All their different branches registered a fall in attendance in the religious census for 1881. Not one out of four of the city's population regularly attended a place of worship. And, as the middle classes moved to the new suburbs and the dormitory towns of Baildon, Ilkley and Harrogate, the fall continued unbroken into the next century. One observer asked, 'What is to become of

Horton Lane Congregational Chapel, once described as Bradford's Nonconformist Cathedral? Things are in a parlous state – no congregation to speak of, no Sunday School worth mentioning, no pastor.'*

Although the rate of growth had slowed down, by the time my father and mother arrived Bradford had expanded its boundaries to increase its population to 300,000, the majority of whom shared in the general rise in living standards in Britain between the wars. Between 1923 and 1937 nearly 20,000 new houses were built and, thanks to an excellent transport system, people were able to move out from the centre to housing estates on the surrounding hills – one reason why health improved and the death rate fell. Bradford had a reputation as a go-ahead municipal government, not only in health services – it was the first local authority to create a municipal general hospital, in St Luke's – but in housing, and also in education. It pioneered in school meals, swimming baths, clinics, nursery schools, camps and special facilities for blind, deaf and other disabled children. At the same time, in 1929 the percentage of children admitted to secondary schools (without fees) was more than twice the national average.

It was, however, still a city in which people had to earn their living, as anyone could see when the working day ended and the crowds poured out from the factories, mills, offices and shops to pack the trolley and motor buses and make their way home. These were not only men: 40 per cent of Bradford women also went out to work.

Like other parts of the industrial North, however, Bradford was a low-wage town when compared with the newer industrial areas in the Midlands and the South. The crucial test was the regularity of employment. Bradford's weakness was its dependence on a single industry. There were newer ones, such as engineering, but at a

---

* I owe this quotation and much else to an outstanding essay by J. A. Jowitt, 'The Pattern of Religion in Victorian Bradford', in *Victorian Bradford: Essays in Honour of Jack Reynolds*, ed. D. G. Wright and J. A. Jowitt (City of Bradford Metropolitan Council, Libraries Division, 1982).

*Chapel Lane Chapel, built in 1867–9,
in the centre of Bradford*

much lower level of pay than in other parts in the country. Far and away the biggest provider of work remained the textile industry, which in 1911 employed 27,000 men and 34,000 women. If men or women lost their jobs, whether because of a slump, sickness or increasing age, they very soon found themselves in difficulties, from which it was hard to recover, especially after the Means Test was imposed in 1931 on those claiming unemployment benefit. Slumps and strikes in the early 1920s were followed by a prolonged depression. Between 1927 and 1932, 400 Bradford textile firms went out of business, and throughout the whole period of 1927–36 the rate of unemployment was often as high as 20 per cent, and sometimes more in textiles. Even for those in work, short time and piecework were widespread; only after 1936 did rearmament gradually reduce unemployment to 10 per cent.

The insecurity created by the threat of unemployment affected far more than those actually out of work. The optimism which had marked the 1850s, 1860s and 1870s had gone. If the majority, in Bradford as in the rest of Britain, had unquestionably improved their standard of living, it was still true – as the nineteenth-century American Unitarian William Channing had written – that 'in most large cities there may be said to be two nations, understanding little of one another, having as little intercourse as if in different lands'.*

III

Chapel Lane Chapel had not escaped the changes which had taken place in the years before my father was appointed. The character of the congregation had altered. They had neither the intellectual confidence nor the financial resources of their predecessors, which had been reflected in the desire to build the new chapel sixty years earlier. The scale of the building and the empty pews were a reminder of what had been lost. In appointing Frank, the chapel

* Channing invented the phrase 'two nations', which Disraeli made famous.

committee no doubt hoped that he would help them to recapture it.

Fortunately, this was the way in which my father and mother saw things. Just entering their forties and full of energy, they looked forward eagerly to the move to a bigger city and chapel. The salary was still a modest one, but brought with it a solidly built terrace house less than a mile from the chapel up a steep hill which had to be climbed after every event. The central site of the chapel was an advantage, but none of the congregation lived as close as their minister and had to make considerable journeys by bus – which fortunately ran on Sundays as well as weekdays.

My mother was as much in the centre of things in Bradford as she had been in Leigh. A born organizer, she had the gift of persuading others to work with her. She found speakers for the Women's League, levied contributions to pay for flowers on the altar, would put on a supper after a special event – all the traditional chores of a parson's wife, including (heaviest of all) the sick-visiting which took her by trolley bus and on foot from one end to the other of a widely spaced-out city. If this book concentrates on my father's ideas and teaching, he would have been the first to recognize that it was my mother's readiness to take on these practical duties, as well as running a home, which made it possible for him to devote so much of his time to reading, writing and delivering so many lectures as well as sermons. No minister ever had a more devoted wife – as much loved by the congregation as he was himself. And, I must add, no son ever had a more devoted mother.

One thing they both missed was a proper garden, but my mother found expression for her own gifts in the arts of embroidery and flower arrangement. Give her a good novel and she was lost to the world, the supper things left on the table and the fire allowed to go out long after Frank had gone to bed, so long as she could finish the story. Her other passion was children. She was no sentimentalist, but she never tired of watching them, and no child ever appealed to her in vain. I am sure the happiest time of her life was when my wife and I presented her with no fewer than five grandchildren, for whom their grandparents became real people.

*

In Leigh, everyone who was at all active had known everyone else; in the much bigger city of Bradford this was no longer true. Frank made no attempt to enter local politics and, besides the chapel where he preached and Channing Hall, where he lectured, his only other platform was the evening institutes run by the city's Education Committee, at which he lectured on literature.

Two initiatives which he made immediately were, first, to secure a place for me in Bradford Grammar School – one of the best of the direct-grant schools, with a good record in winning scholarships to Oxford and Cambridge – and, second, to introduce himself to the Bradford Library and Literary Society, founded by his eighteenth-century predecessor, the Reverend John Dean, of which he was automatically made a shareholder. The Literary Society no longer met, but the Library provided him with access to a fine collection of books, and in due course he became chairman of its book selection committee. Across the street the city's Central Library and the manager of the city's only bookshop were equally helpful in finding books for him, and in due course he was invited to join the selection committee of the city's art gallery.

It was not until after the Second World War that television introduced the age of the media. The 1930s and 1940s, however, were great years for the cinema, and my father saw many of its classic films. He also enjoyed listening to the radio for its comments and talks, especially when the BBC Third Programme started. All these, together with the *Times Literary Supplement* and the *Observer*, helped him to keep abreast of changes in opinion and intellectual fashion.

An invitation to become a member of the Bradford Athenaeum Club brought him into contact with a group of interesting and able men. Founded in 1883 to read and discuss papers on literary, scientific and philosophical subjects, and limited to twenty-four members, it celebrated its five-hundredth meeting in 1939. On this occasion a paper was read by the Reverend Monsignor O'Connor, a Catholic priest who had received G. K. Chesterton into the Catholic Church and was the model for Father Brown, the hero of Chesterton's detective stories. Other members included, over time, doctors, lawyers, parsons, scientists and academics from Leeds and later Bradford universities. Frank's membership helped to break down his isolation and lasted from 1940 to 1957, during which time he gave seven papers and was elected as president for the year 1947–8.

In Leigh, Frank had been a member of an interdenominational fraternity, but in Bradford he had little contact with other religious bodies, who were still liable to consider Unitarians as not Christians at all. The exception was the Jewish community, with whom both my father and my mother came to have a warm relationship. There were some twenty other Unitarian churches in Yorkshire, and their ministers met regularly at Mill Hill Chapel in the centre of Leeds, of which Joseph Priestley had at one time been minister. Frank enjoyed this contact with colleagues and became secretary of the Yorkshire Unitarian Union.

In time he came to discover some of the finest open country in England, the Yorkshire dales and moors. From Bradford an hour's bus ride carried one to Haworth, Ilkley, Skipton. Later, when friends took him by car, he explored Wharfedale and stayed at Kettlewell. This was a great refreshment to the spirit – something he had missed in Lancashire.

This was the time and place. With the move to Bradford in 1926 Frank had completed his apprenticeship. The rest of this book explores what he made of it in the thirty-seven years that followed.

PART II

THE GOSPELS

6

The Role of Jesus

I

Frank's starting point in his sermons was the dissatisfaction felt by so many people: 'The sense of incompleteness in humanity', he wrote, 'is the most telling argument for the reality of God.' For most people who experienced it, this produced disillusionment and depression. But Frank urged them:

Do not turn aside from the waste land, the wilderness, the valley of humiliation. You must cross it, or you will never win peace. Both Buddha and Christ passed through this condition; in the latter case it was called the Temptation in the Wilderness.

The greatest enemy of the soul is false comfort, and flattering hopes. You must endure, realizing that such endurance prepares the soul for a new quality of life, the condition of non-attachment and of selflessness.

Once you have broken out of your preoccupation with self, do not attempt to scale the mountain peaks represented by Buddha and Christ, but turn instead to the high hills of mental and emotional joy that rise above the waste land of the common consciousness and lie within our immediate compass.

These are available to all of us, beginning with the possibility of a new consciousness of nature as this has been revealed to us, for example, by Wordsworth. The beauty of nature and the mysterious process of the seasons are matched by the creations of human genius in literature, art, music and thought, and by the sheer wonder of personality.

Frank distinguished between three levels of truth, or, as he sometimes put it, of ascending consciousness. The first comes to us through the senses; the second through the soul; the third through the spirit, in which the personal and particular give way to the universal.

It was in the senses that the ascent of man began.

The first great religious fact that ever happened to any of us is that we were born and given the mystery of a physical body by which we can hold relationship with the earth and the skies. This started in the earliest stages of evolution, with the ability to touch, taste and smell, all of which, however, bound man closely to his environment.

The first of the great liberations came when life developed the organ of vision, the eye: 'And God said, Let there be light: and there was light' (Genesis 1:3), enabling men and women to look out into the mystery and beauty of the physical world instead of being merely self-regarding. The second and even greater deliverance was when man acquired the ability to hear, and with it the power of speech, the unique gift which distinguishes us from the rest of creation.

If your religion has ever led you to condemn the senses or shut your eyes to the works of the whole great cycle of physical and sensual experience, then you should pray with all your heart to be liberated from so false and damaging a view. The pathway to the eternal begins in the life of the senses.

The instrument of the body, however, wonderful as it is, would be of no value to man's further growth if there were not behind and within it, reaching out beyond it, the even more mysterious life of the soul or psyche. The soul was the focus of all Frank's thinking. 'Have you ever thought', he asked, 'that the soul enables you to interiorize the world of which you are a part, and that your power over the outer world lies in the quality and energy of this inner world of the soul?' In a tradition which goes back to the Greeks, however, he made no attempt to give 'the soul' a precise definition. The Greeks used '*psyche*' to mean soul, spirit or mind, without distinguishing between them, and Frank did the same. Where he found it more appropriate he used 'consciousness' or 'mind'.

The creative energies of the soul are capable of lifting the senses' experience of the world – the world of nature, the world of the arts, the world of history – to the level of those high hills of which Frank spoke earlier. It is the soul which brings these to life and gives them meaning. And it can do more than that. For those who commit themselves and persist, the soul can open the way to the Kingdom of the Spirit, the hidden treasure of a higher consciousness, represented by the mountain peaks of a Christ or a Buddha.

What, then, holds it back? Unlike the physical body, which is born into the world complete, the soul's birth, the achievement of self-consciousness, is difficult, painful and in most cases incomplete. The soul has unlimited possibilities, but there is nothing automatic about their realization.

In its primitive condition the life of the soul remains dark and subterranean until the consciousness of thought arises. The power to think is the light of the soul, the organ of vision whereby it passes from darkness into light.

Birth means a severance from the mother-life in which we were born. The crisis comes when we have to turn away from that spiritually as well as physically and live our own lives from our own centres of consciousness. A great many people never succeed in doing this; all their lives they want security – physical, mental or emotional security – craving a return to the mother image – Mother Earth, Mother Nature, Mother Church. 'The mystery in us is the mystery of divine sonship, the manifestation of a divine life, but as long as we are dependent on the mother image, that life is hidden and frustrated.'

II

Frank saw the world of the 1930s as suffering from an uneasy sense of insecurity, a lack of creativity, a degraded emotional life and widespread scepticism in relation to things of the spirit. Self-consciousness, instead of awakening the soul, had hardened into a self-regarding egoism around which had grown up not only fears and anxieties but pride, ambition and aggression – all emotions which stiffen resistance to the liberation of the soul. This morbid condition could be overcome only by a rebirth of the soul, which would break away from the false self and create a new centre of self-consciousness.

The radical element in my father's thought is best presented in his own words, taken from the two sermons – 'What Shall We Do?' and 'What Do We Know?' – which he preached in October 1938, at the time of the Munich crisis and the prospect of war.

In answer to the first question, 'What Shall We Do?', he urged the need to recognize that the powers of darkness and light, war and peace, destruction and creation are all within the human soul. 'Any appeal to a supposed God outside of ourselves to achieve our deliverance is only self-deception and an escape from our own spiritual responsibility, the recognition that the divine life and power is within ourselves.'

Frank's answer to the second question, 'What Do We Know?', was to quote Paul's challenge in his First Epistle to the Corinthians (3:16): 'Know ye not that ye are a temple of God and that the Spirit of God dwelleth in you?'

But you may say, What then becomes of revelation? Revelation remains what it has always been: an emanation of vision, knowledge and spiritual reality within the mind of man. You can never get beyond that, try as you will. Revelation is an unfolding and unveiling *within the mind of man*, and that revelation includes the knowledge of evil and darkness to a hellish intensity, as well as the knowledge of divinity to the level of the Christ conscious-ness and the Kingdom of Heaven. It is all there in the human mind.

'No man hath seen God at any time' (John 1:18). If man builds a temple, it is his mind that fills it with holiness. If he has found nature in the universe to be the temple of 'the living God', it is his mind that has given form, voice, vision and significance to all the mighty symbols of that temple. Obliterate the mind of man, then all temples are empty, the universe stark and barren. The mind that creates the universe speaks only in the mind of man. Explore its furthest reaches, you will find no God to speak or direct seekers other than in the temple of the mind of man in which that presence can reveal itself.

At first sight it seems to be asking too much of humanity, too great a loss, to surrender the God of theology. But think what God has done within humanity. Think of all the divine creativity which man has revealed, always from the sources of the divine within himself. When we really know this, why do we fear to trust?

The key to understanding this deeply held belief was Frank's view of Jesus. Among those belonging to the mystical tradition with whom he felt a special sympathy were Buddha, St Paul, the author of the Fourth Gospel, Plotinus, Jakob Böhme, William Law, the eighteenth-century mystic who wrote *A Serious Call to a Devout and Holy Life*, and William Blake. But anyone who reads Frank's sermons and lectures cannot fail to be impressed by the unique place which Jesus as a human personality, as well as his teaching, held in both his thinking and his affections.

The primary source for our knowledge of Jesus is the four Gospels, believed to have been written between *c.* AD 70 and the end of the first century. The Gospels undoubtedly have a basis of historical truth, but Frank believed that it was important to recognize that there are other levels of truth – mythological, psychological, imaginative, for instance – a combination of which, together with the historical, gives the Gospels their unique character. Although the other elements take up much the larger part of the Gospels (particularly the Fourth Gospel), without the element of historical truth the Gospels would have made much less impression. With it, they produced the most surprising of all historical facts: the capture of the Roman Empire, and eventually of Europe and the Americas, by a religion founded upon the teaching of a carpenter's son in an out-of-the-way province of the Middle East.

While Frank regarded the Nativity as one of the most beautiful and profound of all myths, he did not take it literally but believed that Jesus was a man, born like other men. He had no doubt about Jesus' historical existence. While it has proved impossible to fix precisely the date of his birth, Roman and Jewish evidence establish independently that a Jewish religious teacher of the name of Jesus was active in Judaea under the Roman Empire and was put to death in Jerusalem during the reign of the Emperor Tiberius (AD 14–37) and under Pontius Pilate's governorship of Judaea (AD 26–36). The best estimate of the date of his birth appears to be c. 7–6 BC, and of his baptism by John the Baptist AD 27 or 28. The death of John – another identifiable historical figure, beheaded by Herod, the tetrarch of Galilee, in AD 28 – is followed by Jesus' death by crucifixion in AD 29 or 30 when he was in his middle thirties.

Like the author of the earliest Gospel, Mark, Frank believed we know nothing of Jesus' life before his baptism by John the Baptist. This appears to have been the decisive event of his life, which led to a sense of mission taking possession of him and, following the arrest of John the Baptist, to the start of a ministry as a wandering preacher which lasted for around two years. Frank believed that the Gospels' account of Jesus' ministry contained many later additions (for example, the miracles) and that it was impossible to be certain how far, when quoting Jesus, they give us his own words.

Overall, however, taking what Jesus said as a whole and not relying upon the wording of particular passages, my father believed it was possible to establish the character of his teaching.

III

Jesus quickly showed his ability to draw large crowds to hear him. He taught not only in the synagogues but in the open air, on the shore of the lake or on the roadside, speaking with a freedom and directness very different from traditional religious preaching. He took his examples not from the Hebrew scriptures but from everyday life, conveying the reality of God in an immediate way and using language and parables which everyone could understand. The authority with which he spoke and which astonished his listeners he drew not from Scripture or the Law but from within himself.

His message was clear. He addressed himself not to the pious, the respectable or the powerful, but to ordinary people, including the suffering, the sick, the poor and the outcasts:

Blessed are those who know their need of God . . . the sorrowful . . . those of a gentle spirit . . . those who hunger and thirst to see right prevail . . . those who show mercy . . . whose hearts are pure . . . the peacemakers . . . those who have suffered persecution for the cause of right; the Kingdom of Heaven is theirs.*

After two thousand years, we have lost the sense of novelty with which Jesus' teaching must have struck his listeners; this was a new voice in the ancient world.

Frank summed up:

While Jesus showed his realism by accepting the world as it was and had no illusions about it, he insisted that it had to be transcended. Men could not reconcile the Kingdom of God with life and the world as they were. The choice he offered was a stark one. Men and women must change their outlook, at all costs – even of family and friends, wealth, position, even of life itself – if they were to develop the spiritual powers within them and be saved.

This was no 'Jesus meek and mild'. He proclaimed 'God is love', but showed no trace of the sentimentality with which his image has since been smothered. A seer and a wanderer, he appears to have been obedient to deep moods and impulses of the spirit. Gentle with the sick and outcasts, he was also given to sudden harsh demands, could show impatience, and had no room for self-pity. Unaffected by mass emotion, he was given to solitary communing. Promising divine forgiveness, at the same time he demanded human forgiveness. Yet there is also a strange element of ecstasy and joy in his preaching, which led his followers later to speak of it in terms of a wedding feast. Scornful of conventional religious observance,

---

* The Sermon on the Mount, Matthew 5:3–10: 'Blessed are the poor in spirit . . . they that mourn . . . the meek . . . they that hunger and thirst after righteousness . . . the merciful . . . the pure in heart . . . the peacemakers . . . they that have been persecuted for righteousness' sake: for theirs is the kingdom of heaven.'

he believed in demons and cast them out. Believing emphatically in the power of the Kingdom of Darkness, of Satan, he believed also in the greater power of the Kingdom of God.

But what did Jesus mean by the Kingdom of God? Sometimes he spoke of the Son of Man coming in his glory and all the angels with him, to judge the nations. At other times he compared the Kingdom to a mustard seed which grows into a tree big enough for birds to roost among its branches; to a treasure lying buried in a field; to a pearl of great value; to a net let down into the sea; to the wise virgins who kept their lamps trimmed and full of oil.

The expectation of the Kingdom of God was widespread among Jews and, by many, was equated with the national hope of a Messiah of the line of King David who would liberate Israel, God's chosen people, from foreign rule. Although fomenting insurrection was the charge against Jesus when he was brought before the Roman governor, Pilate, there is no evidence that he ever thought of the Kingdom in such political terms. In his mind it was an apocalyptic event suddenly breaking into the present world order from the outside and changing it out of recognition.

But when the Pharisees asked him when the Kingdom of God would come he replied, 'The kingdom of God cometh not with observation. Neither shall they say, Lo, here! or lo there! for, behold, the kingdom of God is within you' (Luke 17:20–21).

It was to the impossibility of defining the Kingdom of God that Frank returned as the heart of the mystery, quoting Jesus' teaching recorded by the author of the Fourth Gospel: 'Verily, verily, I say unto thee, Except a man be born again, he cannot see the kingdom of God' (John 3:3).

There was a marked difference between the earlier and the later parts of Jesus' ministry. The opposition to him had become stronger and his challenge to it sharper. At some point he reached the conclusion that he must leave Galilee and bring his mission to a head by going up to Jerusalem, proclaiming the coming Kingdom and confronting the Jewish religious establishment in the Temple.

He appears to have accepted that it might cost him his life, and prepared himself accordingly.

When he came to Jerusalem, large crowds greeted him. Although there is nothing to show that Jesus encouraged their expectations, many are reported to have saluted him as the long-awaited Jewish Messiah who could end the Roman occupation and restore the Kingdom of David. From here on we have no independent historical evidence beyond the bare fact of Jesus' death by crucifixion. We cannot be sure what was in Jesus' mind when he put his faith to the final test of facing death. Did he believe that in the last desperate moment, if he held firm, God would intervene and the Kingdom come? Is this the meaning of the reported cry 'My God, my God, why hast thou forsaken me?' (Matthew 27:46)? We have no answer; we can speculate, but we can provide no proof nor build on it.

There is no need to repeat the accounts of the Passion and Crucifixion provided, with different emphases and details, in all four Gospels. We shall come back to what Frank thought these may have meant. What is certain is the outcome. The first reaction of the disciples must have been one of despair at seeing their beloved Master hanging dead from the Cross, with no sign of the divine intervention on which they (and perhaps Jesus himself) had counted. Yet within a short time (the Acts of the Apostles says forty days) this shattered and disillusioned little community was transformed by the conviction that Jesus had ascended into heaven, and became charged with such energy that it proceeded to carry the gospel of the Risen Christ throughout the Mediterranean world. One can argue about the nature of the experience (the appearance of Jesus to the disciples after his death) which led to this transformation; but no one can question the historical fact of its impact upon the subsequent history of the world.

7

Myths and Mysticism

The major part of the New Testament is taken up with the four Gospels, the earliest of which is the Gospel According to St Mark. But Paul had played his role a generation earlier. Born in Tarsus, a cosmopolitan city on the main east–west trade route, he was brought up as a devout Jew, trained as a rabbi in the Law, and was known as a zealous persecutor of Christians. After the vision on the road to Damascus, however, he felt himself called to become the Apostle of Christ to the Gentiles, breaking down the barrier of prejudice which the Law had erected between Jews and their neighbours. Jesus had seen himself as the heir of the Old Testament prophets and had addressed his ministry to the Jewish people. Paul's widening of his message to include the Gentiles (whom he addressed in Greek, the common language of the Hellenistic world) had a profound effect on the future of Christianity, proclaiming a promise of salvation open to all men and women who accepted belief in the mystery of the Risen Christ, whatever their origins.

The year AD 33 is the best estimate for Paul's conversion, and AD 35 for the start of his missionary activities. He was put to death in Rome in c. AD 62–4, thus filling the gap between the death of Jesus c. AD 29–30 and Mark's Gospel, written c. AD 70. It was at this point, after Jesus' death and as a result of the efforts of Paul and his fellow Apostles, that Christian communities began to organize themselves in the cities of the Roman Empire: Antioch, Corinth, Thessalonica, Ephesus and Rome itself. They were known by the Greek word 'ekklesia', meaning 'assembly' or 'church'. There was no church building in the modern sense, however; in

Rome, for example, they met in the underground catacombs, and they were not open to everybody.

As we know from Paul's letters, there was considerable variety in the rites and creeds of the different Churches. They also shared a number of features in common with the mystery religions dedicated to Dionysus, Demeter and Orpheus, to Isis and Osiris, and to the Persian god Mithras. These became widespread under the Roman Empire and, like the Christians, often included a period of preparation before an initiation, periods of fasting, a sacramental meal, baptism, vigils and the acting out of a sacred drama. In its early stages Christianity was regarded as another such mystery religion. The chief differences were that the Christian communities admitted women as well as men, did not require costly expenditure and so were more accessible, and revealed not a form of secret knowledge (*gnosis*), but a way of life summed up in the Greek word '*agape*', meaning 'brotherly love'.

Jerusalem, the original centre of Christianity, was destroyed by the Romans in AD 70, and the other important centres felt the need to produce Gospels for their own use at a time when Christian belief was expanding throughout the Mediterranean world and naturally developing in the process. With the earliest Gospel, Mark's, dated to *c.* AD 70, and the latest, John's, to the last decade of the first century, or possibly the first decade of the second century, their separate origins account for the differences and inconsistencies between them.

The Gospels were designed not to serve as historical documents, but to expound a 'gospel' (from the Old English version, 'godspel', of the Greek original meaning 'good news'). They were used to instruct and guide the spiritual life of Church members, in preparation for their initiation into the secret, as Paul put it, of 'Christ in you, the hope of a glory to come' (Colossians 1:27).

It was during this same period that the meagre account of Jesus' life and death was elaborated. (Frank noted that exactly the same process of elaboration had taken place in the case of Buddha.) Like Paul, whose whole life was changed by the vision he encountered on the Damascus road, the leaders of the Christian communities felt themselves to be in touch with the Risen Master, spoke in tongues, saw visions, and received illumination by the Spirit. All these elements as well as traditions passed on by the disciples were incorporated into their worship and into the Gospels.

Equally important was the shift of emphasis from the life and teaching of Jesus to his death and resurrection. In his letters Paul shows little interest in the historical Jesus of Nazareth or in what he taught. He regarded Jesus not so much as a person in the past but as a living presence, the Risen Christ, who had converted him by appearing and speaking to him directly in a vision, as he had to others. Paul, of course, like the other disciples, believed that Jesus not only had risen from the dead but would soon appear again in majesty and power to inaugurate the Kingdom of God. It was this belief which enabled him, as my father put it, 'to transform the Cross, that sign of death and defeat, into the great word of hope and light'.

But, as the years passed and belief in the imminent return of Christ faded, something else came to take its place.

The fundamental fact that Paul grasped [Frank said], put into the language of our own time, was that God comes into life by means of the human soul. The power, the life, the illumination are all from within, never from without. This young man, dying on the Cross, represents the divine life within the human soul. A potentiality within the souls of all men and women, its light shines within the darkness, and the darkness never overcomes it. 'Christ in you'.

True to his Unitarian beliefs, my father added that this argument is, however, valid only if we accept the man on the Cross as disclosing the mystery of our own humanity. If he was – and is – different not in the degree of his humanity but in kind from you and me, then for us there is no intelligible word from the Cross. If this was a sham humanity, which was really Godhead and Godhood, then there is no relation between his experience and ours, between the power of his triumph and the promise of ours:

But if the divine power is hidden in our humanity, then indeed the word of the Cross is the word of hope and power, of reconciliation and love for us too, the great pledge and promise, 'Because I live, ye shall live also' (John 14:19).

II

In the ancient world, which Frank described as 'picture-conscious', mythological images and fables were used to represent things which we express in abstract form. An example is the myth describing the beginning of the world in Genesis. Every other early civilization has an equivalent myth, but modern man has replaced these by the concept of 'creation'. In the New Testament, Frank believed, this picture-consciousness applied not only to the Kingdom of God, but also to the Virgin Birth and the Nativity; the Temptation in the Wilderness; the miracles, especially the feeding of the five thousand; the mystery of the Passion (not the fact of Jesus' crucifixion, which is a historical fact, but the significance of it); the Resurrection in the flesh. None of these is to be taken literally as history; what we have to learn to do is to penetrate into their mythological and mystical meaning.

We can learn a great deal if we follow the scholars who have investigated the sources on which the Gospels have drawn. One obvious source is the Old Testament, in which Jesus, St Paul and the authors of the Gospels were all steeped. A second one is the Babylonian, Egyptian, Persian and Greek myths and legends. Israel not only had gone into captivity in Babylon, but even earlier had come into contact with Babylonian myths and culture when the Jews migrated into Canaan.

In the nineteenth-century heyday of positivism, myth came to be equated with fiction or fable; in the twentieth century, however, in the writings of Jung and Mircea Eliade, for example, it has recovered its original meaning of truth expressed in the form of a story, a picture or a symbol. My father described myths as

the imaging out of ideas and beliefs which appear in modern thought in an abstract form but still have power to affect men and women's lives as archetypal patterns in the depths of the unconscious. The literal fact has its place, but its essential value is the effect it has on the mind and imagination. The dry bones of reality are brought to life by the image; 'the letter killeth, but the spirit giveth life' (2 Corinthians 3:6).

The result, in the case of the Gospels, is astonishing: an amalgam of history, myth and mystical vision, produced by unknown authors, which has continued, as no other story has, to speak to the souls of countless millions for two thousand years and has inspired the greatest artists and musicians – think only of Tintoretto's *Crucifixion* or of Bach's *St Matthew Passion*.

But how are we to interpret the Gospels today?

Frank distinguished between four different ways of interpretation. The first, the literal, he found impossible to accept. The second, the scholarly, he regarded as indispensable, but too limited by itself. The third, the ethical, he believed misleading, if taken in isolation, because 'nobody can or ever will practise Jesus' ethics on the basis of common sense, but only after a spiritual rebirth comparable with that which Jesus himself underwent'. This left a fourth, a spiritual interpretation developed by the mystics. Frank never called himself a mystic; that would have seemed to him presumptuous. Suffice it to say that he was a student of mysticism and a believer in what the mystics had to say. From the author of the Fourth Gospel to Plotinus, Jakob Böhme and William Blake, those were his masters, and they played a great part in shaping his life and thought.

Mysticism, however, like myth, with which it is closely connected, has acquired a bad name. It is often confused with magic, with occultism or with spiritualism, with all of which my father had some acquaintance, but which he never regarded as mysticism. In the popular mind it is identified with vague, emotional, irrational beliefs which cannot be proved and which no sane man would take seriously. Frank himself defined it as the claim that human beings can come to a conscious union with God through spiritual discipline. This belief and the practices associated with it have appeared in every religion: in Hinduism, Buddhism and Taoism; in Neoplatonism, in Judaism and in Islamic Sufism; in all the Christian Churches – Roman Catholic, Greek Orthodox and Protestant – and in the nature-mysticism of poets such as Wordsworth. Poetry in fact, which also frequently seeks to 'say the unsayable', provides the closest parallel.

The personal experience of union with God, which, however momentary, is the heart of the mystics' belief, cannot be communicated except by image and analogy, and is not susceptible of proof. It can, however, produce permanent and dramatic changes in attitude and action, as in the case of St Paul, St Augustine, St Francis and St Ignatius Loyola.

Why the mystery, however? Why the initiation? You may think that if something cannot be said straight out, there cannot be much good in it. Well, you *can* tell all about the mysteries if you want to, but you won't do much good because nobody will understand you. It would not, for example, do much good to go and listen to a professor of physics unless you had been initiated into the study of physics first. The mystics say the same of the subject they study: that there are certain great truths which can only be grasped when there has been a certain degree of spiritual growth. All that can be done is to prepare you, leaving the initiation to take place in your own consciousness.

If you are coming to these things for the first time, don't be enthusiastic – listen. Rudolph Steiner used to say, 'You hear these things, and if they cast the shadow of truth in your minds, they will grow; if they don't, they will wither away and you won't be bothered with them at all.'

The unity of mystical experience has been well described by E. G. Browne:

In all ages, in all countries, in all creeds, whether it comes from the Brahmin sage, the Persian poet or the Christian quietist, it is in essence an enunciation more or less clear, more or less eloquent, of the aspiration of the soul to cease altogether from self and to be at one with God.*

* John Ferguson, *An Illustrated Encyclopaedia of Mysticism and the Mystery Religions* (Thames and Hudson, London, 1976), pp. 126–7.

This has set a problem for orthodox Christians who cling to the uniqueness of Christianity, which they see as compromised by sharing the mystical experience with other religions. To Frank, however, the fact that it appeared in all religions confirmed its truth.

What *was* unique in Christian mysticism, he pointed out, was that it gave a historical context for what had hitherto been expressed only in myth. Christianity, for example, took the myths of redemption found in Egyptian and Greek mystery religions (worshipping Osiris, or Dionysus) and in the centre placed the very definite historical figure of Jesus.

First of all you get the myth expressed in the Nativity story. The first Gospel (Matthew) is linked to the Egyptian myth; the fourth (John) to the Greek. These mystery elements are repeated in the crises which follow in the life of Jesus – Baptism, Temptation, Transfiguration, Passion, Death, Resurrection and Ascension. This was no ordinary life story; obviously there is something more than historical elements.

Well, the real doctrine taught by the Fourth Gospel, by the Mark Gospel and by Paul – was what? That the Christ was born in Bethlehem? Certainly not. But that there was a historical person, Jesus, who was born in Bethlehem of ordinary parents in the ordinary way. Then at a given stage in his development, at the baptism in the Jordan, Christ, the Christ consciousness, enters into Jesus, taking possession, for two years, of his body and personality as a vehicle through which to manifest itself – or, as the Fourth Gospel says, 'The Word was made flesh, and dwelt among us' (John 1:14). Then, at the end, the personality of Jesus is assumed back into the universal spirit, and reunited with that divine life which was with the Father 'before the world began' (John 17:5).

This is not merely the story of an individual, but – as the mystics have always known – the story of humanity, just as the Cross is the symbol of the universe upon which the spiritual powers of humanity are fastened, until they too are manifested in a resurrection.

8

The Promise

I

Frank saw his role as like that of the early Christian communities, introducing his listeners to reading and pondering the Gospels in such a way as to uncover for themselves the hidden message which they conveyed. This message is something no one can be taught directly; we can only be awakened to it through a faculty already existing within us if we are ready to learn how to use it. The extra dimension to which this gives access includes things unseen as well as seen, and access is achieved through images which are not to be translated into literal language or treated as no more than the symbolic expression of some trite moral teaching.

The difficulty we have to overcome, Frank pointed out, is that modern readers of the Gospels are preoccupied with the question 'Did this really happen?', whereas their original readers and those who follow the mystical tradition ask, 'How can we discover its meaning?'

As an example he took the account of the Nativity in the Gospels, and in a series of Advent meditations on Sunday mornings in December 1935 he sought to recover its original meaning. He called the first meditation 'The Promise', and took as his text Peter's remark 'Where is the promise of his coming? for since the fathers fell asleep, all things continue as they were from the beginning of the creation' (2 Peter 3:4).

If we could penetrate into that ancient world from which our scriptures have emerged, we should find – in India, in Persia, in Babylon and Egypt, Greece and Rome, and in Palestine – there were always rumours of gods and saviours who would come forth from the unseen realms of reality and bring to men and women light and joy and deliverance. We should find that the last rays of this light focus around the figure of Jesus, concerning whom men felt that there had already been an advent of divine power and wisdom . . .

Then, from the heart of this epoch of hope there comes Peter's utterance of disappointment, 'Where is the promise of his coming?' Gradually, from this point onward, the Advent hope falls into a more or less rigid, conventionalized form, never quite forgotten, yet never quite real to the faith and hopes of men and women, until today the vast majority treat the whole subject as one of beautiful but pathetic illusion, and 'all things continue as they were from the beginning'.

It is a vital part of my belief that the faith and hope of the ages is always nearer the truth than the disappointments and scepticism of men, that no great light ever shines in human history but it brings authentic tidings of spiritual reality. The presence of a great light always casts shadows, and men are more ready to grasp at the shadows than to understand the light. Yet, when we read the ancient scriptures, can we deny that there is in them a light of consciousness? All things have *not* remained the same from the beginning; again and again, at different places and at different points in history, we can see the light of a new consciousness emerge in the darkness. The light of Krishna emerged in India, the light of the prophets in Israel, the light of the Orphic mysteries in Greece, of Mithras in Persia and Rome, and of Christ in Palestine. And the emergence of light is a fact of history, just as much as the wars and the empires, the cruelties and wrongs.

Where did this light come from? Always from within the souls of men and women. We cannot always find the light-bearers, but we know something about the light of Orpheus in Greece, about the prophets in Israel, of Jesus and the light of Christhood, and later of the same light in the soul of Paul.

It would seem then that the light of the Divine Word is always shining and, when the soul is ready to receive it, shines forth in new creative power. This radiance in history is only a reflection of a divine reality hidden as yet from our eyes, but the Advent promise is not an empty promise.

In his second Advent meditation, my father focused on the mother. He pointed out that there was in Mary the same duality as in the case of Jesus the Christ. The human mother, Mary the wife of

Joseph, mother of other children besides Jesus, cannot understand the impulse which sends her son forth on the paths of spiritual adventure. We know very little about her; she is lost in the shadow of the greater mother who gave birth to the Christ in Jesus. Who is *she*?

She appears under many names and forms, even in our scriptures, beginning with Eve in the myth of Genesis, the mother of all things living. Originally she was just the mother earth. In Egypt she appears as Isis; elsewhere she is Our Immaculate Lady, Star of the Sea, Queen of Heaven, Mother of God. In India she is known as Devaki, the mother of Krishna; in Babylon as Ishtar, with stars on her head and her child Tammuz on her knee, or again as the Woman Clothed with the Sun, with the moon under her feet and the stars on her head. In the Zodiac, she is the sign Virgo, in which the sun rose on 25 December; in Luke's Gospel she is Mary, the soul in a state of submission, saying, 'Be it unto me according to thy word' (Luke 1:38). Finally she is the great goddess of the Roman Catholic Church, Mary, Mother of God and friend of sinners.

In none of these images does she really come close to our understanding. Her real secret perished with the ancient Gnostics, because the Church was afraid of the real truth about her. The original Trinity was that natural trinity of Father, Mother, Son. The Mother was the Holy Spirit: the Holy Spirit that brooded as a mother above the waters of Chaos; the Holy Spirit that, in the form of the goddess symbol of the Dove, rested upon Jesus – 'Thou art my Son, this day have I begotten thee' (Acts 13:33).

Frank's third meditation was devoted to the Magi who came from the East. The Magi were in fact a widespread priestly caste who gained a great ascendancy in the Persian Empire and were profoundly influenced by the teaching of Zoroaster, who lived from *c.* 630 to *c.* 533 BC. This ancient faith still survives among the Parsees in India.

The first thing we may notice is the close similarity between the lives of Zoroaster and Jesus. The description 'born of a virgin, saved in infancy from a jealous and powerful foe, confounded wise men by his youthful wisdom, began to preach around the age of thirty after a vision of the open heavens by a sacred river, was tempted by the Devil in the wilderness, cast out demons, cured the blind, and worked miracles, taught that there was one supreme God of truth, light and goodness who would at last establish his kingdom upon earth' – such a description would equally fit both men, at least according to the New Testament in one case, according to the teacher Zend Aveta in the other. The Christian doctrine of Resurrection in a Last Judgement, the Christian images of angels and paradise, to say nothing of the sombre and dramatic image of Satan and a Kingdom of Darkness, are all derived from Zoroastrian sources. These were in a very real way the gifts which the Magi brought to the birth of Christianity, and he is surely the true Christian who knows and rejoices in the inclusiveness of the Christian vision, drawing into himself the power and glory of other myths, rather than he who finds a cause for false pride and security in his alleged exclusiveness.

The cave in which Jesus was born was the subject of Frank's fourth meditation, and forms another link between the Advent legend and other, older, myths. Sir James Frazer's book *The Golden Bough** provided my father with many of his examples, including that

The nativity of the Sun on 25 December is celebrated in Syria and Egypt by the celebrants retiring into an inner cave, from which at midnight they come forth with a loud cry: 'The Virgin has brought forth! The light is born!' In Egypt they even represented the newborn sun by the image of an infant which they exhibited to the worshippers. In the myth of Mithra, the Persian and Roman sun-god, the scene of the sun's nativity is a rocky cavern and the first mortals to adore the infant god are shepherds.

In the Christian mystery of the birth of Christ and of his rebirth from death, both take place in a cave, and the language of the birth legends makes use of images of darkness and light.

The people that walked in darkness have seen a great light . . . (Isaiah 9:2)

---

* *The Golden Bough: A Study in Magic and Religion*, published in 2 volumes by Macmillan, London, in 1890, enlarged to 12 volumes in 1915.

> Through the tender mercy of our God; whereby the dayspring from
> on high hath visited us, To give light to them that sit in darkness and
> in the shadow of death . . . (Luke 1:78–9)

These are no longer ancient dreams but signs and symbols that speak to
our own condition, so that at times even our own inner life seems to be a
cavern of darkness, the abode of wild beasts. And yet the ancient mystery
is true that here in the very heart of the darkness the light is born.

In his final meditation, 'The Birth of Christ', my father summed
up in the 1930s the significance he saw in the Advent story. For
thousands of years, in many lands, men and women have celebrated
the birth of Christ; they have not always called him by that name,
but they have believed passionately in the advent of a divine
humanity which would fulfil the mystery of human suffering,
sorrow and endeavour:

Many generations of men and women have come and gone, and many of
the things they fought for have perished without trace. But the apparently
insubstantial hopes of men and women do not pass but abide when empires
and civilizations have crumbled into dust. Strange though it may appear,
it is a fact that men and women can never give up the faith that this world
is still the centre of infinite possibilities. In face of all the centuries of human
experience, which the cynic summarizes in the phrase 'They were born,
they suffered, they died', that experience has never succeeded in destroying
the faith in the soul of humanity that a divine power works within and
beyond life – a faith of which our own scriptures are only one example.

The divine birth which we celebrate reveals not only the glory
of the Lord but also the glory of humanity – a glory of which
humanity is normally utterly unconscious, but to which, through
light and darkness, hope and fear, it is always giving of its spiritual
substance.

Finally, there is the suggestion that there is a stage in the development of
the individual when he or she passes beyond the unconscious service of an
unknown and unseen purpose and becomes, as Jesus did, aware of the

divine life within his own soul. He or she realizes that their own lives are caught up in the sweep and tide of a divine purpose. They receive the intimation of destiny and immortality, of a power and a life working within their own consciousness – in a word, of 'Christ in you, the hope of glory' (Colossians 1:27).

II

As another example of a hidden meaning, my father took the historical figure of John the Baptist – the first prophet to appear in Israel for three centuries – and asked, 'Why did he go out into the wilderness?'

The wilderness always represents a going out into loneliness – a breaking away from the common consciousness. John, standing on the verge of this new consciousness but not partaking of it, goes into the wilderness, where his task is to 'prepare . . . the way of the Lord' and to 'make his paths straight' (Matthew 3:3; compare Isaiah 40:3: 'The voice of him that crieth in the wilderness, Prepare ye the way of the Lord, make straight in the desert a highway for our God').

John's message was, Change your outlook; don't cling any longer to the petrified religion of the Law. Already the axe is laid to the roots of the trees; and every tree that fails to produce good fruit is cut down and thrown on the fire.

The word 'tree' in the Scriptures always means consciousness – for example the tree of the knowledge of good and evil. Let me read a passage from the prophetic Book of Daniel in the Old Testament: 'I saw, and behold a tree in the midst of the earth . . . The tree grew, and was strong, and the height thereof reached unto heaven, and the sight thereof to the end of all the earth. The leaves thereof were fair . . . and all flesh was fed of it . . . and behold, a watcher and an holy one came down from heaven . . . and said thus, Hew down the tree, and cut off his branches, shake off his leaves, and scatter his fruit . . . leave the stump of his roots in the earth, even with a band of iron and brass . . .' (Daniel 4:10–14).

What Daniel foresaw was a change in consciousness; so did John the Baptist. Frank suggested that this was the meaning of the Virgin Birth: the birth of a new consciousness. The Virgin was the ego, and it was to bear the Christ consciousness. The Christ had chosen the ego to make this the means of men's communication with the spiritual world. Henceforth the ego in Jesus was the Christ – St Paul's 'heavenly man', a spiritual humanity which had descended into the world, the Word (or Logos), which had become flesh in the body and personality of Jesus. This was the new birth granted by baptism.

But how had man come by his ego? What is this self-consciousness? Well, read the story of the Fall. Man is the creation of God in the image of God: he owes a great debt to the divine life for his ego, for his selfhood. But he chose to go on his own, to ignore God's prohibition and eat of the tree of the knowledge of good and evil. It is a tremendous thing to have received the gift of the ego in the first place, and a tremendous chance that humanity has now received to develop it into the divine life. But there is also great peril in this. The ego or self (the two words are used interchangeably) is a necessary stage on the way to the spiritual life, but it can also lead to disaster when men set self above everything else.

It was this that the Devil fastened on in the temptations which followed. After his baptism, Jesus, now the Christ, went into the wilderness to adapt himself to his new experience and be put to the test by the Devil. The final temptation was to show Jesus the kingdoms of the world in all their glory: 'All these . . . I will give you, if you will only fall down and do me homage' (Matthew 4:9). Jesus had no difficulty in resisting this, but all history is there to show how many have surrendered to the temptation to sacrifice everything to self. In perhaps the most famous of his paradoxes, Jesus said:

If anyone wishes to be a follower of mine, he must leave self behind . . . Whoever cares for his own safety is lost; but if a man will let himself be lost for my sake, he will find his true self. What will a man gain by winning the whole world, at the cost of his true self? Or what can he give that will buy that self back? (Matthew 16:24–6)

*

For the most part, Jesus' teaching took the form of parables, which his disciples more than once had to ask him to explain and which my father spent time interpreting to a modern audience. He was particularly interested in the Sermon on the Mount (Matthew 5–7), in which Jesus for once spoke more directly to the inner group of disciples and not by parables. My father believed there were two misconceptions which had to be got rid of before the Sermon could be understood.

Many scholars have treated the Sermon as a collection of Jesus' sayings which the evangelist did not know what to do with. On the contrary, Frank suggested, it was a secret path of discipleship for those who were candidates for the spiritual life – particularly if you matched the Beatitudes of Matthew 5:3–12 with the Woes of Matthew 23:13–36. My father summarized examples of each:

Blessed are those who know their need of God; the Kingdom of Heaven is theirs . . .

Blessed are those who hunger and thirst to see right prevail; they shall be satisfied . . .

Woe, woe unto you, scribes and Pharisees, hypocrites that you are! You shut the door of the Kingdom of Heaven in men's face; you do not enter yourselves, and when others are entering you stop them . . .

Woe unto you, scribes and Pharisees, hypocrites! You are like whitened sepulchres; they look well from the outside, but inside they are full of dead men's bones and all kinds of filth. So it is with you: outside you look like honest men, but are brimful of hypocrisy and vice . . .*

The second mistake was the assumption that the Sermon on the Mount was intended as a system of ethics for this world. On the

---

* Matthew 5:3–6: 'Blessed are the poor in spirit: for theirs is the kingdom of heaven . . . Blessed are they that hunger and thirst after righteousness: for they shall be filled.' Matthew 23:13–28: 'Woe unto you, scribes and Pharisees, hypocrites! because ye shut the kingdom of heaven against men: for ye enter not in yourselves, neither suffer ye them that are entering in to enter . . . Woe unto you, scribes and Pharisees, hypocrites! for ye are like unto whited sepulchres, which outwardly appear beautiful, but inwardly are full of dead men's bones, and of all uncleanness. Even so ye also outwardly appear righteous unto men, but inwardly ye are full of hypocrisy and iniquity.'

contrary, the Gospels constantly stress the conflict between an inflexible system of morality, such as that of the Pharisees, and the new consciousness which Jesus was trying to introduce. Jesus says that he has not come to abolish the Law, but goes on to repeat:

You have learned that our forefathers were told, 'Do not commit murder; anyone who commits murder must be brought to judgement.' But what I tell you is this: Anyone who nurses anger against his brother must be brought to judgement . . . (Matthew 5:21–2)

Ye have heard that it hath been said, An eye for an eye, and a tooth for a tooth: But I say unto you, That ye resist not evil: but whosoever shall smite thee on thy right cheek, turn to him the other also. (Matthew 5: 38–9)

The conclusion was clear enough:

The moral law may be adequate for man's social life, but when spiritual life begins to awaken in him he finds himself in revolt against it. Why? Because the word 'law' perpetuates the conflict between good and evil. Spiritual life and spiritual reality are beyond good and evil.

Frank continued:

You cannot apply this teaching to life as yet, because life has not yet altered the spiritual consciousness. You will look back on your experience, however, and become aware that both good and evil have helped in the development you have achieved.

The Sermon on the Mount is not a law, it is a revelation – a revelation of the spiritual life and how it will redeem good and evil. We have been hopelessly wrong in treating the Sermon on the Mount as a sort of second edition of the old Mosaic law. It is not a law given from outside but something that is going to emerge from inside.

III

One of the most striking features of the Gospel drama is that the incarnation of Christ is not followed by his triumph. When he set out after the Last Supper, Jesus told his disciples that they would desert him and, when Peter protested that he would never disavow him, Jesus replied, 'I tell you, tonight, before the cock crows, you will disown me three times' (Matthew 26:34).

Jesus himself was deeply troubled. In the garden of Gethsemane 'anguish and dismay came over him', and he said to the disciples, 'My heart is ready to break with grief. Stop here and stay awake with me,' and a little later, 'My Father, if it is possible, let this cup pass me by. Yet not as I will, but as thou wilt' (Matthew 26: 37–9).

Jesus had already told the disciples 'in deep agitation of spirit' (John 13:21) that one of them was going to betray him. When asked who it was, he had replied by dipping a piece of bread in a dish and handing it to Judas. 'As soon as Judas had received it Satan entered him.' This was a tremendous moment, the incarnation of Christ in Jesus matched across the table by the incarnation of the Prince of Darkness in Judas:

As soon as Judas had received [the bread], Satan entered him. Jesus said to him, 'Do quickly what you have to do.' . . . Judas, then, received the bread and went out. It was night. (John 13:27–30)

My father continued:

Satan represents the spiritual energy expressed in the realization of egoism. This selfhood has been born out of evolution; all the forces of evolution over millions of years have been building up and leading towards this self-consciousness in all of us. It is indispensable to human development, but it cannot rest there. Not evil in itself, it always tries to express itself at the expense of others; it seeks to dominate, and if not changed will end by destroying man. On the other hand, the mystic believes that until this lower selfhood has been manifested, a higher selfhood cannot be born. It must be born out of the lower. It is this that the Christ consciousness seeks to achieve and that Satan summons all the forces of darkness to prevent.

Whatever the circumstances surrounding the historical fact of Jesus of Nazareth's crucifixion, by the time the Gospels came to be written down the Passion had acquired the stylized form of a mystery play. Jesus the Christ had accepted that he must go through the ordeal of execution:

Every step in it has a reference not merely to the historical events of the Crucifixion, not merely to the initiation of the Christ, but to the initiation of the human spirit, which has to replicate the Passion in his or her own individual consciousness, in the dark night of the soul, and be nailed to the cross in the Place of the Skull, Golgotha.

9

The Fourth Gospel

There are, of course, important differences between the first three Gospels, but the differences between them and the Fourth Gospel are of a more fundamental character. This was of particular interest to Frank because, while there are mystical elements in all the Gospels, the Fourth has generally been recognized as a more mystical work from beginning to end. In Frank's view the Fourth Gospel was without an equal among all the books of the New Testament, and its author perhaps the greatest of all mystics.

But who was its author? There has been no more controversial question debated by biblical scholars over the past 150 years, with no agreed outcome. Although attracted to the traditional belief that the author was John, the son of Zebedee, Frank wisely concluded that the question could not be answered and concentrated instead on the text. The sixty years since he gave his lectures in the 1930s have not advanced the debate further except to establish with reasonable certainty that the Fourth was the last of the Gospels to be written, in the last decade of the first century, between AD 90 and 100, or possibly early in the second century.

There were several features distinguishing it from the three other Gospels which attracted my father's interest. The first was the famous prologue, in which the unknown author provided a framework in which to set the Gospel. It has been said of the author that he stood at the confluence of two great spiritual and intellectual worlds, the Hebrew and the Greek, combining the religious inspiration of the Hebrew prophets with the philosophical mysticism of Plato and the Neoplatonists. This is seen in his use of the Greek word '*Logos*' (Word), identified with Christ as the self-expression of God in Creation, the link between transcendent deity and the material universe. To provide the framework he needed, John went back before the Creation, when 'the Word already was. The Word dwelt with God, and what God was, the Word was.' When the will of God turned towards creation, it was through the Word that all things were created. 'All that came to be was alive with his life, and that life was the light of men' (John 1:1-4).

The world, then, owed its being to the Word. But when Christ entered the world, although it owed its being to him, the world did not recognize him. At last came a time when the Word itself became flesh, when that hidden light revealed itself in the consciousness of Jesus of Nazareth. This was the background outside time against which the life and death of the Jesus of history had to be set.

The three other Gospels are primarily concerned with the story of Jesus from a human point of view, tracing the preparation of a human soul to become the bearer of the Christ. The Fourth Gospel is not interested in the story of Jesus as such but in the Christ. It tells us nothing about the birth of Jesus or his life before the moment when the Christ enters into him at baptism; nor does it tell us anything about the Temptation in the Wilderness, which is concerned with the adjustment between Jesus and the new consciousness which has taken possession of him. The eternal Christ knew perfectly well what he was going to do, but the human being Jesus had to work out how he was to come to terms with this new and tremendous role.

No less striking is the Fourth Gospel's presentation of Jesus the Christ in terms of glory, as the Lord who speaks with a confidence not to be found in the other Gospels. There is none of the agonizing in the Gethsemane garden described by Mark and Matthew. In place of that, the Fourth Gospel reports Jesus learning that some Greeks have come to see him. Frank saw their arrival as awakening Jesus to the realization of what might be achieved by his death, in a breakthrough to the great Gentile world outside the Jewish nation, leading him to declare

'The hour has come for the Son of Man to be glorified. In truth, in very truth I tell you, a grain of wheat remains a solitary grain unless it falls into the ground and dies; but if it dies, it bears a rich harvest . . . Now my soul is in turmoil, and what am I to say? Father, save me from this hour. No, it was for this that I came to this hour. Father, glorify thy name.' A voice sounded from heaven: 'I have glorified it, and I will glorify it again.' (John 12:23–8)

Similarly, when Judas left the Last Supper and went out into the night, Jesus did not flinch but declared, 'Now the Son of Man is glorified' (John 13:31). A little later he tells the disciples, 'I shall not talk much longer with you, for the Prince of this world [i.e. Satan] approaches. He has no rights over me; but the world must be shown that I . . . do exactly as [the Father] commands; so up, let us go forward!' (John 14:30–31).

The other Gospels still held out the hope, dear to the Jews, of an apocalyptic Second Coming to be realized in the future. In the Fourth Gospel, however, this is interpreted in a spiritual not a literal sense. In place of the Kingdom of God being established in this world, Christ makes clear that he is returning to the Father, sending the Holy Spirit as advocate and comforter in his place. Eternal life is represented as already present for the individual believer, and the raising of Lazarus demonstrates that the power of resurrection is already possessed by Christ, and is not something still to manifest itself in some future time.

One question which intrigued Frank was the identity of 'the Beloved Disciple', a character who does not appear in any of the other Gospels, but makes five, possibly six, appearances in the Fourth Gospel as an actual eyewitness of the Passion and the Resurrection. At the Last Supper, when the disciples are bewildered by Jesus' declaration that one of them will betray him, he is 'the disciple [Jesus] loved', who is 'reclining close beside Jesus' and whom Peter calls upon to ask Jesus who it is he means (John 13:23–5). The Beloved Disciple is again the only one of the disciples who is mentioned as present at the Crucifixion, and whom Jesus entrusts with the care of his mother, Mary (John 19:25–7). After Jesus' death, when Mary Magdalene discovers that the tomb is empty, it is the disciple 'whom Jesus loved' who outstrips Peter in reaching the tomb first (John 20:2–4). Again, after the Resurrection, when Jesus appears on the shore of the Sea of Galilee, he is the first to recognize Jesus when the other disciples fail to. Finally, when Peter asks the Risen Christ what will happen to 'the disciple whom Jesus loved', he receives the mysterious rebuke 'If it should be my will that he wait until I come, what is it to you?' (John 21:22).

Frank was attracted by the idea that the Beloved Disciple might have been the author of the John Gospel, but abandoned this in favour of the stronger case that can be made out for identifying the Beloved Disciple as a surviving eyewitness of the Passion on whose testimony the unknown author of the Fourth Gospel drew. He also speculated that the Beloved Disciple might have been Lazarus, whom Jesus raised from the dead, the brother of Mary and Martha, who appears only in the John Gospel and who is the only other man of whom it is said that Jesus loved him dearly. However arresting an idea, this is one for which there is no evidence, one way or the other.

II

After the prologue, the Fourth Gospel divides into two parts, with the raising of Lazarus in Chapter 11 as the hinge which holds the two together. The culmination of the prologue is the statement that the Word, the Logos, became flesh and dwelt in the world. The first part which follows recounts the ministry of the Word in the flesh – that is, the ministry of Jesus Christ, who 'must work the works of him that sent me . . . the night cometh, when no man can work' (John 9:4). The most important of these works are the seven signs or miracles, beginning with the changing of water into wine at the feast in Cana and reaching a peak in the raising of Lazarus. Each is a sign for those whose minds are prepared to receive its hidden message that Jesus truly is the Christ sent by God.

In Lazarus's case, his sickness, as Jesus said, was 'not unto death, but . . . that the Son of God might be glorified' (John 11:4). When he died, Jesus intervened and demonstrated for the first time the truth of his claim 'I am the resurrection and I am life. If a man has faith in me, even though he die, he shall come to life; and no one who is alive and has faith shall ever die' (John 11:25–8). It was not physical but spiritual life and death of which Jesus was speaking.

In the Old Testament, when Moses asked God for his name, God replied, 'I AM THAT I AM' – the ultimate expression, which there is no getting beneath or behind (Exodus 3:14). In the Fourth Gospel Christ takes over God's answer and matches the seven signs with a sevenfold affirmation of the Eternal Logos: 'I am the bread of life . . . the light of the world . . . the door of the sheepfold . . . the good shepherd . . . the resurrection and the life . . . the way, the truth, and the life . . . and the true vine' (John 6:35, 8:12, 10:8, 11:25, 14:6, 15:1).

As in the case of the seven signs, each of the 'I am' affirmations conceals a mystery which the initiated can read.

At some point in man's spiritual history, he absorbed the consciousness of self. Not 'I am', but for the most part 'I want'. This was what Buddha saw. His diagnosis of evil was that man was possessed by a passion of desire, an eternal hunger, always reaching out to draw things unto himself. This is the counterfeit of the real self. The *real* self is the 'I am', the tree of life, while the false self is the tree of death. Your hunger is never satisfied until you have passed from the false self, which always says 'I want', to the knowledge of the Eternal Self which says 'I am'. Take the affirmation 'I am the light of the universe.' All the darkness in our lives comes, as Blake says, from the little self 'that stands in the light and casts a shadow'. Just as the 'I am' is the light of the universe, so that false consciousness is the little shadow that makes all the darkness in the universe. You must recognize that consciousness of self which casts its shadow, in order that you may come to know the true self, which is the light of the universe.

Frank saw a parallel in the teaching of the Hindu Vedanta scriptures, in two sentences which recur again and again: 'I am Brahma' and 'That art Thou.' The root of every soul is Brahma, God, the great reality at the heart of the universe; but Brahma is veiled. All that you can say when you see the sunlight is 'That art

Thou.' Christ turns it the other way and says, 'I am the light.' When you turn to the *Bhagavadgita*, the *Song of the Lord*, the best-loved of Hindu scriptures, you find that Krishna, the Logos of that particular scripture, repeats, 'I am the Sacrifice', 'I am the receiver of the Sacrifice', 'I am the duration in the heart of him who offers the sacrifice.'

The raising of Lazarus marked the turning point for Jesus' ministry. The chief priests and the Pharisees decided that, if they left Jesus alone, 'the whole populace will believe in him. Then the Romans will come and sweep away our temple and our nation' (John 11:48). 'So from that day on they plotted his death' (John 11:53). With Chapter 12 of the Fourth Gospel it is no longer day, but 'the night cometh, when no man can work'.

III

The Passion which follows appears from the outside as unrelieved tragedy. From the inside, however, for Jesus Christ, who was 'well aware that the Father had entrusted everything to him, and that he had come from God and was going back to God' (John 13:3–4), it is the supreme moment of glorification. When Judas goes out into the night, Jesus, knowing what is to follow, declares, 'Now the Son of Man is glorified, and in him God is glorified' (John 13:31–2). His object in the brief time remaining is to prepare the disciples for what is to come and for what will happen to them.

Chapters 13–17 (which my father believed had been arranged in the wrong order and should be rearranged with greater effect in the order 13, 15, 17, 16, 14) are among the most moving in the whole of the New Testament.

On one side are the disciples bewildered and struggling to understand why their Master should leave them – 'Lord, what can have happened, that you mean to disclose yourselves to us alone and not to the world?' (John 14:22) – on the other, Jesus comforting and reassuring them – 'Let not your hearts be troubled ... A new commandment I give you: Love one another; as I have loved you ...' (John 13:34). 'Dwell in me, as I in you ... I am the vine, and you are the branches. He who dwells in me, as I dwell in him, bears much fruit . . .' (John 15:4–5). 'The hour is coming . . . when you are all to be scattered, each to his home, leaving me alone. Yet I am not alone, because the Father is with me. I have told you all this so that in me you may find peace. In the world you will have trouble. But courage! The victory is mine; I have conquered the world' (John 16:32–3).

Finally, the Christ, recalling the prologue, prays, 'Father the hour has come . . . I have glorified thee on earth by completing the work which thou gavest me to do; and now, Father, glorify me in thine own presence with the glory which I had with thee before the world began' (John 17:1–5).

There is no parallel in the other Gospels to these discourses, as they are known, in which Jesus reveals himself to his disciples, but, once the narrative reaches the arrest of Jesus, from there to his death the author of the Fourth Gospel keeps close to the same order as the other Gospels.

As Jesus had forewarned the disciples, Frank wrote, 'That which is manifested by rapture and joy on the spiritual plane changes, when it is translated on to the physical plane under the limitations of time and space, into the tragedy and suffering of human life.'

Jesus – 'knowing all that was coming upon him' (John 18:4) – was not perturbed when he and the disciples moved from the upper room into the night, and did not hesitate to confront those who had come to arrest him and declare himself to be the man they were searching for. When the impulsive Peter drew his sword, however, and sought to protect him, Jesus intervened: 'Sheathe your sword. This is the cup the Father has given me; shall I not drink it?' (John 18:11). He made no attempt to use the powers which he had earlier displayed, or to defend himself in the three trials which followed.

Brought before the Jewish High Priest and Council and asked 'You are the Son of God, then?' Jesus replies, 'It is you who say I am' (Luke 22:67–70). Before Herod he remains completely silent. Only when the Roman governor, Pilate, puts the question 'Are you the king of the Jews?' is he roused to ask, 'Is that your own idea, or have others suggested it to you? . . . My kingdom does not belong to this world.' When Pilate asks, 'You are a king, then?'

Jesus replies, '"King" is your word. My task is to bear witness to the truth. For this was I born; for this I came into the world.' For a moment, my father said, you feel that Pilate is on the edge of a vision, only to turn away with the dismissive remark 'What is truth?' (John 18:33–8).

It is probable that because of anti-Jewish feeling, especially in the Fourth Gospel account, and out of a desire to win favour with the Romans, all four Gospels show Pilate in a sympathetic light – three times saying that he can find no case against Jesus and only reluctantly acceding to the demand of the Jewish authorities, and the crowd they have stirred up, to put Jesus to death.

In practice it made little difference. The Gospels follow a symbolic pattern, a mixture of the historical and the mystical which came naturally to earlier ages – as late as the seventeenth century – but which modern man finds hard to accept. Thus the seven stages of initiation begin with Christ's washing of the disciples' *feet*, the scourging of Christ's *body*, the placing of the crown of thorns upon his *head*. This immediately recalls Genesis and God's curse on the ground that shall bring forth nothing but thorns and thistles for man. This leads to the parable of the sower and the seed which fell among thorns and was choked by them. These are followed by Christ's seven last words on the Cross, starting with 'Father, forgive them; for they know not what they do' and ending with 'Father, into thy hands I commend my spirit' (Luke 23: 34–46). It is notable that neither Luke nor John includes the cry of anguish, 'My God, my God, why hast thou forsaken me?' (Matthew 27:46; Mark 15:34).

Frank saw Jesus as the central figure in a mystical drama, at once victim, priest and offering. The disciples, as Jesus had foretold, scatter and appear to be moving through the drama like men in a sleep. Only the Beloved Disciple is named by the Fourth Gospel as present at the Crucifixion, and according to Luke it is one of the two thieves crucified with Jesus, not one of the disciples, who grasps what is taking place and calls to him, 'Jesus, remember me when you come to your throne' and receives the answer 'I tell you this: today you shall be with me in Paradise' (Luke 23:43).

IV

The final act of the drama, the Resurrection, begins in the Fourth Gospel with the initiation of Mary Magdalene, the Beloved Disciple and Simon Peter into the mystery of the empty tomb. But it is Mary, with the power of love – Mary who, weeping, says, 'They have taken my Lord away, and I do not know where they have laid him' (John 20:13) – who is the first to see Jesus, although she does not immediately recognize him.

We must avoid any suggestion [Franks said] that the manifestation of Christ after death was the same in any sense as our manifestation in a physical body. The physical body was assimilated into the spiritual . . . What was the nature of this resurrected body? It was matter spiritualized, or even spirit materialized, not a body belonging merely to the physical dimension, but one which could move in and out of it. Luke tells the story of two Apostles who were walking on the road to Emmaus and who became aware of a figure walking beside them without realizing that it was Jesus. He talked at length with them, but it was only in the evening when they sat down together and Jesus blessed and broke bread with them that their eyes were opened. No sooner had they recognized him, however, than he vanished from their sight (Luke 24:13–31).

The Apostles returned at once to Jerusalem and told the rest of their company their experience.

As they were talking about all this [Luke continues], there he was, standing among them. Startled and terrified, they thought they were seeing a ghost. But he said, 'Why are you so perturbed? Why do questionings arise in your minds? Look at my hands and feet. It is I myself. Touch me and see . . .' They were still unconvinced . . . for it seemed too good to be true. So he asked them, 'Have you anything here to eat?' They offered him a piece of fish they had cooked, which he took and ate before their eyes. (Luke 24:36–43)

It took time for the disciples to grasp what had happened, and the note of doubt is repeated by the three other Gospels. When

Jesus appeared to the disciples in Galilee, 'they fell prostrate before him, though some were doubtful' (Matthew 28:17). When the last, Thomas, was convinced and cried out, 'My Lord and my God', Jesus said, 'Because you have seen me you have found faith. Happy are they who never saw me and yet have found faith' (John 20:26–9).

According to Acts 1:3, Jesus appeared to his followers over a period of forty days, teaching them about the Kingdom of God and the role they were to play as apostles of the Risen Christ.

Then suddenly he parted from them, never to return in the flesh. Yet there was no despair or sorrow in their hearts. They understood that in his unseen life the personal Christ had become one with the Ever-Living and the Eternal. From henceforth he was absorbed into Godhood. That was a very different thing, however, from saying that the Jesus of Nazareth who walked on this earth was God.

Before he left, Christ communicated the divine life to the Apostles by breathing upon them and saying, 'Receive the Holy Spirit! If you forgive any man's sins, they stand forgiven' (John 20:23).

Frank pointed to the parallel with Genesis, where God breathes into the nostrils of Adam and 'man became a living soul' (Genesis 2:7), adding the comment 'This was a new creation in a new expansion of reality.'

What will the character of reality be? It will be neither matter, soul nor spirit, but all three blended. Our consciousness functions in such a way that we see matter in separation from soul and spirit. It is only when we come to a certain stage of mystical awareness that we find these things credible, can enter into the new state of consciousness and know all three as one with the Father.

Frank ended his lectures on the Gospels with what he called the Gospel within the Gospels, returning to the need, however difficult, to bring together the historical and the mystical elements in them. This was the unique character of the Christian gospel. It borrowed freely from the other mystery religions – the journey of the Magi from the Zoroastrians, the birth in the cave and the shepherds from Mithras, the changing of the water into wine from Dionysus – but it alone related these to a historical episode: the ministry and crucifixion of Jesus of Nazareth.

Were the authors of the Gospels aware of the fact that they were transcending the different visions of the ages and presenting a universal gospel which had the sanction of the deepest traditions of the human spirit for its assurance and its reality? I think they were profoundly aware, and I suggest two passages which I believe support that view.

One is taken from that remarkable book which we do not fully understand, the Revelation of St John, or the Apocalypse:

> And I saw an angel flying in mid-heaven with an eternal gospel to proclaim to those on earth, to every nation and tribe, language and people. (Revelation 14:6)

It is an everlasting gospel which has no beginning in time and is not affected by the passing of history, and it is designed for all people upon earth.

The other passage is taken from Paul's first letter to Timothy:

> For there is one God, and also one mediator between God and men, Christ Jesus, himself man, who sacrificed himself to win freedom for all mankind . . . (1 Timothy 2:5–6)

> And great beyond all question is the mystery of our religion:
> God was manifested in the body,
> > vindicated in the spirit,
> > > seen by angels;
> > preached unto the Gentiles,
> > > believed in throughout the world,
> > > > glorified in high heaven.   (1 Timothy 3:16)*

This is the process by which God is made manifest in the flesh, the

---

* 1 Timothy 3:16: 'He who was manifested in the body, vindicated in the spirit, seen by angels; who was proclaimed among the nations, believed in throughout the world, glorified in high heaven' (New English Bible); 'God was manifest in the flesh, justified in the Spirit, seen of angels, preached unto the Gentiles, believed on in the world, received up into glory' (Authorized Version).

process by which humanity achieves the putting on of Godhood. To us modern people perhaps it does not sound a very exciting kind of programme, but to the ancient world it was the goal of their most passionate desire, the only consummation of human life and history that was worthwhile. They believed that man was of God, who had come forward into manifestation within the limitations of time and space and matter and preached the gospel, the vision and hope that man could put on Godhood once more.

It was not taught as something outside of humanity, as a sort of miracle story that was presented to a humanity so desperate that it was for ever doomed, but it was taught to humanity that had within it the possibility of Godhood. That is the basis of our whole Unitarian faith: that man has within him the potentiality of Godhood. Man has always been a spiritual being, and behind all his history there lies a spiritual tradition.

Well, they say this is an everlasting gospel. Wherever there are men lost in the abysses of time – and remember they believed in the plurality of worlds – wherever this pilgrimage begins, then those who begin it must ask, What is the goal? How can man put on Godhood once more? The Gospels were written to answer that question, and it is a moving thought that we gathered together tonight in Bradford, talking as we are, are at one with those little groups scattered over Asia, Greece and Rome nineteen centuries ago.

PART III

THE ANCIENT WISDOM

10

Buddha, the *Bhagavadgita*, Plotinus

I

As a young man, my father had rebelled against the Calvinist orthodoxy in which he had been brought up. He next turned to late-nineteenth- and early-twentieth-century rationalism, only to become disillusioned with the insubstantial idealism which was all that it offered:

I felt very much like the ass who was 'fed on the east wind'. About that time I heard a famous Hindu proverb: 'The mind is the slayer of the real; slay the slayer!' We Western people have been taught to trust the intellect – which is what the Hindu proverb meant by 'mind' – only to discover that, although a superb instrument, the intellect, when allowed to become master, can weaken and finally destroy the primary instincts on which our powers of intuition and imagination depend. I felt I was in danger of becoming imprisoned within the web spun by the intellect, yet was convinced that there must be some other way of approaching truth and knowledge.

After a long search, and after following many false lights (and there are many modern intellectual charlatans), I found that there had been in almost all ages people who had the gift of interior illumination. They did not learn from books; they did not approach a subject in an intellectual way, but their minds became illuminated from within and their knowledge was intuitive, without the processes of thinking.

From these and others, Frank came to recognize the existence of a great fund of knowledge known as the Ancient Wisdom. This includes the Hindu Upanishads, the Buddhist scriptures and the Hebrew scriptures, to mention only three. These draw on still older sources (for example, the Babylonian myth of the garden, which becomes the Garden of Eden) and in turn were drawn upon by later writers, such as Blake and W. B. Yeats, who preserved and added to the tradition.

It did not matter where I came across traces of this Ancient Wisdom, they always told the same thing, although for the most part they were unaware of each other. What was the method it used? They did not think in any analytical way; they thought in symbols, and their great key was that of correspondence between man and the universe, man in himself as an epitome of the whole mystery of the universe. They conveyed this correspondence of that which is within and that which is without by the use of symbols and images, which are to be found in all records of the Ancient Wisdom.

Frank believed that the barrier to our understanding of the Ancient Wisdom is our projection of our modern consciousness on to the past.

We have been trained to think historically, in terms of cause and effect, with a very deep consciousness of time. But these ancient peoples had very little, if any, sense of history. When they began to think back at all, they thought in terms of mythology not of history. The story of beginnings for them – whether you go to China, India, Egypt, Greece or Scandinavia – was in each case a mythological story.

In addition to the Gospels, the New Testament provided other striking examples of the Ancient Wisdom in that visionary master-piece The Revelation of St John, which had a great attraction for my father, and in the Epistles of St Paul, from which it was possible to reconstruct the gospel of St Paul – the so-called Fifth Gospel. Each of these was made the subject of a series of lectures.

At the same time, Frank's Unitarian beliefs allowed him, while remaining in the Christian tradition, to appreciate the insights and truth of other religious traditions. Among those which he chose to lecture on and explore further were Buddhism, the Hindu Upanishads and *Bhagavadgita* (the *Song of the Lord*), the *Hermetica*, and Plotinus and the Neoplatonists.

*

Buddhism was founded in the sixth century BC in India, from where it spread all over Asia. Buddhist tradition tells how Gautama Siddhartha (*c.* 563–483 BC), born a prince and raised in luxury, renounced the world at the age of twenty-nine to search for a solution to the problem of suffering innate in the human condition. After six years of spiritual discipline he achieved enlightenment ('Buddha' is the Sanskrit word for 'the Enlightened One') and spent the remaining forty-five years of his life teaching and establishing a community of monks and nuns to continue his work.

Buddha taught:

Everything has a cause. Wherever there is sorrow, there is something that accompanies sorrow, and wherever there is no sorrow that thing is absent. What is that thing? Desire. Desire is always present where there is sorrow. Desire, therefore, is that which binds us to unhappiness, to suffering. Moreover, this desire causes ignorance, and that is the great cause of the world's suffering. To know the cause of suffering and to cease from the cause of suffering is to find release from ignorance and darkness.

Buddha came into a world full of gods, with a priestly caste deriving their authority from an ancient scripture. He swept all these aside and declared:

'No authority for me, no scripture, no priest; by my mind I can see the truth, and the truth can make me free. Because I am a man, and have my gift of mind, if I look deeply enough, and search keenly enough, this wisdom and knowledge can give me illumination.'

What did he mean by 'the truth'? [my father asked]. I will put it this way. Buddha says that the ultimate truth you have to grasp is that self – your idea of yourself, of your personality, of your individuality which you set so much store by – this is the great illusion which binds men and women to the wheel of passion, suffering and death.

To Western people this comes as a great shock. So much of Western teaching is built up on the idea that I am to realize myself, to express myself.

Yet Jesus taught: 'He that saveth himself shall lose himself, and he that loseth himself shall find himself' (Matthew 10:39).* What is it that brings all the antagonism into life? Is it not my *self*? The moment I have that deep-rooted instinctive feeling of self, I am in antagonism with everybody.

A selfish person is one who is obsessed with hunger and desire for things. What is more, that hunger and thirst cannot be satisfied. His selfishness is against the real facts of life. Only when he acknowledges that selfishness is an illusion will he be liberated and know the end of all hunger and desire.

'He has no consciousness anywhere; he is utterly well.' Buddha used these words about a monk who had died and, he believed, had attained nirvana, the state of supreme bliss. What did he mean?

Primitive man had no knowledge of self-consciousness. He had an unself-conscious relationship with the cosmos, the sun, earth and stars, and knew a completeness of life which we have never attained.

But there came a time when man could no longer remain in that relationship, and, in the way described by the legend of the Fall of Man, he ate of the tree of the knowledge of good and evil, and took upon himself the burden of self-consciousness. Since then the question which has preoccupied all religions is man's destiny. Whence does he come? Whither does he go?

My father was very impressed with the way – the very modern way, as he thought – in which Buddha dealt with these questions. Buddha grasped, even then, 2,500 years ago, that people would eventually find their self-consciousness an intolerable burden which would destroy them unless they could find a way of deliverance.

Buddha sought for that way of release in a very characteristic way. He did not turn back to any ancient scripture; he did not invoke the idea of some God who would give a revelation. He said the way of deliverance must be found in a scientific way, by looking for the cause of the trouble. In fact he was the first psychologist in history.

The answer he arrived at was to see the mind as a flowing stream of consciousness connected with the body and giving rise to the image or

---

* Matthew 10:39: 'He that findeth his life shall lose it: and he that loseth his life for my sake shall find it.'

illusion of self. And what controls that stream of consciousness which flows through you is a law which Buddha calls the law of karma, or the law of consequences.

The way of escape, Buddha says, is to release yourself from the stream of consciousness. The Buddhist way of achieving this is by releasing all the psychic energies of the mind, soul and body which have been focused around the self, and by gradually destroying the image of the self. Then you will find that all those energies that have made the stream of consciousness will now flow in another direction and you will know the liberation which Buddha sees: 'He has no consciousness anywhere; he is utterly well.'

II

The *Bhagavadgita* (the *Song of the Lord*) is the most famous of Hindu scriptures. It takes the form of a dialogue between the warrior Prince Arjuna and the god Lord Krishna embodied as the driver of Arjuna's chariot. It takes place on the eve of a battle in which Arjuna is faced with fighting and killing kinsmen on the other side. He asks, Can that be right on Hindu principles? The Lord Krishna answers him:

Thou grievest where no grief should be! thou speak'st
Words lacking wisdom! for the wise in heart
Mourn not for those that live, nor those that die.
All that doth live, lives always! This that irks
Thy sense-life, thrilling to the elements –
Bringing thee heat and cold, sorrows and joys –
'Tis brief and mutable! Bear with it, Prince!
As the wise bear. That which is
Can never cease to be; that which is not
Will not exist. To see this truth of both
Is theirs who part essence from accident,
Substance from shadow.
But for these fleeting frames which it informs
With spirit deathless, endless, infinite,
They perish. Let them perish, Prince!

Life cannot slay. Life is not slain!
Never the spirit was born; the spirit shall cease to be never;
Never was time it was not. End and beginning are dreams!
Birthless and deathless and changeless remaineth the spirit for ever;
Death hath not touched it at all, dead though the house of it seems!

Frank fastened on the question, What is this innermost light and life that nothing can touch or affect, and, knowing which, the soul has deliverance from fear, death and all the evils of this world?

First of all there is the Absolute, the unmanifested, that the human mind knows nothing about. From that there emerges in Hindu thought – and in the New Testament too – a second god, or, if you like, a manifestation of the unmanifested, which is here called the Lord and in the New Testament the Logos.

In the *Bhagavadgita* the Logos or eternal self descends upon man and manifests itself for the purpose of enlightening humanity. This spiritual manifestation has taken place not because the individual has attained to the spiritual qualifications of the Logos, but because the Logos wishes to manifest itself for the purpose of aiding humanity. As the Gospel says, 'The Word [the Logos] became flesh, and dwelt among us' (John 1:14).

Frank was particularly impressed by the Hindu view of matter (*prakriti*), which insists that deity has two sides to its being: the spiritual and the material, the completion of God's being. As an illustration, he took the example of an electric bulb. In every lighting circuit there are two forces, positive and negative. When they are joined together there is light; if you separate them there is darkness. For the light to shine forth there must be the union of the positive and negative, of spirit and matter.

My father asked:

How can we come to this kind of illumination? I suggest that in order to know this inner light you must withhold a fraction of your consciousness; in all experiences, maintain a hold on your consciousness.

Let us take love and friendship. You can make these intensely personal experiences – it is *your* friend, *your* lover. You give yourself utterly, and your friend or lover must do the same. You can make that entirely a personal experience, but if you do you will never see the light and life in the experience. Suppose, however, that you train yourself to feel the universal speaking, caressing, touching you through the personal. Then you will understand how all beauty, all delight reaches us through the particular. Through the personal comes the great incoming tide of life, beauty and delight. At that stage you will have reached such a consciousness that it stands above the particular, and feels the universal through it . . .

In the experiences of pain, sorrow, death, you must seek to eliminate the personal. It is the great impersonal manifestation of universal law that heals us, and when we realize that, we begin to see the light and shadow of the extremes in life; then we come to that saying 'The darkness and the light are both alike to thee' (Psalms 139:12). The eternal comes to us through the darkness as well as through the light.

III

Philosophy was the greatest gift of the Greeks to Western culture – above all, Socrates, Plato and Aristotle. There are elements of mysticism in Greek philosophy; the best-known perhaps in Plato's *The Republic*. It was not, however, until six hundred years after Plato that Plotinus (AD 205–70) carried Plato's thought further and developed the mystical doctrine of Neoplatonism.

The core of Plotinus' teaching was the question, What is the relation between this visible world of physical matter and the invisible worlds of soul and spirit? What is the relation between 'here' and 'yonder'?

The truth, Plotinus claimed, was that things were arranged in upward order of perfection:

First the world of matter, which forms, orders and maintains in being the material universe, and then above that the world of soul, which uses matter to express itself . . . Above the world of soul in turn is the world of spirit or nous. Just as soul uses matter to express its hidden beauty, so the world of spirit uses the soul to bear *its* image.

The world of matter is made in the image of the soul; the world of the soul is made in the image of the spirit; and finally there is the One, the world of the Absolute, which uses the spirit to bear its image.

In so far as the soul turns away from the vision of the spirit, imperfection enters. This, says Plotinus, is the temptation of the soul: to look down towards sense (or nature) rather than up to spirit. How has this happened, how has evil crept in? It is within the soul, within *ourselves*, that we are confronted with evil, that the soul has turned aside from the vision of spiritual perfection and has forgotten God – the Absolute.

Why? Because men have begun to revel in free will and have taken their own path. They have lost the knowledge that they sprang from the divine One. All evil, according to Plotinus, is a forgetting of men's selves, whence they have come and where they belong. Man in himself is not evil; he is of divine origin, only he forgets himself.

Plotinus denies that we are ever cut off from God. At the core of our being there remains a spark of the divine light which has never been extinguished by sin or evil – nor ever can be. To those who have fallen, it is essential to remind them whence man comes – as the prodigal son was reminded when he came to himself and said, 'I will arise and go to my father' (Luke 15:18). Hope lies in reminding them of this, not in any threats of punishment. The whole universe is seen as a vast organism, an immense living being, held together by the power and Logos of God, so that all existence – men and things – is drawn by a kind of centripetal attraction towards him.

Plotinus himself never became a Christian, but nonetheless came to exert a unique influence on Christian as well as Islamic and Jewish mysticism. This influence extended from the tough-minded St Augustine to the Platonic Academy in Renaissance Florence, the Cambridge Platonists of the late seventeenth century, the Londoners William Blake (1757–1827) and Thomas Taylor (1758–1835), and the American Ralph Waldo Emerson (1803–82).

11

The Book of Job

Centuries before the birth of Jesus and the composition of the New Testament, Judaism had developed as a mystery religion in its own right. This religion found expression in the Old Testament, and the Jewish people outlived defeat, captivity and the loss of their national independence largely because these writings enabled them to preserve their identity, their history and traditions. The finest of them – the Book of Genesis, the Book of Job, the Psalms, the Book of the Prophet Isaiah – are unsurpassed in their power of vision and literary genius, and the linking of the Hebrew Bible with Christianity – to which it is as basic as it is to Judaism – gave them a universal currency. Without the Old Testament the New Testament could never have been written and there could have been no man like Jesus; Christianity could not have been what it became. And without the New Testament this small people could never have made their unique contribution to the religious painting, drama, art and music of Western civilization.

The Hebrew genius was particularly well adapted to make such a contribution. By comparison with other religious traditions, such as those described in the previous chapter, the Hebrew scriptures express a profoundly religious rather than a philosophical consciousness, aware of the senses and of a presence in nature – mountains, trees, streams – and with a vast and vivid repertoire of images. And above all dramatic – alive to crisis, history and destiny.

Every people has its creation myth. The Jews wrote down their version in the eighth century BC, although the myth itself had taken shape in their consciousness many years before.

The ancient seers' image of Creation was a tree, the roots of which go deep into the spiritual. The tree of life represents man's spiritual perceptions and powers, but there is a second tree, the tree of the knowledge of good and evil, representing that knowledge in relation to selfhood. Man was free to eat of the tree of life, which sometimes appears as the true vine. The only tree he was forbidden to eat of was the tree of the knowledge of good and evil, because, when man comes to the knowledge of selfhood, there is a separation from the harmony and unity of life, a descent into the limitations which we know today. In our experience there is the tree of life which links you up to the great power of the universe, the tree of life whose leaves are 'for the healing of the nations' (Revelation 22:2); but there is also the other tree, the tree of selfhood and the knowledge of good and evil.

Besides the image of the trees, there is also the image of the serpent, and just as there is more than one tree, there is more than one serpent. The serpents of life or cherubim (the word means 'winged serpents') guard the Garden of Eden. Jesus bids his disciples to be 'wise as serpents, and harmless as doves' (Matthew 10:16). The serpent of death, 'more subtil than any beast of the field which the Lord God had made' (Genesis 3:1), is the image of egoism, the subtle consciousness of self which tempts Eve and Adam, and awakens desire in their souls. It too is of divine origin.

Note also that the serpent approaches the woman first – the woman who represents the higher faculty of intuition, associated with emotion and desire. When you crush emotion, you are destroying the greatest power of the soul. You will never be saved by your intellect, but by your intuition.

What was the result? Adam and Eve ate of the tree of the knowledge of good and evil, and immediately their eyes were opened and they knew that they were naked – that is, literally unclothed, expelled from the consciousness of unity, no longer clothed with the forces of immortality. 'And the Lord God called unto Adam and said unto him, Where art thou? And he said, I heard thy voice in the garden, *and I was afraid*' (Genesis 3:9–10).

We still feel naked and are afraid. The more deeply we eat of the knowledge of good and evil, the more we become self-conscious – and if you want to know what that means, read the writers of the late nineteenth century, Nietzsche, Strindberg and Ibsen. They realized that humanity was naked, and they were afraid. It seemed an intolerable burden to bear, this burden of self-consciousness, of self-direction.

As an account of how human life began, this fragment from the past has an obvious interest for later generations. But the reason why it catches the imagination is because, at the same time, it has become a symbol of some earlier state of beauty, happiness and freedom from evil which we feel we have left behind us and lost. Mankind rebels against the shadow of evil and death; we refuse to believe that the suffering of the world expresses the original intention of God. There remains in human memory the concept of a Fall, a decline from earlier heights which this legend dramatizes.

Frank ended with two lines from Browning:

> Is it a dream? – Nay, but the lack of it a dream,
> And missing it – all the world a dream.

What I have been telling you is a truth that still holds in the modern world.

When a member of his audience asked if there was any evidence in Genesis itself that it was related to a more ancient wisdom, my father replied:

Yes, indeed. In the eleventh chapter of Genesis, when it speaks of a time when 'the whole earth was of one language, and of one speech'. Ancient man retained the memory of a time, since lost, when all men had lived together in unity and spoke one language. The story of the Tower of Babel is another version of man's fall from grace and expulsion from paradise, leaving behind his spiritual consciousness and descending to the lower, divided, state of self-consciousness. This is the sin of Titanism, 'the greatest evil of our time', as the Protestant theologian Karl Barth called it, of man seeking to make himself the equal of God, creating a substitute in the human consciousness for that spiritual wisdom which was his original guide.

When the Lord saw that Adam and Eve had eaten the forbidden fruit of the tree of the knowledge of good and evil and sought 'to be as gods'

(Genesis 3:5), he drove them out of the Garden of Eden. So when he sees man building the tower that will reach the heavens, the Lord declares, 'Behold, the people is one, and they have all one language; and now nothing they have a mind to do will be beyond their reach' (Genesis 11:6). This time, in order to prevent man from obtaining spiritual power to bolster up their egoism (and that can be done, men have used spiritual forces for that end) the Lord confuses their language – 'That is why it is called Babel because the Lord there made a babble of the language of all the world and from that place scattered men all over the face of the earth' (Genesis 11:19).*

The counterpart in the New Testament, as Frank did not fail to point out, was the Day of Pentecost, when the Apostles were all together 'And there appeared to them tongues like flames of fire . . . resting on each one. And they were all filled with the Holy Spirit and began to talk in other tongues, as the Spirit gave them power of utterance' (Acts 2:3–4). And the crowd drawn from every nation on earth were amazed and exclaimed, 'Why, they are all Galileans, are they not, these men who are speaking? How is it then that we hear them, each of us in his own native language?' (Acts 2:7–8). For a moment the lost unity was restored.

II

My father's second example of the Ancient Wisdom in the Hebrew scriptures was the Book of Job, written c. 500 BC, but in this case interpreted – in effect reworked, as the Ancient Wisdom is capable of being – by the great English visionary, poet and artist William Blake.

Blake's series of twenty-one illustrations to the Book of Job, engraved between 1823 and 1825, was one of the last and greatest of his works, the fruit of a fascination with Job which went back

---

* Genesis 11:6–9: 'Behold, they are one people, and they have all one language; and this is what they begin to do: and now nothing will be withholden from them, which they purpose to do . . . Therefore was the name of [the city] called Babel; because the Lord did there confound the language of all the earth: and from thence did the Lord scatter them abroad upon the face of all the earth.'

to the 1790s. There are two versions of the Book of Job. The Hebrew original stands out as a dramatic masterpiece. Blake's version, the basis of his engravings, follows the main outline of the story as presented by the unknown Hebrew author, but Blake does not hesitate to offer his own view of its meaning.

The prologue begins with the Lord offering Satan the example of Job – a man who 'was perfect and upright, and one that feareth God, and eschewed evil' (Job 1:1). Satan at once retorts:

Doth Job fear God for nought?

Hast thou not made an hedge about him, and about his house, and about all that he hath on every side? thou hast blessed the work of his hands, and his substance is increased in the land.

But put forth thy hand now, and touch all that he hath, and he will curse thee to thy face.

And the Lord said unto Satan, Behold, all that he hath is in thy power. (Job 1:9–12)

Blake first shows Job united with his family, in a scene of peace and prosperity; then the calamities which befall him, destroying his family and all his possessions. Although overwhelmed with disaster, Job still trusts in God, saying:

Naked came I out of my mother's womb, and naked shall I return thither: the Lord gave, and the Lord hath taken away; blessed be the name of the Lord. (Job 1:21)

When Satan is shown trampling on Job and smiting him with sores from head to foot, Job's wife says, 'Dost thou still retain thy integrity? Curse God and die.' But Job answers, 'Shall we receive good at the hand of God, and shall we not receive evil?' (Job 2: 9–10).

When three friends visit him, they cannot recognize him; for seven days and nights they sit beside him without saying a word, 'for they saw that his grief was very great' (Job 2:13). Then at last Job's resignation and trust give way to bitter lamentation and reproach – a scene which Blake's drawing captures superbly:

Let the day perish wherein I was born, and the night in which it was said, There is a man child conceived. (Job 3:3)

When his friends remonstrate with him, he replies:

Oh that my grief were thoroughly weighed, and my calamity laid in the balances together! For now it would be heavier than the sand of the sea: therefore my words are swallowed up . . . Teach me, and I will hold my tongue: and cause me to understand wherein I have erred . . . I have sinned; what shall I do unto thee, O thou preserver of men? why hast thou set me as a mark against thee, so that I am a burden to myself? . . . If I justify myself, mine own mouth shall condemn me: if I say I am perfect, it shall prove me perverse. (Job 6:2–3, 6:24, 7:20, 9:20)

The intervention of Job's friends drives him first of all to a perfect torrent of self-pity. They in their turn are exasperated by his indignation and stubborn self-righteousness, urging him to admit his fault and respect the discipline of an Almighty who cannot err. Never, says Job:

God forbid that I should justify you: till I die I will not remove my integrity from me. My righteousness I hold fast, and will not let it go: my heart shall not reproach me so long as I live. (Job 27:5–6)

To his friends this is blasphemy: his obstinacy in asserting his innocence is nothing less than an indictment of God. Job has the last word, however:

Oh that one would hear me! because my desire is, that the Almighty would answer me, and that mine adversary had written a book. Surely I would take it upon my shoulder, and bind it as a crown to me. (Job 31:35–6)

So we reach the bottom of the pit. Job has rejected his friends and, in Blake's terrifying vision, is shown lying upon his narrow bed in utter isolation from all human fellowship. He becomes a prey to the hideous phantoms of his own creed and sees in terror that the deity he has been worshipping is none other than the Great Selfhood of Satan, worshipped as God by the soul in its blindness. Below, three devils seek to drag him down into the flames of hell – 'Hell which is all self-righteousness.' Above, two stones represent the tablets of the prohibitive law, the ideal of which is the punishment of sin, rather than the liberation of man's passion out of which all human good is born. The deity who overshadows Job and offers this alternative is actually Satan, as we see by his cloven hoof. But he is Satan in the likeness of Job, alone with his selfhood, shut up in himself. Coiled round Satan is the serpent symbolizing Satan's alternatives – the Hell of Sensuality or the Hell of Self-Righteousness.

The next illustration (No. 12), calm after the storm, shows that the crisis is past. A young man, Elihu, has appeared, expressing anger that Job should make himself out to be more righteous than God and that the three friends had found no answer to Job, but had let God appear in the wrong. He breaks the spell of self-pity and self-obsession and opens Job's eyes to the greatness of God, to the vastness of his design, which far exceeds the understanding of man:

Lo, all these things worketh God oftentimes with man. To bring back his soul from the pit, to be enlightened with the light of the living. (Job 33: 29–30)

This in turn leads up to the climax – the appearance of God himself in the whirlwind:

Who is this that darkeneth counsel by words without knowledge? . . . Where wast thou when I laid the foundations of the earth? . . . Who laid the measures thereof, if thou knowest? . . . or who laid the corner stone thereof; when the morning stars sang together, and all the sons of God shouted for joy? (Job 38:2–7)

Job is overwhelmed by God's anger:

Therefore have I uttered that I understood not; things too wonderful for me, which I knew not . . . I have heard of thee by the hearing of the ear:

but now mine eye seeth thee. Wherefore I abhor myself, and repent in dust and ashes. (Job 42:3–6)

Blake's designs, each not much bigger than a man's hand, match the magnificence of the language – God in the whirlwind, the morning stars singing together, the creation of the world beneath man, represented by Behemoth and Leviathan, who 'is a king over all the children of pride' (Job 41:34). In all three plates in which he appears, God is shown in the likeness of Job, as earlier, in the pit, Satan had been. This is the sign that the conflict has taken place in Job's soul, and is followed by the casting of Satan out of heaven. Jesus said, 'I beheld Satan as lightning fall from heaven' (Luke 10:18). With him, in Blake's engraving, are cast out the evil selves of Job and his wife as they had been embodied when they were enslaved to the Great Selfhood.

In his last but one design, Blake shows Job reunited with his daughters; in the margin, Blake has engraved:

> How precious are thy thoughts unto me, O God,
> How great is the sum of them!
> (Psalms 139:17)

> If I ascend up into Heaven thou art there
> If I make my bed in Hell behold Thou art there.
> (Psalms 139:8)

Finally, Job is seen once more restored to peace and prosperity with his family beneath the patriarchal oak, as in the first illustration, but this time joining in a symphony of praise to heaven which mingles with the song of the morning stars.

III

Summing up Blake's vision of the Book of Job, my father focused on Blake's belief that

126

The divine within man is clouded by a great and destructive error, which is none other than the subtle and dominating consciousness of self, which man first worships as God, creating God in his own image, although he does not realize what he is worshipping. This is the dark satanic presence which must first be made manifest and then cast out.

Blake believes it cannot be cast out unless it is made manifest. He shows Job passing through the fires of experience into the pit of his own spiritual darkness and selfhood, until Elihu awakens him to pass beyond the thought of himself and Job enters into the vision of the universe illuminated by the same spiritual life as himself.

With little formal education, Blake read deeply in the Bible and the mystics, from the Hebrew Kabbalah and the *Bhagavadgita* to Dante and St Teresa. *The Everlasting Gospel* (to the scandal of the godly) and *The Marriage of Heaven and Hell*, with its 'Proverbs of Hell',* show the brilliance of which he was capable. His major works, however – *Vala*, or *The Four Zoas, Milton* and *Jerusalem* – take up 475 pages of his completed works and require a concentrated effort to master – an effort which my father never regretted.

Single-handed, Blake developed a doctrine of fourfold vision as the basis of his mysticism. Single vision is spiritual blindness, the uninformed work of the eye, a mechanical, material, Newtonian outlook. Twofold vision is *through* the eye, not of it. It is the perception of a spiritual reality, described in four magical lines:

> To see a World in a Grain of Sand,
> And a Heaven in a Wild Flower,
> Hold Infinity in the palm of your hand
> And Eternity in an hour.†

---

* Among the best-known of the Proverbs (in Plate 7 of *The Marriage of Heaven and Hell* (*c.* 1790–93)) are: 'The road of excess leads to the palace of wisdom', 'Prudence is a rich, ugly old maid courted by Incapacity', 'He who desires but acts not, breeds pestilence', 'Eternity is in love with the productions of time', 'If the fool would persist in his folly, he would become wise', 'Damn braces. Bless relaxes.'
† 'Auguries of Innocence' (*c.* 1803).

Threefold vision is associated with the life of the moon – what Blake calls Beulah, the state of eternity, and his name for the unconscious as the source of creative art. Fourfold vision represents the mystical ecstasy in which God and man and the whole world become one.

It was this vision which sustained Blake in face of poverty and neglect. In his later years, when he was engraving *Job*, he and his devoted wife worked, cooked, ate and slept in a single room off Fountain Court, Strand. An old man now, suffering much pain from gallstones, the bitterness of unrecognized genius had almost entirely left him. *Job*, when published in 1826, proved to be one more failure, but this did not for long disturb his serenity. As Joseph Wicksteed wrote, 'He sat or lay in his earthly home, and drew and sang and dreamed of heaven.' A century later he was at last recognized as an indisputable genius.

12

The Relevance of the Gospel
in the Modern World

I

During Lent 1936, Frank made a determined effort to break through
the theological controversies which surround the figure of Jesus
and to present him in a way which modern men and women can
understand.

What nobody seems prepared to accept is that Jesus reveals the ultimate
possibilities of human nature, including alleged miracles and resurrection,
not as an exception but as the normal unfolding of latent powers in every
man and woman. Yet this is precisely what Jesus appears to have taught:
that what he revealed and experienced is at some time possible for us all
and certainly possible for the future of humanity.

Do we then accept the Gospels, with all their difficulties and contradictions, as history? Well, what do you mean by history? History is made up
of two orders of reality: outward fact and inward consciousness. We may
call them history and mystery, the mystery of the hidden side of things,
that is present in us, in our consciousness. The Gospels are great because
they present both orders of reality and recognize that in the end they are
not two things but one. The difficulty for those who live in modern times
is that we think and speak of the hidden side of things in abstract terms,
while in Jesus' time (and long afterwards) they thought and spoke of them
in symbols, signs and images, in a picture consciousness.

Frank then turned to the Sermon on the Mount. Jesus' new
consciousness, following his baptism and the Temptation, the new
power which it gave him and the eager response of the multitudes,
produced a sense of urgency in his own soul.

For a short time there appeared the vision of the end of history, the advent of a new order of reality in which all things should be consummated in the Kingdom of God on earth. That is the glory which shines over these Galilean days, and it was under the glow of this great hope that he summoned his disciples to ascend the mountain with him. There he revealed to them, in the Sermon on the Mount, the character of the Kingdom of God which he believed was about to be realized on earth. That did not happen, the end of history did not come, but the promise of the Kingdom and the Beatitudes remain as an eternal part of the gospel.

The turning point came in the episode of the feeding of the five thousand, following the beheading of John the Baptist. Jesus sought to retire to a lonely place, but the multitude followed him wherever he went, drawn by the healings he performed. The more he forbade those he cured to tell anyone, the more they published it. 'They had no leisure even to eat,' Mark says, 'so many were coming and going.' An attempt to escape by boat failed. 'When [Jesus] came ashore, he saw a great crowd; and his heart went out to them, because they were like sheep without a shepherd; and he had much to teach them' (Mark 6:31–4).

It was then that the so-called miracle occurred, the feeding of the five thousand, when Jesus took the five loaves and two fishes which was all they had and with them fed the multitude. What Frank saw in this was no piece of commonplace magic but a manifestation of the Kingdom of God, a release from self, in which man ate of the bread which cometh from above and drank of the living water of the spirit. For a moment all things seemed possible, the Kingdom trembled on the edge of manifestation – and then, suddenly, the shadow fell. The multitude had misunderstood. 'Surely', they said, 'this must be the prophet that was to come into the world.' But 'Jesus, aware that they meant to come and seize him to proclaim him king, withdrew again to the hills by himself' (John 6:14–15).

From this time on, abandoning any hope that history would end and be replaced by the Kingdom of God immediately, Jesus began to teach the disciples that he would first have to undergo great sufferings and be put to death. But this too they did not understand, and they were afraid to ask him what he meant.

My father's account of the Passion has already been given. What caught his imagination was the symbol of the empty tomb, the point at which history is replaced by mystery – a symbol with an infinite suggestiveness. The first reaction of the disciples was an overwhelming sense of loss and bewilderment, slowly giving way to wonder and the gradual realization of the mystery of the risen life – a consciousness beyond the assessment of history, which may note its effects but cannot measure its substance.

And yet if we think about it, we shall not cry miracle, a breach of the natural order, but will recognize that the law and order of Nature and the law and order of the Kingdom of God are at one in their triumph over death. The empty tomb is the law of Nature. In her unresting if unhurrying process, Nature takes all things back into the great mystery of life and brings forth a million new forms of flower, grass and leaf to proclaim, this Easter morning, the evangel of the empty tomb.

Poetry can understand what theology quarrels about. Think what theology has done with that empty tomb and the mystery of the risen life. It has used it to proclaim the falsehood that Nature is sin and death, and condemns the natural life as the darkness of evil. Instead of surrendering the ringing hope of the gospel and the symbol of the empty tomb to the arguments of unbelief, we should celebrate them as the affirmation that, in the Kingdom of God as in the Kingdom of Nature, life is eternally triumphant.

II

A stranger visiting Chapel Lane Chapel in 1935 might well have been surprised to find that four morning sermons in the spring were devoted to the Hindu scriptures and four more in the autumn to Buddhism. Frank would have nothing to do with the claim that Christianity had a monopoly of truth. He was fascinated by the discovery that the Ancient Wisdom was to be found in a score of different civilizations, which constantly threw up parallels and borrowings from each other. There was, however, never any doubt that for him – the inheritor of a Christian, not a Hindu or Buddhist tradition – the centre of his development, the foundation to which he could relate his own experience and what he learned from other traditions, remained the mystical interpretation of the life, death and resurrection of Jesus Christ. He never tired of returning to and finding fresh inspiration in the New Testament. An example is the two sermons he preached in 1936 on the mind of Christ. He took his text from Matthew's account of Jesus' reception in his home town:

> Whence hath this man this wisdom, and these mighty works? Is not this the carpenter's son? is not his mother called Mary? . . . Whence then hath this man all these things? And they were offended in him. (Matthew 13:54–7)

The people of Nazareth were not the only ones offended by the mind of Christ, not least because of its deeply rooted historical reality. Many people could accept an ideal Christ, but the son of Joseph and Mary has been too much for orthodox Christianity. Instead, they got rid of Joseph and made Mary into a goddess, ignoring the fact that the whole of the gospel of Incarnation is that Christ came along the pathway of normal human existence.

Frank continued:

Jesus was not an intellectual; he created no philosophical system as Plato did. His mind was apocalyptic, vivid, concrete, aphoristic, poetic, a startling manifestation of mental powers to our rationalistic expectations. We begin to realize that this is the primal structure of the human mind. We treasure it still in myth, poetry and proverbial wisdom. Jesus' mind never deals in abstractions, deals always with immediate reality in brilliant flashes of imagery and swift decision, breaking through the shams, conventions and different mechanisms of complacent minds, presenting them with a crisis in which they must decide and act.

Jesus responded to originality in others. When a Canaanite woman sought help for her daughter he rejected her plea, saying that he was sent to help the lost sheep of Israel and them alone. 'It is not meet to take the children's bread and cast it to the dogs.' 'Yea Lord,' she answered: 'for even the dogs eat of the crumbs which fall from their masters' table.' Jesus responded at once: 'O woman, great is thy faith: be it done unto thee even as thou wilt.' And from that moment her daughter was restored to health (Matthew 15:21–8).

He makes no compromise with evil. Suffering, disease, inhumanity are manifestations of a spiritual Kingdom of Darkness. This frank acceptance of dualism is another cause of offence. But Christ does not hesitate: 'Get thee behind me, Satan' (Matthew 16:23). Nor does he show any sentimentality: 'It were well for [a man] if a millstone were hanged about his neck, and he were thrown into the sea, rather than that he should cause one of these little ones to stumble' (Luke 17:2). Yet he can also show great tenderness. To the prostitute who kissed his feet and anointed them with myrrh: 'Thy sins are forgiven ... Thy faith hath saved thee; go in peace' (Luke 7:48–50). To one of the two thieves who were crucified with him: 'To-day shalt thou be with me in Paradise' (Luke 23:43).

Finally, there is his courage, his open challenge to Jewish religion and Roman power, knowing it will lead to his death.

Frank pointed out that, so far as we know, when Christ died not a single word of his teaching had been put on record. It was the overwhelming impression made by his followers' experience of the Risen Christ, whatever that experience was, that led them to turn their sense of tragedy into a gospel of hope for all men.

The Gospels in which this was expressed are not literary creations of genius like Greek or Shakespearean tragedy. They became literature almost by accident; they are unconscious literature, revealing the mind of Christ as not destroyed by death or the last cry of despair, 'My God, my God, why hast thou forsaken me?' (Matthew 27:46), but alive, creative and dominant beyond death.

The effect was to replace the shadow of fate over human life by the conviction, which the example of Christ inspired, that there was no limit to the power of the human spirit to grow and create. The proof was the extraordinary achievement of this small body of men in starting a movement which captured the Roman Empire and eventually the whole of Europe.

No one contributed more to this than Paul. His preaching of Christ's message to the Greek and Roman cities and the letters he addressed to them constitute what has been called the Fifth Gospel but in fact was the first, pre-dating Mark's Gospel by several years. Unfortunately Paul appears never to have set down his teaching in written form, and it has to be reconstructed from the scattered references in his letters,' which were written *c*. AD 48–61.

Paul insists that he did not derive his knowledge of Christ from any human or historical source. 'I certify you, brethren, that the gospel which was preached of me is not after man. For I neither received it of man, neither was I taught it, but by the revelation of Jesus Christ' (Galatians 1:11–12).

Paul's powerful statement was later recorded in Acts as the vision on the Damascus road.

Frank concentrated on three fragments of Paul's original Gospel which he saw as central to his teaching: the first and third from his letters to the Corinthians, the second from the letter to the Romans. Corinth was a Greek city, and the members of the Church there prided themselves on their intellectual attainments. These, however, had brought strife and division into the community, and Paul charges the brethren with being puffed up with knowledge.

God has made the wisdom of this world look foolish . . . (1 Corinthians 1:27)*

The Jews require a sign, and the Greeks seek after wisdom: But we preach Christ crucified, unto the Jews a stumblingblock, and unto the Greeks foolishness; But unto them which are called, both Jews and Greeks, Christ the power of God, and the wisdom of God. (1 Corinthians 1:22–4)

Frank continued:

Paul is not talking about physical resurrection at all, but about a profound change of consciousness. To begin with it would seem like death; then there would come a change. 'Behold I shew you a mystery; We shall not all sleep, but we shall all be changed, in a moment, in the twinkling of an

---

* 1 Corinthians 1:27: 'God chose the foolish things of the world, that he might put to shame them that are wise.'

eye . . . for the trumpet shall sound and the dead shall be raised incorruptible, and we shall be changed. For this corruptible must put on incorruption, and this mortal must put on immortality . . . Then shall be brought to pass the saying that is written, Death is swallowed up in victory' (1 Corinthians 15:51–4). It is still wisdom in a mystery – a hidden wisdom.

The second expression of Paul's on which Frank fastened was the Greek word '*dikaiosune*' – a word which appears no less than seventy-eight times in Paul's letters, and which the Authorized Version translates as 'righteousness', in 'they which do hunger and thirst after righteousness', which the New English Bible gives as 'those who hunger and thirst to see right prevail' (Matthew 5:6). Frank suggested that, whatever the literal meaning of the word, the idea which both Paul and Jesus had in mind was not morality or justice but harmony with the divine creative forces in the universe.

If we could penetrate deeply enough into the fundamental problem of both humanity and nature, we could say that what all things hunger and thirst after is harmony and that it is the achievement of this which produces the state of blessedness of which Jesus spoke.

Paul's argument was that Adam, that is mankind, fell out of this divine harmony, and with man Nature also fell. The natural law had become distorted and corrupt, the divine image had become deformed, while the law revealed in the Ancient Wisdom brought only despair: men could not keep the harmony or attain the righteousness revealed by the divine law. The divine law had become for man – because of his corruption – the law of sin and death, the law of consequences.

What then is Paul's remedy? Men and women, Paul says, must begin to live from another centre – from the centre of the spirit, not of the senses. As the text says, harmony or righteousness is 'fulfilled in us, who walk not after the flesh, but after the Spirit' (Romans 8:4). So Paul passes from a vision of despair to one of hope. 'For we know that the whole creation [which] groaneth and travaileth in pain together until now . . . shall be delivered from the bondage of corruption into the glorious liberty of the children of God' (Romans 8:22, 21).

*

To the last of his meditations on Paul, Frank gave the title 'The Nothingness of Man', and he asked whether Paul's constant insistence on the vanity and frustration of life, sin and death is not exaggerated.

When we think of the inexhaustible emergence of new life in the endless generation of man and nature, of the vast unfolding of history, the creative energies revealed in great personalities, in sacred art, music and literature, we resent Paul's pessimistic vision.

But is he wrong? Let us look a little further. Can you get any real foothold in history? Corruption and decay overtake every institution. What was the dominant fact before Paul's eyes as he moved about that great Roman Empire? Abundance of life to create, but no power of life to sustain. Over all things falls the shadow of death – over the planet, over the world of nature, over ourselves.

We shut our eyes, but when we face the facts and grasp the inevitability of the end, we are ready to listen to a gospel which affirms that there is in man the seed of a life of the spirit which, emerging out of the experience of death, bears life forward into a kingdom where no shadow falls. 'But some man will say, How are the dead raised up?' 'Thou fool,' Paul replies, 'that which thou sowest is not quickened, except it die' (1 Corinthians 15:35–6).

Frank concluded:

There is a kingdom of spiritual humanity which through the ages has been called by many names, and in the New Testament is called Christhood. That kingdom was operative in Jesus; he passed out of the Kingdom of Death into the Kingdom of the Spirit. Paul had touched that Kingdom, when Christ appeared to him on the Damascus road, and proclaimed it with passionate eagerness.

'For since it was a man who brought death into the world, a man also brought resurrection of the dead. For as in Adam all die, even so in Christ', another man, 'shall all be made alive' (1 Corinthians 15:21–2). This is the great affirmation of Paul's Fifth Gospel.

III

The second theme in Frank's sermons was the crisis which he believed afflicted the Western world in the twentieth century. In the sermon already quoted and entitled 'What Shall We Do?', delivered in the autumn of 1938, immediately after the Munich crisis, he told his congregation:

These events have not arisen from any immediate political causes and cannot be settled by the expedients of statecraft, however skilful. They are the symptoms of a profound psychological and spiritual crisis in man's consciousness and, deeper still, in our unconscious, which will go on working itself out despite any temporary relief of tension.

The oppositions, the drama, the tragedies of violence and conflict which are everywhere manifest in our world are the projections on to the screen of history of division, tragedies, frustrations and conflicts of volcanic intensity which stir and rage within the hidden life of humanity.

Philosophy, science, the whole of the modern temper of mind has been inclined for the last hundred years to the conclusion that man is just an animal with superior instincts, emotion and mental capacity, which *mean* nothing.

Or, as Macbeth puts it:

> Life's but a walking shadow, a poor player,
> That struts and frets his hour upon the stage
> And then is heard no more
> (Macbeth, V.v.26–8)

The crisis of society has been reflected in the crises of individual lives: the feeling that life has no meaning, no purpose, no end. No one expressed this more clearly than T. S. Eliot in his two poems *The Waste Land* (1922) and *The Hollow Men* (1925):

We are the hollow men
We are the stuffed men
Leaning together
Headpiece filled with straw. Alas!*

Between all we desire and all we are a shadow falls:

This is the way the world ends
Not with a bang but a whimper.†

Elsewhere Frank spoke of an unrest which revealed itself as an uneasy sense of insecurity in relation to material things, as a lack of creativity in relation to things of the mind, and as fundamental doubt in relation to things of the spirit. The religious faith which, in the past, had provided security and assurance had lost its power.

The outbreak less than a year later of the Second World War – a war in which some 30 million died in Europe and the Soviet Union and half as many again in Asia – confirmed Frank's forecast of a crisis, fuelled by the violence and conflict in the hidden life of humanity, which nothing could stop until it had exhausted itself.

Even before the war began he was asking 'What Can Be Done?', searching and hoping – as he continued to for the rest of his life – for the sort of fundamental change in human attitudes that had occurred from time to time in the past (the Renaissance, the Reformation, the Enlightenment), only to be driven back to the conclusion that, for his lifetime at least, the only answer that could be given was in terms of individuals or at most small groups.

What sort of answer could be given at that level? What was needed? What was possible? Frank addressed himself to those who felt that the vitality of the original religious experience, as this had been known to Jesus or Paul or Luther, was becoming exhausted. They were looking for a religious experience of their own. What

---

* *The Hollow Men* (1925), in T. S. Eliot, *The Complete Poems and Plays* (Faber, London, 1969), p. 83.
† Ibid., p. 86.

would be the main elements in such an experience? His starting point was his recognition that the life in him was part of the life of the universe.

The thought in me, with all its impulse to range and hope, is part of the thought that built the universe and sustains it. I know that this is a thinking, creative, aspiring, sympathetic universe because the power of thought, creation, inspiration and sympathy in my soul are born out of the life of the universe.

Time and space are illusions of my surface consciousness. In a profound sense I can answer the challenge of the Book of Job and say, 'I *was* there when the foundations of the earth and of the universe were laid.' That which is to be my ultimate being was and is a part of the universe from its beginning.

In thought and imagination – which are powers given me by the universe – I can realize these things, but as yet in my experience I cannot. I am still subject to limitations of body and conscious thought, and strangely enough I have to realize that this limitation is also in the purpose of the universe. In the power of thought and feeling we are gods; in the experience and realization of our powers we are but children.

Beloved, now are we the sons of God, and it doth not yet appear what we shall be: but we know that, when he shall appear, we shall be like him. (1 John 3:2)

After the living soul of humanity and the living universe, Frank came to the living God, affirmed in his creativity and in his formlessness. In these two affirmations he believed we come as near to the heart of the mystery of religion as can be expressed in words.

The creativity of God is expressed in the universe, but to appreciate it we must escape the shadow of self and see nature as a whole, including life and death, joy and sorrow, power and pain, emergence and dissolution, ebb and flow. That manifestation will give us confidence and hope.

But we are not merely spectators, we are a part of this universal life, and its most intimate creativeness comes to us, in the last resort, in our own lives, expressed in a thousand images, felt in a thousand subtle relations, ranging from the first report of the senses up to the highest ranges of mental vision. This creativity has produced all the scriptures, all the myths, legends, poetry, art and music that have flowed out through the soul of humanity.

Last of all, God comes to creative manifestation in the mysteries of personality and will. But at no moment must we say, 'This is God' or 'That is God'; not even the universe itself is God. He is the formless exposed in all the forms, the light behind the shadows, the eternal background of life against which death is only a process of his creativeness.

13

Stages of the Inner Life

I

Another subject Frank explored in his sermons was the nature of the inner life. The deepest minds in all ages, he pointed out, have always known instinctively that the inner life of man follows the same great rhythms of life and death, birth and rebirth, submergence and re-emergence as are followed by the life of nature.

Take for instance the fact of death. As long as a man only sees this objectively, it appears to have an absolute power over life. This is how the materialist sees it. Very often he is more honest and disinterested than those who condemn him. What he lacks is inner experience, the awareness of an inner life. He can as yet only read the face of things, and his philosophy follows from what Blake would call single vision.

On the other hand, awareness of the inner life will often result at first in emotional confusion, morbidity and self-centredness.

In the end, however, the man who comes to real knowledge is not very disturbed by the phenomenon of death in the outer world; and he knows that in the soul there is a system and unity of life which carries birth and death within itself as a process and is not deeply affected thereby.

Frank projected four stages, or horizons, of inner growth. The first two were individuality and community.

We are slowly beginning to realize that the soul contains resources and possibilities of development to which most of us have little access. These only become accessible through the focus point of consciousness we call self-consciousness. That, however, is the same self which we are so afraid of, out of which emerges the conflicts of egoism and selfishness. That is a side of individuality which requires constant attention. Mere selflessness, which many talk about, is not only impossible, but undesirable. What we need to understand is that the self in man is intended to grow, not to play possum and sham death, nor to express itself in outward acquisitiveness. 'What shall it profit a man, if he shall gain the whole world, and lose his own soul?' (Mark 8:36). Instead, with infinite patience, through the growth and inner enlargement of the self, men may enter into the possession of their souls.

Many men and women have attained to some degree of individuality, but one of the major failures of mankind has been its inability to create a lasting community. In fact, no one can attain complete individuality without sharing in a communal life, and it is the distorted version of individuality, identifying it with egoism and self-assertion, which makes this impossible, leaving some of the finest elements of our humanity starved and underdeveloped. The second horizon of the inner life is therefore to recover the lost capacity for a spiritual community, by cherishing appreciation and a sense of loyalty towards all who share in any degree the mystery of spiritual life.

Individuality and community are at least familiar to us as ideas. But of the two other horizons the first was so unfamiliar that Frank had to invent a word, Naturehood, to describe it, and the second, Godhood, is frankly incredible to most people as the goal of human destiny. From this point on he was speaking the language of mysticism.

In one sense, of course, we are all a part of nature, but, with the growth of self-consciousness, man became conscious of a division between nature and himself, came to see nature as something indifferent and was captured by the idea of exploiting and fighting against nature.

Frank saw the reversal of this attitude, the recovery of a sense of being part of nature, as a goal that could not be achieved in one lifetime. He was equally certain, however, that the beginning of such an initiative had to be made during our physical incarnation. He found support for his idea of Naturehood in the Gospels, and particularly in the figure of Jesus.

It is very revealing [he wrote] what men have chosen for emphasis in the image of the Christ – his goodness, his alleged theology – but how little attention they pay to the great nature mystery in the Gospels. Jesus alone on the mountain, alone on the sea, commanding the storm, are proof not of theological divinity, but affirmations, if only in legend, of man's oneness with nature. This is an image of nature the ever-living, the ever-creative, with a life that ages of death cannot touch in its central depths.

Frank described Godhood as the furthest horizon of human destiny, where the human merges into the unknown. Any attempt to make this mystery credible to our normal way of thinking ran into disbelief on two very different grounds. Religious orthodoxy regarded the claim to Godhood on the part of any human being as presumptuous and blasphemous, accepting it only on very special terms in the case of the Christ, rejecting it even in the case of Buddha. Agnosticism saw man as a chance emergence from the animal kingdom achieved in face of an indifferent, even hostile, universe.

Far from being deterred by this blank unbelief, Frank declared his unshakeable belief in the affirmation of Godhood, as in the case of Christ and Buddha, as 'a far-off goal of possible destiny for every human soul who seeks this path of divine fulfilment'.

He found the foundations of such a faith in two directions. The first was in the nature of the universe and in the nature of man, both of which he saw as essentially that of mind and spirit. At first man is under Nature and under necessity, but as he grows he learns from Nature the secret of his divine sonship, making him the heir of her whole vast estate of wisdom and power.

The second was in the direction of a universal tradition in which he found traces of this same great word of destiny expressed in all the scriptures and in the greatest literature and art of the human race.

Once the call has been received [he concluded], the great pilgrimage begins with a profound change of mind and emotion, and the slow acceptance of a great discipline. We set aside conventional standards, orthodox dogmas; we learn to trust the great word of life that speaks in our hearts; we set forth towards the goal that the divine in us may become at one with the divine in the universe.

II

In contrast are three sermons which Frank delivered at the end of 1937 on the personal experience of religion. He began with faith, remarking that the cliché that the modern world had lost faith was silly. Men and women had plenty of faith in many things – in themselves, in science, in communism, in democracy. What was really meant by loss of faith was that the overworld of spiritual values, of the Kingdom of God, which at one time was mediated through the images of the Bible, the legends and myths of religion, the credo and rituals of the Church, was now veiled from us. This meant, Frank argued, not that the overworld no longer existed but that it was necessary to seek a new way of approach, along the line of recognizing the spiritual nature of our own humanity and the spiritual nature of the world we live in. Abraham looked into the stars and saw the vision of a divine humanity; we may look into the stars for ever but that vision will be veiled from us. The early Church looked into the Gospels and saw the manifestation of the Kingdom of God in miracles and signs. These same miracles and signs are a stumbling block for us. On the other hand we can look into the Gospels and see the mind of Christ, and the psychological and spiritual depth of his wisdom. Why is it, Frank asked, that we can appreciate one but not the other? Because, he answered, the latter follows the direction of the modern consciousness. The authenticity of the Bible no longer lies in its manifestation of miraculous powers, but in a spiritual consciousness, and it is through that consciousness that we can recover our faith.

In a second sermon, under the title 'Knowledge of God', Frank asked whether the ordinary man could have direct experience of God, and answered that he believed he could. The fundamental fact in all experience is the fact of consciousness, the preliminary condition of any experience at all. The direction of consciousness is always towards a more compulsive awareness of reality and the universe; in that unfolding there emerge in every man's experience what can only be called moral and spiritual values.

If we are wise [Frank said], we realize that these values are not absolute. At first we incline to see things as good and evil, but in the end we pass beyond the condemnation of evil to feel its tragedy and realize that our goodness is ultimately futile unless it can redeem evil by changing both good and evil into a larger whole. This, in the language of Jesus, is the Kingdom of God. That is what I would call the divine presence in our consciousness; it will not let us rest in anything less than the vision of redemption. 'The Son of man is come to seek and to save that which was lost' (Luke 19:10). 'God sent not his Son into the world to condemn the world; but that the world through him might be saved' (John 3:17).

God eternally commits himself to the responsibility of Creation, and works within the thought and will of men, even with their doubts and questions. Remember Emerson's great lines 'They reckon ill who leave me out ... I am the doubter and the doubt.' I think that in my own experience God has slowly become the eternal creative background against which my personality, thought, feeling, faith and emotion have their eternal sanction and support. And I find in the words of the psalmist – 'Whither shall I go from thy spirit? Or whither shall I flee from thy presence?' – that all I need is a confession of faith.*

For his third sermon, preached in the Advent season, Frank chose a phrase from Paul's Epistle to the Hebrews (6.5): 'And have tasted ... the powers of the world to come'. Dismissing conventional ideas on a future life after death, he declared that a really intellectual and spiritual faith in a future life was perhaps the most desperate need of religion today. The first condition of such a faith must be a new awareness that it must grow out of life and reality as we experience these here and now, in this present world and time.

Frank argued that the evidence for a future life was to be found in the nature of the self.

---

* The first quotation is from Emerson's poem 'Brahma' (1867); the second from Psalms 139:7.

Can anyone believe that the powers of the self in any of us are realized and exhausted in the present world order? Surely not. We accumulate powers which are surplus to the life we live now, and the cause of the ennui which attacks the spirit of modern man is his abandonment of the hope of growth beyond his present limitations, which he accepts as final – no wonder he despairs. In what realm, then, is the urge to growth to take place? The answer is that the powers of the world to come are already in man, in the horizons of his inner life.

From silent growth and dim intimations of possibility, the life in man has built the body he now uses, the brain, the organs of speech, vision and hearing with which he makes contact with reality and gains dominion over his world. If, then, at this stage, he still becomes aware of further silent inner growth, why not accept the prophecy of experience and believe that these accumulated surplus powers of the soul will build bodies, organisms, instruments of finer sensitivity, vision and being which will correspond with wider ranges of reality and gain dominion over a greater world of life and power? That is the significance of this Advent sermon – a birth in man of a life and power which shall inherit by natural right the Kingdom of Eternity.

III

A word which Frank made much use of was 'reality': the real state of affairs underlying appearances. In 1936 he made the different levels of reality the subject of a series of five sermons, starting with the power of vision and the experience of light which not only the New Testament but practically all the great religious scriptures have seen as the key to spiritual growth.

Frank warned against claiming to see more than we can and against mistaking a personal and private fantasy for the true vision.

The only way to decide this is by the practice of mental and emotional detachment. Give up your system of thought, your traditional inheritance of thought; live always in the expectation of new apprehensions of reality. Then, speaking from my own experience, I suggest that what will happen is that you will slowly begin to apprehend a deeper relationship in life than you have ever expected; you will become aware of a kingdom of reality, at different levels, something beginning in time and space which transcends both.

Frank saw the mark of true vision in awareness that all things are related by invisible bonds, related in ascending levels, or kingdoms, of reality. The first of these he called the Kingdom of Time. The mark of the person without vision is that he or she is imprisoned in time. So far as they can see, time is a single line moving from birth in an ascending arc to mid-life and then in a descending arc to death. As long as our personal lives are identified with this simple line of time, we have no genuine awareness of being and there is a tremendous emotion of sadness related to time and our consciousness of it.

Wordsworth likened that consciousness of time to the 'shades of the prison-house' beginning to close around us.*

It is little wonder that man has always struggled in his thought against this line of fate. He has tried to supplement it with the idea of evolution, which is only the image of an indefinitely longer line in time, millions of years into the past, millions into the future.

Another line of attempted escape has been the extension of the line of time into the invisible. The conventional view of life and reincarnation after death is really this. The part of the line we can see we call time; the part we cannot we call eternity, but it is still an indefinite extension of time.

When Jesus was tempted in the wilderness, he saw the kingdom of this world in a moment of time and rejected it for another vision of reality. Masked behind time and moving within it are the powers and forms of eternal creativity and newness, and this deeper realm is apprehended by our emotion rather than by intellect. To it Frank gave the title the Kingdom of Life. This Kingdom is manifested in time, but both its origins and destinies lie beyond time.

In fact when we speak about life most of us think only of the

---

* 'Ode, Intimations of Immortality', v (1807).

surface stream of events, the patterns life has made in time. We have no vision of that fountain of life hidden in God which, if we would only let it, would rise eternally in the soul.

Frank continued:

If you are in any way aware of that Kingdom of Life, then indeed you are growing in vision, and the Kingdom of Time and the surface pattern of life will not trouble you much, because you will be aware of a power that can transcend time at any moment and rise clear above the pattern of ordinary life in new creativeness.

For the fourth sermon in this series, Frank chose a passage from the Book of Daniel (Daniel 7:13–14) in which the prophet has a vision of the Son of Man descending from heaven and establishing an everlasting kingdom which shall not pass away or be destroyed. Frank called this the Kingdom of Humanity or the Kingdom of the Son of Man. As he remarked, the author had no reason to take an exalted view of human nature. His account is full of human folly, cruelty, pride, violence and war. To use Daniel's own phrase, he saw the human empires he described as empires of the beast. Then clear beyond all that he sees the Kingdom of the Son of Man:

One side of the picture remains constant: the empire of man has always been the empire of the beast; all these elements are present in our world today. In what sense is the other side of the vision true? How can we men and women, living in the Kingdom of Man, find our enfranchisement in the eternal Kingdom of the Son of Man, of spiritual humanity? It is the question of double vision, as Blake called it: the things of time and the things of eternity.

Perhaps we can best understand the mystery if we recall the image of Jesus: men and women seen as seeds. They have no form as seeds, but they have a hidden life in them which, when it begins to awaken and open out, links them to another kingdom, the Kingdom of Humanity. Jesus even said that the sower of the seed was the Son of Man, the eternal and spiritual humanity, and I remember a sentence of Goethe: 'To die and rise again is the mystery of Humanity.'

The process by which men and women enter the Kingdom of Humanity is by a new birth, the beginning of a new life of thought, feeling, emotion and vision. That new life may be very weak by comparison with the 90 per cent still imprisoned in time and absorbed in the surface pattern of life, with only a fraction in the newness, the vague inarticulate desire for truth and beauty and love. But it is that slender thread which links us to the Kingdom of the Son of Man.

The two texts Frank chose for his fifth sermon, on the Kingdom of Heaven, chose themselves:

The kingdom of heaven is like unto a treasure hidden in the field. (Matthew 13:44)

Except a man be born again, he cannot see the kingdom of God. (John 3:3)

In the previous talks there was something to build on in our ordinary ideas, however inadequate, of time, life and humanity. When we come to the Kingdom of Heaven we may feel that we have no corresponding experience of reality with which to begin. We must dismiss immediately the assumption that the Kingdom is related to a life beyond death.

It is obvious from the words of Jesus that the Kingdom of Heaven is actually hidden in life itself 'like unto a treasure hidden in the field' (Matthew 13:44). It is not beyond death; it is not hidden in the future as a reality unrealized, but actually exists with all its beauty, power and significance in life itself. But to see and enter it demands a new birth, new organs of perception growing out of the soul, a new direction to life energies.

Secretly but inevitably it weaves its silent pattern in history and nature, in personality and character. Generally speaking, it is a hidden kingdom. It has its own secret cycles of life, and again and again puts forth its beauty and power in time. It is indeed the river of life; by its waters grows the tree of life whose leaves are for the healing of the nations. 'Seek, and ye shall find; knock, and it shall be opened unto you' (Matthew 7:7).

PART IV

THE EMERGENCE OF
CONSCIOUSNESS

14

'There is nothing in the mind which is not first in the senses'

While my father never departed from a spiritual view of life, and found great satisfaction in taking a church service and preaching, he was well aware that the trappings and language of traditional religion, even in a Unitarian church, created barriers between him and many to whom he believed he might have something to say, if only he could reach them.

Channing Hall, an annexe of Chapel Lane Chapel, originally used for Sunday school, with a separate entrance and nothing to recall religious associations, provided the answer for what might be called 'an alternative ministry'. When Frank spoke in its Lower Schoolroom there were no prayers, hymns or lessons, he wore no gown (he never wore a clerical collar), and the atmosphere was that of a lecture room rather than a chapel. He never attracted or sought to attract large numbers – between twenty-five and forty was the usual audience – but besides church members he drew in strangers who might never otherwise have heard him. Not least of the advantages was the freedom to develop his thoughts in the expanded time of an hour, and in series frequently of twelve, sometimes of six or nine, sessions. Many of the lectures were given on Sunday afternoons in addition to two Sunday services – a punishing schedule; after the war, they were moved to a weekday evening.

Thanks to Miss Thorpe, a devoted lady who had retired from business and acted as chapel secretary, there are verbatim records of no less than sixty-nine series of lectures (600 lectures in all) given by my father in Channing Hall between the autumn of 1928 and the end of 1951. She would make several copies, which were available for those who had missed a session.

Frank's starting point was the propensity of men and women to ask questions, even before they expressed them in words. Their questions were stimulated by necessity: the need to find ways of protecting themselves against wind and storm, cold and heat. But from an early time, surely, some men – and some women – went further and pondered such questions as who created the sun and the stars, why the seasons always followed the same order, what happened when they grew old and died. A very important part of being human was this urge to seek understanding, to go behind immediate experience and try to discover what caused it and what it meant.

The earliest attempts to find answers to these questions were mythological. Every early civilization has its creation myth, of which Genesis is only one example, and myth-making, which enables men and women to bring events and experiences that disturb them into a relationship with themselves, remains an inde-structible activity of the human mind. From myth developed religion, literature, the arts and philosophy. With the rise of ration-alism, however, these were no longer alone in offering answers. By my father's lifetime they had become overshadowed as an approach to life by a secularized philosophy increasingly reliant on the discoveries and explanations of science.

Applied to the physical universe, science has had an unparalleled success, but the attempt to use its methods in the study of the human mind (the mind on which that success depended) has run into a maze of difficulties. As long ago as the seventeenth century, Descartes, the French mathematician and scientist as well as philos-opher (1596–1650), argued that the world is made up of two different kinds of thing: one extended and physical, of which our bodies are made, the other unextended and mental or psychic (from the Greek word for soul), of which our minds are made. These are subject to completely different principles of operation, and how to reconcile the two (the so-called mind–body problem) has remained a central issue of controversy ever since.

An alternative to Descartes's dualism which has attracted support in the past two hundred and fifty years has been one form or another of materialism: the view that the only reality is the physical universe, and that mental processes – feeling or thinking – are by-products of purely physical changes in the brain and the central nervous system.

My father regarded the mind–body problem as a man-made difficulty, recalling the remark of the eighteenth-century Bishop Butler: 'Men first raise a dust and then complain they cannot see.' Relying on his own experience, which corresponded with the common view of mankind throughout history, he was as much convinced – at times even more so – of the reality of the inner world of consciousness, with its emotions, thoughts and doubts, as he was of the reality of the external world. Obviously the two were different, but he could see no reason to assume a fundamental incompatibility or discontinuity between them, still less to seek escape from such an impasse by reducing mental phenomena to a shadowy reflection of physical processes. It seemed obvious to him that the two interacted with each other, the mind influencing the body – and the observer's view of the physical world – as well as the body influencing the mind. The fact that science could not yet explain *how* this took place was not a reason for declaring dogmatically that it was an impossibility.

More than thirty years after Frank's death in 1964, the debate on consciousness remains as sharp as ever. Some of the leaders in the field of neuroscience, however, have turned away from the preoccupation with computer models of the brain which attracted so much attention in the 1950s and 1960s and have moved in a quite different direction, bringing them closer to the position which Frank had adopted instinctively. An example is Gerald Edelman, who in 1993 published *Bright Air, Brilliant Fire: On the Matter of the Mind*, an account of an inquiry which he and his colleagues at the Neuro-Sciences Institute of Rockefeller University in New York had been pursuing since 1978. Following earlier work which had developed a radically different view of how the body's immune system worked and won him a Nobel Prize, Edelman set out to discover whether a similar model could be developed for the nervous system which would show how it is able to categorize the whole

sensory experience of life, and what is the relation of the categoriz-
ing mechanisms to such functions of brain and mind as perception
and, finally, consciousness.

Edelman's theory of Neuronal Group Selection is the answer
which he and his colleagues have worked out in detail, offering a
biological basis for individual human consciousness – both primary
consciousness, which we share with animals, and higher-order
consciousness. In Edelman's own words:

Primary consciousness is the state of being mentally aware of things in the
world – of having mental images in the present. But it is not accompanied
by any sense of [being] a person with a past and a future . . . In contrast
higher consciousness involves the recognition by a thinking subject of his
or her own acts and affections. It embodies a model of the personal, and
of the past and future as well as the present . . . It is what we humans have
in addition to primary consciousness.

In the nineteenth century, many people denounced Darwin's dem-
onstration of evolution by natural selection as reducing man to the
level of the apes and destroying religious belief. In contrast, my
father made evolution the framework on which to develop a psychological approach to human life that never lost sight of men and
women's spiritual potential. He was able to do this because he saw
that the most important fact about evolution was not that it began
in the primeval mud but that it has culminated – so far – in the
emergence of the human species and the human mind, thereby
fundamentally changing the nature of the evolutionary process.

The first to grasp that the operation of the law of natural selection
was no longer universal, but henceforward would be rivalled by
human selection, was Alfred Russel Wallace, in 1864.* It was not,
however, until the middle of the twentieth century that it became
generally recognized that, with the human ability to pass on all
newly acquired knowledge and experience directly to later generations by means of the spoken and printed word – now by computer

---

* See the lengthy quotation from an article of that date by Wallace published in Sir
Alister Hardy, *The Divine Flame* (Collins, London, 1966), pp. 35–8.

as well – evolution had entered a new stage, which Julian Huxley named the 'psycho-social' phase.

My father argued from the fact that the universe, although in incessant motion and change, did not collapse in chaos, but showed order and pattern at every level – that it was governed not by chance but by purpose. He believed that this purpose, although beyond human power to comprehend, gave evidence of an intelligence, a mind at work.

He was well aware of the strong resistance to the idea of purpose in the universe, and the conclusion of many, overwhelmed by the sheer size of the universe, that the human race was a chance creation on an insignificant minor planet, without a future. On the contrary, he argued, the extraordinary combination of circumstances which alone makes possible life on this planet and protects the human race from being destroyed could be taken to suggest that the earth had been selected as an incubator, a testing ground for an experiment in the evolution of life. There might well be comparable experiments on other planets of other stars.

Life of some sort is believed to have been in existence for at least 2,000 million years; it took nearly the whole of that vast period of time for *Homo sapiens* to emerge, not much before 50,000 BC. It was not only the human body, but the human mind as well that emerged. My father never lost his sense of wonder at the extraordinary achievement this represented, the marvellously adaptable human hands and eyes being matched with the imaginative power which allows, for example, the painter not only to represent the external world but to express the inner world of human consciousness.

The achievement has been not only lengthy but painful, involving much effort, conflict and waste, and these were increased when an element of freedom of choice was added in the form of human *self*-consciousness. That was a turning point, since when the pace of evolution has quickened. There was no reason, Frank believed, to suppose that the limits of human development had been reached and evolution had stopped when the experiment had not yet reached a conclusion. Recalling Aristotle's dictum 'look to the end', not just to the origins, Frank applied it to Jung's belief that the tensions in man's present psychological situation are not merely related to his past but represent the pull of an unknown future, the further expansion of human consciousness in ways that cannot yet be foreseen, only imagined.

In his classic study, *On Growth and Form*, Sir D'Arcy Thompson underlined the importance of teleology, explaining phenomena by their being directed towards an end, and shaped by a purpose. 'All the while,' he wrote, 'like warp and woof, mechanism and teleology are interwoven together and we must not cleave to the one or despise the other, for their union is rooted in the very nature of totality.'* On the timescale of evolution, the five thousand years of recorded history are a short period in which to carry out an experiment. There have been important changes in human consciousness even between the Bronze Age and the twentieth century. Why suppose that the experiment has been abandoned?

II

It was against this background that Frank, in his lectures given over thirty years, explored different stages in and facets of the history or, as he often referred to it, the adventure of consciousness, constantly refreshing and deepening his treatment of it from his reading in modern literature and mythology as well as in psychology.

He was fascinated by the extraordinary complexity and subtlety of the evolutionary process, which built up from single cells to create the incredible richness of plant, insect, animal and finally human life. But, where the majority of scientists described that process in terms of mechanism and chance,† he saw it as proof of a guiding intelligence and purpose.

It was in instinct that he found the directing power and energy

* *On Growth and Form* (Cambridge University Press, Cambridge, rev. edn, 1942).
† 'Man is the result of a purposeless and materialistic process that did not have him in mind' – Dr G. G. Simpson, late director of the American Museum of Natural History, in the Terry Lectures delivered at Yale and quoted in Sir Alister Hardy, *The Living Stream* (Collins, London, 1965), p. 14.

which drive life on, so that as soon as one manifestation is achieved, life reaches out to achieve another. Much of man's life (for example, breathing) remains instinctive and unconscious, and men and women share with plant and animal life the same three primary instincts: self-preservation and the search for nutrition; self-reproduction; and the social instinct to hold together and preserve the group. Upon these depends the continued existence of every species, including the human.

Such a view, he argued, was entirely compatible with the competition and conflict between different life forms which is the basis of natural selection, constantly discarding those which failed – 'a continuous Judgement Day' which extends to certain types of humanity as well.

Similarly, he accepted that fear and aggression are a necessary part of the continuous testing of the strength of an organism's instinctive urge to life, the instinct of self-preservation. Those plants and animals which fail to respond to the test eliminate themselves. The same primal instinct prompts every organism to search for that which it needs to feed and nourish its life. There comes a point, however, when it suffers a check, when it cannot find the nutrition it needs and for the first time feels hunger. Frank saw this frustration as the beginning of consciousness, the reaction to the need for food. If hunger cannot be satisfied, it leads to death, but if it can, a rhythm of hunger and satisfaction is established. 'A great deal of a successful organism's cleverness in relation to its environment comes from the primary urge for nutrition and the consciousness aroused by the check.'

In birds and the higher animals, instinctive patterns of behaviour can be modified by learning, but only to a very limited degree. Much of men and women's behaviour too remains unconscious, but in their case the instincts are capable of profound transformation. An example is breathing, which for most of the time is unconscious but which (in yoga, for instance) can be developed through exercises, and has been developed by both Christian and Eastern mystics, to produce a psychological liberation from their environment. The sex instinct can be sublimated into the aesthetic sense, that lasting pleasure in artistic as well as natural beauty which outlives the physical, reproductive, stage. The instinct for self-preservation, to take another example, can be transformed into an overriding care for other lives even at the sacrifice of one's own. Curiosity also plays an important part in the instinct of self-preservation and, starting from that, is a prime factor in human development at all levels, including the development of intellectual life. We owe the greatest discoveries of mind, including the greatest scientific discoveries, to our deep-rooted instinct of curiosity.

A cardinal point in my father's teaching was 'Never despise the instincts, the senses or the body.' The Buddhist tradition was as distrustful of the body and its senses as the Christian: 'Despise the body utterly,' Buddha said; 'give all your attention to the powers of the mind. Only then can you be delivered from the corruption that is in the body.'

Frank would have none of it. Against St Paul's outcry 'I know that . . . in my flesh dwelleth no good thing . . . O wretched man that I am! who shall deliver me out of the body of this death?' (Romans 7:18–24) he quoted Paul's later declaration 'Know ye not that your body is a temple of the Holy Ghost?' (1 Corinthians 6:19).

Against the separation of mind and body he set the concept of their unity, reviving, against both idealism and materialism, the Greek, Neoplatonist and Renaissance image of the microcosm, the 'little world' of man in which the macrocosm or universe is reflected. The ancient idea (for example, in Plato) of a world-soul animating the universe (Frank's 'directing intelligence') had as its corollary the human body as a miniature universe animated by its own soul.

The whole meaning of life [he wrote] is an ever closer correspondence, through the body and its senses, between the individual and the universe out of which you and I have been born . . .

What are your lungs but a correspondence between your body and the air? What is your blood but a mysterious correspondence between your body and the powers of the tide and the moon? Your eye is the one focus of light in a dark universe, built in order that there should be light. In being given light you are also given space – light space. What would you know of the stars if there had not been created that mysterious correspondence which is the eye?

Four of the senses – taste, smell, sight and hearing – appear to be extensions of touch, the fundamental sense in which instinct first expresses itself. Sight and hearing in particular represent a great expansion of human powers. Without sight and the power of observation of the external world in which we live, neither science nor the visual arts would be possible. Hearing leads to the development of speech, which in turn opens the way to the inner world of emotion and thought.

Nonetheless, Frank pointed out, there are millions of people who regard themselves as educated but who have never learned to appreciate and make proper use of their senses, simply allowing them to be passive and respond to traditional stimuli:

Don't shun your senses. What do you think they were given you for? What do you think millions of years were spent evolving them for? You have been living in a mental and emotional hothouse; the time has come to open the windows and let in the air. You are going to allow your mind to be actually aware of the mystery of life as it is there in the hedgerow, in the bird, in the cloud, in the light and shade falling across the landscape . . .

What is the mark of people who liberate their minds and senses in this way? It is a marked simplicity and stability; they have become aware of the elemental power around and within them. They are 'spared and delivered from a multitude of bondages and frustrations'.

The senses can be cultivated by concentrating your attention, and that you can learn to do through mastering the art of breathing. Thus, a musician is taught above everything else to concentrate on listening; such concentration makes it possible for him or her to combine the senses of hearing and touch and so achieve an awareness of sound far beyond anything most of us have ever experienced.

Frank saw no conflict or separation between, on the one hand, the body and the senses and, on the other, the inner world of feeling and thought, quoting a famous sentence from the greatest of medieval philosophers, Thomas Aquinas: 'There is nothing in the mind which is not first in the senses'. Body and mind, he believed, are inseparable. It is the quickening of the mind that intensifies the senses, and it is the life of the senses that quickens the mind. Take the case of your hand. The separation of the fingers and thumb was a great step forward not merely for the hand but for the mind. A painter's eye and hand are dependent on his imagination, but so is his imagination on what he can see with his eye and paint with his hand. Without the senses there would be no art and no science.

III

We know that life began with single-cell organisms like the amoeba. These cells are receptive of impressions and respond to stimuli, as a result of which, for example, they join up with other like cells. But it would be hard to describe their behaviour as evidence of the beginning of consciousness. Frank suggested that it was not until frustration arose that consciousness was born. Human beings certainly share this awareness with animals and just possibly, he thought, in an elementary form, with some plants.

In the course of an immense period of time, consciousness became increasingly sophisticated, until in the human race it passed the crucial threshold of self-consciousness – of being conscious of one's self being conscious. In the preceding stage, however, which lasted many thousands of years, primitive people developed not an individual but a communal consciousness, which each individual shared with the other members of the tribe.

From surviving fragments of ancient literature and law, and from the anthropologists' study of primitive peoples in the modern world, Frank thought it possible to make out the main characteristics of this common consciousness. Those who shared it thought and acted as a group, not as individuals, and could not break away or survive outside that group. They evidently suffered from no inner conflicts or individual sense of guilt. Indeed, they appear to have had no consciousness of an inner life, projecting their awareness of the psychic element in life outward into the external world.

They saw everything there – rocks, caves and trees as well as animals – as endowed with psychic life and inhabited by spirits who possessed magical powers. Some of these spirits were friendly, some hostile. It was of the utmost importance to be able to distinguish between these, and to propitiate them with sacrifices, the performance of ritual ceremonies and the observance of taboos. The tribe was composed of both the living and the dead. The latter had to be kept in remembrance and measures had to be taken to secure their protection and goodwill; in China and elsewhere, this took the form of ancestor worship.

In such circumstances both magic and myth flourished. In order to try to enter into relationship and unify themselves with the life around them, as expressed in the plants, the crops, the sun and stars, men and women learned to practise magic. Dancing may have been the first expression of this. The cave drawings provide another striking example. By far the greatest of the mysteries was the magic of words (the Greek for 'word' is 'logos'), bringing men and women into direct communication, as the Greeks felt, with the living powers and energies around them – a magic which survives into our own time in poetry as it does in music and the visual arts.

Wherever this communal consciousness developed it expressed itself in myths. The first god man knew was the sky, the Father; the earth was the Mother. The bull became the representative of the Great Father, the cow of the moon and of earth. These were creations of the collective imagination, powerful formative images, which men saw not as part of an inner life they had not yet developed, but as something outside themselves.

It is through these myths that we can still secure an insight into primitive man's collective mind. With the growth of self-consciousness, the myths sank into the unconscious, but they still retain their vitality, on which artists and writers of our own time have continued to draw – Picasso, for example, and James Joyce in *Ulysses*.

Frank speculated that it was the 'medicine man', the 'witch doctor' or – another possibility – the outcasts of the tribe who began to feel themselves cut off from the common consciousness and became the first individuals, conscious of themselves. At first, self-consciousness was felt as an intolerable burden. This is still repeated at that stage in childhood when we too first become aware of ourselves.

Those who opposed abandoning the community resorted to an intensification of ritual in an effort to preserve the old pattern of life, while those who broke away were conscious not only of loneliness, but of loss, suffering for the first time inner conflict and a sense of guilt.

Frank pointed out that this was the central theme of the second great myth in the Book of Genesis: the Fall of Man, the expulsion of Adam and Eve from paradise because they had eaten of the tree of the knowledge of good and evil and sought to become as gods. He used two other myths of Genesis to illustrate the consequences: Cain's murder of his brother Abel, and the life of a lonely wanderer to which he was condemned, and the fate of those who sought to build the Tower of Babel, 'a tower, whose top may reach unto heaven' (Genesis 11:4), and who were punished for their presumption by being scattered over the face of the earth and losing their ability to understand each other's speech.

But the sense of loss was more than compensated for by the excitement of discovering one's own identity as an individual self and by the opening up of new ranges of thought and feeling to which this led. Frank speculated that in India this took place at the time when the Vedas, the Hindu scriptures, were written down in Sanskrit, around 1500 BC, and in Greece when the oral poems dealing with the Trojan War were composed, to be written down later as the *Iliad* and the *Odyssey* in the second half of the eighth century BC.

Both Hindus and Greeks were fascinated by the conscious power of thought; the Hindu word for man is 'the one who can think', while the Greeks made the idea of the Logos – 'that which speaks', and so gives expression to thought – a central concept of their philosophy.

The difference which conscious thought made comes out clearly in the changed attitude to myths, the most characteristic expression of the collective unconscious. Myths did not lose their power, but, instead of repeating them, men began to think about their meaning. In India, for example, the first great system of Hindu thought, the Vedanta, no longer treats the images in the Vedic hymns as historical but starts to reflect on their meaning and to develop them. In Greece the myths become the material out of which the dramatists make their plays. Among the Jews, however, community conscious-ness remained strong for a longer time, as the Old Testament shows. It is the struggle between community consciousness and self-consciousness in St Paul's mind and the guilt which he felt at abandoning the Jewish community law which still gives such power to his letters.

The human advance to self-consciousness remains the greatest achievement, to date, of the evolutionary process. To it we owe all the riches of the imagination and intellect expressed in music, art, literature, science and speculative thought. Without it men and women would never have developed that inner life – not only thought and emotion but our awareness of ourselves thinking and feeling – which is mankind's most precious and distinctive possession. It is this power of 'interiorizing' the external world, of making our experience of it personal, which transforms the universe into an environment to which we can respond with our minds and not be overwhelmed.

The word which Frank used to describe the mysterious change from community consciousness to self-consciousness was 'reflection'.

Our consciousness has acquired the power of casting back so that we can see again the experiences we have passed through and feel again the emotions we felt. You cannot really think until you can begin to reflect. The change which produces that power of reflection is the slight inhibition between the impulse and the act. It was out of that break between the vision and the action that you eventually got speech.

15

Psychology and the
Unconscious

I

It could well have been the American psychologist William James who first aroused Frank's interest in psychology and religion. In 1890 James had published a masterly two-volume *The Principles of Psychology*, but in the next decade his interest centred on religious experience – the nature and existence of God, immortality, free will and determinism – culminating in his famous Gifford Lectures, *The Varieties of Religious Experience*, published in 1902. A classic, still in print today, it made all the greater impression because of the richness of the material James assembled and the caution with which he treated it, before coming down in favour of the view that the record of religious evidence pointed to the existence of reserves of energy similar to consciousness on which men and women could draw in times of trouble.

It was not until the 1920s that Freud's ideas – his theory of the unconscious and of psychoanalysis as a method of treating mental disorders – began to penetrate the English-speaking world, giving him an influence in the modern world – on literature and the arts as well as psychology – comparable with that of Darwin and Marx.

The fact that Freud remained implacably opposed to any form of religion and insisted on the sexual basis of neurosis meant that Frank learned more from Carl Gustav Jung, who had broken with Freud in 1914 and developed his own system of analytical psychology. My father was introduced to Jung in translation by Frank Pearce Sturm (see Chapter 4), who gave him a copy of his *The Psychology of the Unconscious*. Frank was impressed by Jung's increasing readiness to consider a new approach to psychology which took account of mythology and religion.

The achievement of individual consciousness meant for the first time a differentiation between the conscious mind and the unconscious. For primitive man, there was no such distinction: he lived in the unconscious. But, when individual consciousness was born out of the unconscious, the relationship between the two became of crucial importance, both for the individual and for society. During the millennia which had passed since then, men and women had experienced the power of the unconscious, often as an irrational force erupting into their lives or, if they were artists or prophets, as the mysterious source from which they drew their inspiration – without in either case identifying it as a part of themselves.

It was left to Freud to recognize it as 'the fourth dimension of the human mind', although, as he himself said, 'The concept of the unconscious has long been knocking at the gates of psychology, asking to be let in. Philosophy and literature have often toyed with it, but science could find no use for it.'*

The use which Freud found for it was to describe what Jung later called 'the personal unconscious', that part of the mind (or, better, psyche) to which we banish those impulses (especially infantile impulses), those experiences and actions in our individual lives, which we find it painful to recall and seek to repress – often with harmful consequences which find expression in neurotic behaviour. Jung, however, differed from Freud in going on to distinguish this personal unconscious from what he called 'the collective unconscious', the most original but also the most controversial of his ideas.

While the personal unconscious [Jung wrote] is made up essentially of contents which have at one time been conscious but which have disappeared from consciousness through having been forgotten or repressed, the contents of the collective unconscious have never been individually acquired but owe their existence exclusively to heredity. Whereas the personal unconscious consists for the most part of complexes, the content of the collective unconscious is made up essentially of archetypes.

* 'Some Elementary Lessons in Psycho-Analysis' (1940), in *The Standard Edition of the Complete Psychological Works of Sigmund Freud* (Hogarth Press, London, 24 vols.), vol. 23 (1964), p. 286.

These, Jung continues, are 'patterns of instinctual behaviour . . . inborn and universally present . . . They comprise a second psychic system of a collective, universal and impersonal nature which is identical in all individuals.'*

Another way of putting it, suggested by Anthony Storr, is to say that the human infant is born with a number of innate, inherited predispositions, probably embedded in the nervous system, which condition the child's response to parents, to the opposite sex, and to basic human situations like having children, separating from parents in adolescence, and finally death.†

According to Frieda Fordham, what Jung called 'archetypal' is the tendency – one might say the necessity – to apprehend and experience life in a manner conditioned by the past history of mankind. Archetypes are 'the pre-existent forms of apprehension' which Jung thought were formed during the thousands of years when the human brain and human consciousness were emerging from an animal state. But their representations are modified and altered according to the historical era in which they appear.‡

The unconscious has a logic of its own, quite different from that of the conscious mind; its surrealistic character is familiar to us from mythology and dreams. The archetypal images through which it communicates may take the form of a figure, a creature, a situation or a symbol. Examples of the first are the Hero, the Great Mother, Satan; of the second, a serpent or a horse; of the third, the situation in which Oedipus found himself; of the fourth, the sun wheel, a tree, a cross, a circle known by the Sanskrit word 'mandala', a magic circle.

The power of such images is particularly noticeable in typical and highly charged human situations such as birth and the rituals

* From a lecture delivered at St Bartholomew's Hospital in October 1936, reprinted in *The Portable Jung*, ed. Joseph Campbell (Viking, New York, 1973), p. 11.
† Anthony Storr, *Jung* (Fontana, London, 1973), p. 49.
‡ Frieda Fordham in her *An Introduction to Jung's Psychology* (Penguin, Harmondsworth, 1959) points out that Jung was inconsistent in his use of the word archetype, sometimes using it when he meant archetypal image, at others using it to cover both archetype and image (pp. 24–5).

of adolescence, extreme danger and triumph over obstacles, and awe-inspiring experiences and death. 'In these circumstances an archetypal image that might have been drawn in the caves of the Auvergne will often appear in the dreams of the most modern of men.'*

Jung claimed that it is in dreams that we most commonly encounter such mythological images. He came to regard our experience of them while asleep (as we are for up to a third of our lives) as the natural and spontaneous expression of the collective unconscious, even if much practice and skill are required to interpret their meaning. He found that such images played an even greater, at times dominating, role in the dreams and hallucinations of his mentally disturbed patients.

From this starting point, Jung embarked on a lifelong exploration of the mythological imagery of other cultures and other periods of history, in a search for parallels. He found them in such profusion that he became convinced that mythological images were expressions of an innate human capacity for image-making, to be found in a great variety of forms in all peoples and all times. They appeared to have a power and energy of their own, and an ability to move men and women to action, independently of and often against their conscious intentions – action which could be at times creative, at other times destructive: a work of art or an outburst of mob frenzy. 'They are', Jung wrote, 'the hidden treasure upon which mankind has continually drawn, and from which it has raised up its gods and demons, and all those potent and mighty thoughts without which man ceases to be man.'

My father's first encounter with Jung's ideas was as fruitful as his meeting with Sturm. Here was a thinker coming from a quite different background – a German-speaking Central European, educated in a scientific-medical tradition, a psychiatrist with ten years' experience in mental hospitals in Zurich and Paris, initially closely associated with Freud – who shared Frank's own interest in mythology and symbolism, and his conviction of the relevance of what Frank called the Ancient Wisdom to the experience of modern

* Fordham, *An Introduction to Jung's Psychology*, p. 25.

man. Sadly, my father never met Jung, but he bought and read all his books that were translated and published by the Bollingen Foundation up to Jung's death in 1961. While he owed and acknowledged a great debt to Jung, however, he was able to absorb this and draw encouragement from it to continue developing his own ideas.

The relationship of the unconscious to the conscious mind can be suggested only in metaphors. Frank compared consciousness to a wick drawing the oil that sustains its light from the great reservoir of the unconscious, both personal and collective. At other times he followed Jung in comparing the unconscious to the sea out of which consciousness rises as an island, with the self, the ego – the knowing, willing 'I' – at its centre. We see only what appears above the water, but below it is a vast underwater world of which the island of consciousness is only the tip.

Out of that hidden sea emerges not only our consciousness, but all the energies and forms of human life in their multitudinous variety – all the energies that are expressed in history, the whole of human experience and the living part of creation, the world of plants and the animal kingdom:

> In the beginning God created the heaven and the earth. And the earth was without form and void; and darkness was upon the face of the deep. And the Spirit of God moved upon the face of the waters.
>
> And God said, Let there be light: and there was light. And God saw the light, that it was good: and God divided the light from the darkness . . . And God made the firmament, and divided the waters which were under the firmament from the waters which were above the firmament: and it was so. (Genesis 1:1–7)

II

As late as the sixteenth century the majority of the inhabitants of Europe accepted the answers which the Christian Church had provided to questions about the purpose of human existence and the place of man in the universe. It is only since the seventeenth century, and with growing effect since the middle of the nineteenth, that men have ceased to believe those answers, without finding adequate alternatives. As a result, a substantial number of men and women have become so disturbed by the failure to find an answer as to create a psychological and spiritual crisis which my father believed underlay and added powerfully to the economic and political crises affecting Europe in the 1930s.

We cannot go on living as we are, with all our traditions destroyed, with all our faith uncertain, with all those forces of ours bottled up in ourselves. There will be a burst somewhere. If we could, we would begin to build for ourselves a new relationship to the universe, to religion, to the conduct of life . . . But everything is in chaos. We do not know what to do or what to believe . . . It is all in the melting pot, and unless we can bring out of ourselves – out of our own souls – a new consciousness, and unless we can relate ourselves in a new way to the universe and to the realities of religion – well, we know what is going to happen. We shall perish. That is the crisis affecting our European world at the present time [October 1934].

There were plenty of others engaged in the same quest,* beginning with Rudolf Steiner (1861–1925), the founder of Anthroposophy, and extending to Jung and his *Modern Man in Search of a Soul*; Count Hermann Keyserling (1880–1946) and his *Travel Diary of a Philosopher*; the Russian philosopher Ouspensky (1878–1947);† and the English poet and novelist D. H. Lawrence (1885–1930), for whom Frank had the highest regard. My father read them all, picking up ideas but going his own way, distrustful of systems, convinced that it was a new world in which he and they were living, from which there was no return to the world in which they had been born, but still drawing inspiration from such older figures as Blake and Böhme and from the Ancient Wisdom. What he did between the beginning of the 1930s and the end of that decade with the outbreak of war in the autumn of 1939 was to try

---

* See Chapter 4.
† J. B. Priestley, the Bradford-born playwright, made Ouspensky the centre-piece of one of his 'Time' plays, *Johnson over Jordan* (1939).

out in his lectures a variety of bases – 'a new consciousness', 'new patterns of thought', 're-education and rebirth', 'explorations and adventures in reality' – on which to start building in the world of the twentieth century a new relationship with God and the universe comparable to – although different from – that which the wisest men and women had achieved in earlier times.

Opening his series on 'New Patterns of Thought' in 1936, Frank said:

You may think I am going to give you a new system of ideas, or a hotchpotch of a bit of my own and a great deal of other people's, but I am not going to do anything of that kind. Systems of ideas cut us off from reality, we get imprisoned in them; what we are after is an approach to reality, not to build up a system of ideas . . .

He concluded the same series:

There are many people who will say, 'Is it not an inevitable thing that people will try to explain, however much you say the word "Mystery" . . . ?' Yes, indeed, we have got a mania today for explaining . . . Nature, Life, Death, Sex, God or Religion – these are the mystery words.

But there is *no* explanation of life. There is no explanation of death. There is no explanation of God. There is no explanation of nature. There is no explanation of sex; you may know all about the physical function of sex, but you have not explained it. These mysteries are profound realities, creative realities, realities which are eternal. Explanations are calling you away from these realities. What we gain in this exteriorization of feeling and intellectualism we pay for by the cutting of our roots, by the withdrawal of our deep-rootedness in the mystery of life.

'Reality' was a word of which my father made much use. Starting from the use of the word 'real' to describe any thing or event which has an objective existence, independently of our perception of it, he went on to conceive of reality as the totality of all such things and events – both the external world and the world within.

He did not believe that it was possible to grasp, still less define, reality as a whole. Nor did he believe that our perception of it can ever be wholly objective, if only because our access to the world 'out there', no less than to the world within, is through our own experience. This is fleeting and subjective, in the sense that we cannot get behind 'how it seems to us' to 'how it really is' – we are ourselves part of 'reality'.

Granted these limitations, he believed that there were four ways in which we can attain partial knowledge of 'reality'. They are: through our sense impressions; through memory; through the intellect; and through the imagination.

Enough has already been said to make clear the importance Frank attached to the first of these:

We could not know anything about the life of the mind, or the life of the emotions or about spiritual reality, if we did not have the instrument of the body and the senses. It is through their development that we graduate to the awareness of consciousness, which brings the widest range of reality within the power of our perception.

The experience of reality through our sense impressions is pouring in on us at such a rate all the time that it would be impossible for us to absorb more than a fraction of it, if it were not for the faculty of memory, which Proust explored with such insight in *Remembrance of Things Past*. Memory is a prime source for the unconscious, and no less important for our consciousness. Both consciousness and the self depend on memory for the continuity which gives us our personal identity.

Whatever its physiological basis, which was still in dispute in Frank's lifetime, memory can be divided into voluntary and involuntary memory. The former can be cultivated, particularly in areas where there is a strong motivation of interest – musicians, actors, scholars, for instance, all have an obvious interest in developing their power of recall.

In contrast, we have no control over our involuntary memory, which can often startle us by the recollections it throws up. All our personal experience, even from the prenatal state, passes into and is stored up in our personal unconscious. Add to that the experience of the race which is preserved in the collective unconscious, and you have some idea of the riches to which our involuntary memory gives us access. Imagination draws deeply upon memory, without which it would hardly exist. A great artist not only sees and remembers, but by the interplay of memory and imagination he is enabled to create new forms and new experience instead of producing a mere copy.

Frank regarded intellect as the supreme instrument of self-consciousness: 'When it first develops, it has an almost hypnotic effect, it gives such a sense of magical power, the power to impose order on external reality.' What man has accomplished with it is extraordinary, both in practical terms – in creating the complex civilization in which we live – and in understanding the structure of the physical universe, from the particle and the cell to the celestial bodies in the outer reaches of space.

But this success has led many to equate the mind with the logical, analytical methods of the intellect, making the latter the sole arbiter of what can or cannot be accepted as the truth about the nature of 'reality' and the meaning of life. The effect of this has been to devalue or suppress the other faculties of the mind, such as feeling, memory and imagination, and to identify 'reality' with abstract systems of thought, from theology and philosophical idealism (Plato to Hegel) at one end of the spectrum, to scientific realism and Marxist materialism at the other. Each has identified a particular aspect of reality and added to human knowledge of it. Provided we understand that none of these systems can offer a final, complete or exclusive account of reality, but that at best they are shadows of it, they can provide a form of training for an approach to reality. But history shows that too often they become strongholds of dogmatic intolerance barring the way to knowledge of a reality which (Frank was convinced), like nature, was always specific, not generalized, always concrete, not abstract, and ever-changing, not static in its manifestations, and so not susceptible of being captured in a set of intellectual concepts or scientific formulae.

III

My father believed that 'consciousness reaches its highest power when it is expressed and realized in imagination'. In saying this he drew a sharp distinction between imagination and fantasy. Fantasy has a part to play in childhood, when it veils the stresses and strains which are to come later and gives time for the child's powers to develop before he or she is confronted with the sterner things of life. But addiction to fantasy after childhood Frank described as a self-indulgent form of day-dreaming, wishful thinking in which our dreams and hopes all come true, a form of escapism which encourages illusion and weakens the mind's grasp of reality. 'The very opposite is true of imagination. Instead of dissipating, it gathers together all our mental powers, quickening our senses, stimulating our intellectual forces, strengthening our will.'

Imagination, unlike fantasy, was as much a part of thought as the intellect. It worked in a different way from intellect, however: not by dividing and analysing, but by combining images and ideas to create new insights and by releasing the energy to realize them in new forms – in art, in poetry and music, in religion, in philosophy and not least in the imaginative leaps of scientific thought. In doing so, the imagination integrated the unconscious and the conscious mind, drawing on the first for the material and the energy for the creative process, relying on the second (here was the true role of the intellect) for the discipline (including self-criticism), the concentration and the skill needed to carry the process through to the finished work of art or scientific theory.

When imagination combined in this way with the other powers of the mind – intellect, emotion and memory – then consciousness rose to its greatest height and came closest to knowledge of, and participation in, reality.

My father more than once used the striking phrase 'Man has a hunger for the apprehension of reality.' Primitive men and women were moved to ask who or what created the stars, the sea, the earth. The Book of Genesis was an attempt to answer that question by creating a god in man's own image as the power behind reality – as all mythologies have done. Later, the Greek philosophers speculated that this power was something like their own minds, and this too they called '*logos*', meaning 'thought' or 'reason'. Frank himself, following Coleridge, saw the power creating and sustaining reality as something like imagination – 'but another name', Wordsworth wrote, 'for absolute power . . . And Reason is her most exalted mood'.*

What light did these answers throw upon the nature of reality? 'All three', Frank pointed out, 'are images taken from the human psyche. There is no getting away from that. The human psyche can only conceive of reality in terms of its own experience, created by something like itself and psychic in character.'

But what did he mean by 'psyche', the Greek word for 'soul'? For many people it is a word, like 'mysticism', which has dubious associations – with the supernatural; with occult powers such as spiritualism, telepathy and clairvoyance; with irrational beliefs and faked experiments. While Frank, like his friend Sturm, had at one time been interested in such phenomena, this was not the sense in which he now used the word. For him, the psyche and the psychic were the subject matter of psychology, the study of the human mind. 'Mind' and 'mental', however, in common usage, refer to the conscious activities of the human mind. He needed a word which would embrace the unconscious as well as the conscious life of human beings, and, following Jung, he found it in the word 'psychic'. 'All that I experience,' Jung wrote, 'is psychic. Even physical pain is a psychic event that belongs to my experience. My sense-impressions – for all that they force upon me a world of impenetrable objects occupying space – are psychic images and these alone are . . . the immediate objects of my consciousness.'†

There are, of course, different levels of reality, but Frank conceived of reality in all of them in terms of energy – an energy which fills the universe with ceaseless activity and manifests itself in myriad different forms. Despite their outward differences, he believed there

* *The Prelude* (1850), Book xiv, lines 191–3.
† *Modern Man in Search of a Soul* (Routledge & Kegan Paul, London, 1933), p. 219.

was no essential distinction between the energy which generates inanimate forces, such as magnetism, and that which creates living forms; between physical and psychic energy; or between the life energy expressed in plants and animals and that expressed in human beings. This is not far from the view of Sir Charles Sherrington (1857–1952), the great Oxford physiologist who laid the foundations of the study of the nervous system, and who spoke in his Gifford Lectures of 1937–8 of the concept of energy 'unifying our whole perceptible world, what it is and what it does ... in a concerted system', of which man himself is part.

Because it is the total sum of everything, reality must include unreality and delusion, evil as well as good, frustration and fear, the incomplete, the unbalanced and the imperfect. It can do this because it is in a state of continuous creation and evolution. This is the reason why intellectual systems of thought can never be imposed on it: it continually breaks up old forms and creates new. The famous phrase which we owe to the early Greek philosophers – 'All things are in flux' – describes the unceasing change of an energy-based reality. Creation is never finished or truth final. There are no unchanging absolutes; the future is always open-ended.

The dynamic nature of reality is balanced by the web of relationships which sustains reality and gives it unity. Its movement is towards greater integration, towards binding diversity into wholeness. Our imperfect apprehension makes it appear infinitely complex; as we understand it better, we realize that its richness is matched by its simplicity.

16

Psychology and Mysticism

I

My father's growing interest in psychology did not lead to any reduction of his interest in mysticism. Between 1929 and 1939 he devoted eighty-five lectures – a third of his output – to mystical topics. It is remarkable that he was able to make so inherently difficult a subject – ranging from two series on St John and two on the mystical tradition in the Gospels to Plotinus and Jakob Böhme – sufficiently interesting to hold his audience.

The difficulty is due to the fact that the discussion of mystical experience and mystical literature has always been conducted in a language which the majority of listeners or readers cannot understand. This was true not just of my father but of all the great mystical teachers, from Buddha to Blake.

You may ask, 'Why the mystery? If something cannot be told straight out, it cannot be much good.'

Well [my father said] as a matter of fact there *are* many things which you cannot say outright. The words 'mystic' and 'mysticism' come from the Greek word '*muo*', to close the lips or shut the eyes, a reference to the mystery religions, the secrets of which were revealed only to the initiated. The mystics say there are certain great truths which can only be grasped when there has been some degree of spiritual growth. You have to allow the mind to grow by revelation.

As a guide for those approaching the study of mysticism for the first time, my father suggested three principles.

First, although appearing in endless variety, most myths, world-wide, fall into one of three main groups: the myth of creation, the myth of man and the myth of redemption.

Second, mystical insight depends upon the principle of analogy, summed up by Jakob Böhme as 'As above, so below.' What happens in this world is a dramatization of what is happening in the invisible; conversely, what is happening in the invisible is a dramatization of what happens here.

The third principle is that of recapitulation, of repetition, turning in an upward spiral round and round but always, the mystic hopes, at successive turns a little higher, a little nearer to God.

The symbol that most excited Frank was *word* – in Greek, *logos*.

Have you ever thought what *word* is? It is breath modified by matter; breath comes up and is modified by various organs to produce speech. The symbol of breath is that of the spirit. 'In the beginning was the Word', spirit moving through all kinds of forms, the creative energy making a pattern and giving identity – the whole object of creation.

When we want to manifest ourselves, we *speak*. Shakespeare makes Prospero say, 'I endowed thy purposes with words' (*The Tempest*, I.ii.359–9), and the account of the Creation in Genesis begins, 'And God *said*, Let there be light.' The act of creation was 'speaking a word', repeated seven times in the first chapter and matched by a second act of speech: 'And God *called* the light Day . . .' repeated five times.

The mystical tradition has always taught that man was involved in the Creation; this too was by an act of speech: 'And whatsoever Adam called every living creature, that was the *name* thereof' (Genesis 2:19). No other living creature is able to do that, to utter words.

From Genesis you can turn to the opening words of the Fourth Gospel and read: 'In the beginning was the Word [Logos], and the Word was with God, and the Word was God . . . And the Word was made flesh, and dwelt among us' (John 1:1–14).

And what did God *say*? He *called* into being the earth and the heaven – the firmament – and the sun, moon and stars, separating out the sea and the dry land, dividing the light from the darkness and creating man in his own image.

*

This is the first great myth: that of creation. The second is the myth of man, a collective name for the human race and the universe in which it lives. Originally man was a part of God, living in perfect unity, but his destiny – his self-chosen destiny – was to fall out of that unity and seek a new life in separation and freedom.

The mystics have always held that it is man (as a part of God) who made the universe, breaking up the original unity, creating a universe in which he could manifest his potentialities and achieving this by successive acts of separation, separating out of eternity into time and space, out of life into kingdoms – mineral, vegetable, animal – separating the two sexes and their desire for each other, the cycle of birth and death. 'By man came death' (1 Corinthians 15:21).

The mystics say that man came out in order to create a new being who was free, who could live his own life and achieve fulfilment in free will. The last separation that took place was the separation of the consciousness: man *knew* himself to be alone. That point of consciousness shrank until it burns like a little flame in you and me, shrinking at last, as William Blake put it, into a little root five feet long. Man is a God who has died; a God has died into man.

Here is the basis and substance of all human tragedy, the death of a God. What was the story Aeschylus took but that of Prometheus, the god who died into man, the god who flung the lightning flash into the abyss in the certain hope that some day that spark would redeem the darkness. Every religion has it. Do you wonder that the centre of the Christian religion was a dying God? It does not mean that God died for you; it means that you are the God who died.

But as by man came death, by man came also the resurrection of the dead. The destiny of man does not end with the myth of the Fall. There had to be a fall because without it there could not be a redemption, the third of the great myths. Man is not only the being who went out to realize his own freedom and self-will; he is ultimately the being who, of his own free will and by an act of freedom, turns back to seek unity with the divine life. It is better that man should choose to go out rather than, under compulsion, remain within. In the end he will come to the knowledge of his divinity, or as Blake put it will 're-assume his ancient bliss'.

Man is a God who has chosen the way of separation, but at some point he has to halt his fall or he will be carried on down and down into the abysses of annihilation – the danger that the intellectual faces, portrayed by Dostoevsky in *The Brothers Karamazov* in the figure of Ivan, who refuses to set any limit to his questioning and falls into nihilism. Another genius, William Blake, grasped that God had set a boundary and provided a point of arrest in matter, in materiality. Matter was not all evil, as Zoroaster's mystical doctrine claimed; on the contrary, Blake wrote, 'matter is the ultimate mercy of God'.

II

In the series of lectures 'Re-education and Rebirth', which my father gave in January–March 1937, he drew a distinction between novelty and originality. Novelty immediately attracts attention but fails to retain it. The original thinker goes back to a tradition which is ages old. Whether you go to Buddha, to the teachings of Jesus in Palestine, to the poets and philosophers in Greece or to the older thought in India (the Vedanta), you realize that every one of those teachers has drawn from the same source, and that it is this which gives their teaching power. There *is* novelty in the universe, but the fundamental character of the universe is not novel at all. Truth itself is never new; real truth is eternal.

My doctrine [Frank wrote] is not mine but his that sent me. I am a servant of an eternal tradition, a poor servant who does not understand it with the clarity with which many great teachers have understood it. Like you I am also a learner, but within my capacity I serve an original truth that lies at the foundation of the universe and reality.

We cannot hope to grasp the truth in one utterance; we need to go over the same ground again and again. That is why Jesus and Buddha repeated their teaching in aphorisms, with the intention that the mind would go back to these sayings again and again. The sense in which I want to use the word 're-education' is the act of re-knowing, not something that we are going to acquire for the first time, but something that we are going to know again, a bringing back of something we have lost sight of.

Recognition may take place suddenly, when you read a passage in the Scriptures, suddenly see its meaning, and ever afterwards always remember it. Rebirth, however, is a much slower process. You become discouraged, sometimes you find satisfaction, at other times it seems incredible that you could ever have been interested in such things. Do not worry: recognition will come again and with it, finally, rebirth. 'The water that I shall give him', Jesus said, 'shall become in him a well of water springing up unto eternal life' (John 4:14). Thomas à Kempis, the fifteenth-century author of *The Imitation of Christ* said, 'He to whom the Eternal Word has spoken, is sped and delivered from a multitude of opinions.'

My father pointed to the importance, from first to last, of Jesus' sense of destiny: the feeling that, whatever they entailed, certain things must happen. It is not some exterior force which has drawn you into things; the ultimate meaning of destiny is 'For this cause came I into the world' (John 18:37). You have come into a given situation, into a given world, for a given purpose. The moment you accept that, liberation begins. Jesus carried his consciousness of this into death itself. That is the meaning of Christian initiation – that it integrates death itself into the human consciousness.

Jesus' action is deliberate from beginning to end of his story. When one of his disciples betrays him and another denies him, and when all are going to forsake him, he does not repudiate their allegiance, but looks into their faces and says, 'Ye have not chosen me, but I have chosen you' (John 15:16). He accepts the whole situation as having been deliberately chosen by himself, not forced upon him from outside.

Jesus *knowing* . . . that he was come from God, and went to God . . . (John 13:3)

And Jesus, *knowing* that Satan had put it into the heart of Judas Iscariot to betray him . . . (John 13:12)

Jesus *knowing* that the Father had given all things into his hands . . . (John 13:3)

I have power to lay [my life] down, and I have power to take it again . . .
(John 10:18)

For this cause came I into the world . . .

When you see that Jesus takes upon himself the full responsibility for the situation in which he finds himself, and understands that situation as the instrument by which he is going to achieve his purpose, then you begin to understand the mystery of liberation. For what Jesus did lights up the ultimate destiny of every man and woman: at some point, to accept the responsibility for all the limitations in their lives, and thereby that truth which alone can make them free.

Resurrection, or rebirth, is the greatest mystery, and one which we can never fully understand. One way of approaching it is through a common experience upon which our lives depend – the experience of sleep, which has many analogies with death. Five minutes before death there is some principle that holds the body together, and five minutes after death the life forces begin to turn into death forces and carry that which is the most marvellously coordinated machine, the human body, back into the elements from which it came. In sleep there is no such dissolution, but the consciousness has gone from the body, which returns to a plant-like state, is released from the tensions of the self and renewed. Jacob, in the Old Testament, shows what can happen. Here was a man of the ego-type, the supplanter who would set anything aside to have his own way and would reject any spiritual impulse while he was awake. But when he was asleep the grip of his self-consciousness was relaxed and he became aware of other claims upon him. When he awoke he was afraid and said, 'This is none other but the house of God, and this is the gate of heaven . . . If God will be with me, and will keep me in this way that I go . . . then shall the Lord be my God' (Genesis 28:17–21). What happened to Jacob can happen to other men: in the night they are renewed, and in the morning return reborn.

The same pattern is followed by nature. In the winter, when the great objective life of nature sleeps and renews itself, the subjective, spiritual forces follow a much more intense life, beginning in the autumn. This great rhythm is always taking place – night and day, sleeping and awake, spring and summer – and in the inner life also there are similar periods of awakening, and periods of darkness and obscurity.

When we come to a complete rebirth, what makes it utterly different from all that has gone before is that 'death hath no more dominion' (Romans 6:9) over the reborn person. What happens then?

Behind all human life, indeed behind all life, there is a hidden thing which is never manifested completely, a hidden reality that holds the whole thing in manifestation, the Fatherhood of God. If there is to be a complete rebirth, then there has to be a passing back into the Fatherhood, into the life of God. Read the passages about death in the Fourth Gospel, especially those about Christ in the upper chamber, and you will find that he never mentions death. Instead he says 'I am . . . going to the Father' (John 16:28), dying into the Father so as to be born again.

This is the merest outline of a great mystery, a long way from being realized. But the message of hope this Eastertide is Christ is 'the firstfruits of them that are asleep' and 'since by man came death, by man came also the resurrection of the dead' (1 Corinthians 15:20–21).

III

There have been mystics in every generation and every culture, from the ancient Greeks and the Buddhists to the present.* I have chosen two very different figures, both favourites of my father.

The first, Dante Alighieri, was famous in his own lifetime, and has remained so ever since – through his political writings and

---

* Two anthologies were published in English and were used by my father. The first was *The Perennial Philosophy*, edited by Aldous Huxley (Chatto & Windus, London, 1946); the second was *Mysticism in World Religion* (Penguin, Harmondsworth, 1963), edited by Sidney Spencer, a Unitarian minister.

activities; through Italian history; through his place in the history of the Italian language; as a poet, ranking with Shakespeare and Goethe as the greatest in European literature; as the author of the supreme *summa* of medieval thought and civilization; and, like his contemporary Giotto, as a forerunner of the Renaissance. But the supreme moment of his life was the mystical vision which is the climax of his great poem *The Divine Comedy.**

The *Comedy* was probably composed over a period of fifteen years at the beginning of the fourteenth century and completed shortly before Dante's death in 1321. It is autobiographical in form, beginning:

> In the middle of the journey of our life I found myself
> in a dark wood where the straight way was lost.†

It unfolds as a vast fresco of medieval life to depict Dante's journey. Led by Virgil through hell (the *Inferno*) and purgatory, he is rejoined by his beloved Beatrice, who accompanies him into paradise.

As they enter the Empyrean, the highest heaven in ancient and medieval thought, Beatrice tells him that it is made of 'pure light, intellectual light full of love, love of true good, full of happiness'.

Accompanied now by St Bernard of Clairvaux, the great mystical theologian of the twelfth century, Dante is allowed to look on the Godhead. It is full of light, and, although he cannot describe it, he recognizes it as the source of 'the love that moves the sun and the other stars' in famous lines:

> As is he who dreaming seeth, and when the
> Dream is gone the impression stamped remaineth,
> And naught else cometh to the mind again;

* It was called a comedy because it ended happily; the adjective 'Divine' was added after Dante's death.
† Translations from *The Divina Commedia: The Inferno, The Purgatorio, The Paradiso* (Temple Classics, Dent, London, 17th edn, 1932).

Even such am I; for almost wholly faileth
My vision, yet doth the sweetness that
Was born of it still drop within my heart

. . . .

O grace abounding, wherein I presumed
To fix my look on the eternal light
So long that I wearied my sight thereon.

Within its depths I saw ingathered,
Bound by love in one volume
The scattered leaves of all the universe.*

There could not be a greater contrast with Jakob Böhme, born in Silesia in 1575. The Reformation had by this time lost its initial impact and the Lutheran Church had fallen away from its original fervour into a barren orthodoxy with which Böhme was in conflict for much of his life. Making a living as a shoemaker, he had had only a rudimentary education, which added to his difficulty in expressing radical and disturbing ideas.

In 1600 he had a religious experience which lasted no more than a quarter of an hour but changed his life and gave him an insight into the nature and life of the universe. Sitting in his kitchen, he was looking at a pewter plate on which the sun's rays were reflected. As he looked, the whole universe opened to him. He claimed to see into the inner mystery of roots, plants, trees, animals, grass, sun and stars. Not altogether trusting this experience, he got up and went outside. But, instead of passing from him, the experience deepened and intensified:

I fell into great melancholy and sadness when I beheld the mighty depth of this world . . . for I saw evil and good, love and anger in all things. I considered also that little spark of light, man, and what he might be worth before God in comparison to this great fabric of heaven and earth.

* *Paradiso*, canto xxxiii, lines 58–63, followed by 82–7.

The Scriptures could not comfort me and often the Devil would give me heathenish thoughts . . .

In this affliction I raised up my spirit . . .

And when in my zeal I stormed as hard on God and all the gates of hell as if my life depended on it, suddenly my spirit burst through with the innermost birth of Deity, and there I was embraced with love as a bridegroom embraces his bride . . .

I was obliged to work out this great mystery like a child going to school. I was pregnant with it for twelve years . . . Finally, it overwhelmed me like a cloud-burst . . . Whatever I could grasp sufficiently to bring into outwardness, that I wrote down.

Böhme's account of his experience (*Aurora*, 1612) brought him into further trouble with the orthodox Lutheran clergy, and he was branded a heretic. A period of silence followed, during which his ideas matured and a circle of neighbours and friends who were impressed by his intellectual abilities helped him to find the books he needed. Among them were the writings of Paracelsus (1493–1541), whose alchemical and mystical views inspired Böhme's interest in nature mysticism and provided him with the terminology which he needed for his final period.

Between 1619, when he resumed writing, and 1624, when he died, Böhme poured out a flood of pamphlets and books, the most important of which was the two-volume *Mysterium Magnum* (1623). My father added translations of *Aurora*, *Mysterium Magnum* and *De Signatura Rerum* to his small library, but he had the same difficulty as German scholars in reducing to a coherent pattern of thought the prolix and confused writings of a man who was essentially a visionary.

Böhme would have nothing to do with the idea that it was God who gave man freedom. No, Böhme says, God did not give him freedom: man was born free. Man comes from an abyss of reality that lies over opposite to the world of light, and his body and consciousness are the product of the interaction between these two abysses, or worlds – light and darkness. Man is the only creation who can bridge the two abysses and can manifest in himself the unity of these two eternal worlds. Böhme saw everything in the universe as being created by will and imagination – not God's will and imagination, however, but the separate entities of plants, of matter, of beasts, bird, man; all of them, says Böhme, have independent wills.

You don't live in a universe just made by one mind but in a universe that has been created by millions of minds and wills. If I ask you who is at the root of all this mischief – it is man. For, says Böhme, man was created in the light world, that is where his spirit had its being, but he *imagined* himself into the abyss – that was the Fall of Man.

Böhme believed that man had imagined himself into the whole vast scheme of things which we see now. When the imagination works in the abyss, he describes it as fantasy. When the imagination creates truly, then it is illuminated from the world of light. Böhme insists, however, that the imagination is the active and creative expression of the will. The darkness, the sorrows, the problems are all created by the imagination; it is a self-will, it springs out of the darkness. It has to change. It has to penetrate into the light world. 'Out of the heart proceedeth all the issues of life, for as man thinketh, so is he.'

Do not think, Böhme adds, that by imagination is meant some trifling fantasy. Imagination is something much more profound. It is an unconscious action in you: 'As a man thinketh in his heart, so is he', or 'As the imagination of a man is, so is the reality around him.' The problem is, How can the imagination be changed?

According to Böhme, there are seven stages of development. When Creation begins with the interaction of the two eternal powers, the dark and the light, the first three forms or stages – Astringency, Attraction, Bitterness – lead up to the crisis which Böhme called Fire. There is a choice, however. You can at that point, if you so wish, turn your imagination right back into the dark world – and become, once again, involved in its conflicts and frustrations. Or you may turn your imagination into a new direction; this is the key, the direction of love. Love draws people together, draws the mind together in a new way, and the first word of Creation is 'Let there be light' – the Light of love, the fifth stage.

He who makes that choice moves from the world of love and light to the penultimate stage of Sound – the Logos, the Word – and finally to Figure or substantiality, motion, harmony and the complete manifestation of the Kingdom of God.

It says all the more for Böhme that, despite the difficulties in his writing, there is a general agreement that he was the most original of Protestant mystics, with a profound influence on such later movements as idealism, romanticism, German pietism and the Quakers (notably William Law), Schelling and Hegel, Schopenhauer and Coleridge. 'When people ask me where have I got these things?' Coleridge wrote, 'I say that I have drunk deeply from the great well of Boehme.' In fact the twentieth century has seen a reprint of Böhme's complete works in modernized German and a continuing series of biographical and specialist studies.

PART V

THE STRUCTURE OF
THE MIND

17

Development of the Self

I

The war which broke out in September 1939 came as no surprise to my father. He believed that the succession of crises – the First World War, the Great Depression, the rise of extremist movements of the Left and Right, the Second World War and later the partition of Europe and the Cold War – was accompanied by, and in large part was the expression of, a deeper psychological crisis, vividly reflected in twentieth-century art and literature.

Widely read in modern literature, from Nietzsche, who had proclaimed the death of God, to Kafka, Strindberg and the T. S. Eliot of *The Waste Land*, Frank was convinced that Western men's and women's experience in the first half of the twentieth century had opened a chasm between them and orthodox religion which was unbridgeable. If they were ever to regain access to the spiritual dimension of life, the loss of which he believed to be the source of their distress, it would be not by a return to traditional religion but only by discovering a new approach – an objective summed up by Jung in the title of his book *Modern Man in Search of a Soul*.

It was this which my father had already set out to explore during the years before the war. The winter of 1942–3, however, brought an important change. As a form of war service, for three years Frank had visited and talked to the young men and women called up for service in the Army and the RAF and stationed in camps around Yorkshire. In all he travelled 30,000 miles. His visits were organized by the University of Leeds Extra-Mural Department, which soon discovered his gift for talking to 'ordinary people'. He offered a number of subjects on which he was prepared to speak, but the subject on which he was asked to talk again and again had the intriguing title of 'Self-Knowledge'. Uprooted from their ordinary occupations, confused and often unhappy in the situation in which they now found themselves, the young men and women he met responded at once to a speaker who offered to help them understand themselves better and so adapt more successfully to their new environment.

There is no record of these talks, but they led him to give three series of Channing Hall lectures in 1943–4, the first of which he called 'Self-Culture'. For, as Frank said, it was not only men and women in the services but most people who found themselves faced with the problem of how to adapt not only to growing older but to the drastic changes brought by the war. My father's own views had not changed. He remained for the rest of his life committed to mysticism, but his approach changed. He turned it round, starting not with his own views but with the psychological difficulties felt by the men and women who came to listen to him. Setting aside the technical jargon, theories and controversies which put most laymen off the study of psychology, he drew on his own experience, as well as a lifetime's reading, to offer practical suggestions as to how to make adjustments to life more effective and less painful.

The first question he asked in his 'Self-Culture' lectures was 'What is the Self?' His own answer was that the self is the feeling of self-identity born out of our habit of referring all experience to ourselves. We know who we are, and feel that we are responsible for certain things.

There are, however, two major obstacles to our developing this sense of identity and responsibility. The first is the difficulty we have in accepting ourselves as we really are.

It is not easy to acknowledge that we can lie on occasion, can pose, and not always find it easy to be fair-minded. The way to overcome this is by practising the discipline of self-examination, learning to accept yourself as you really are, without becoming indignant or ashamed or bitter with yourself.

The second obstacle is the habit, which many people fall into as they approach middle age, of accepting themselves as set and fixed. Never regard yourself as finished and incapable of further growth and change, however old you may be. Have you never noticed how strongly such people resist new ideas and regard any suggestion of change of mind as a threat to their security? They are already succumbing to a kind of mental death before their physical death. You should learn to regard yourself, your consciousness, as a kind of seed which remains capable throughout life of unfolding into something finer.

Each decade, from our twenties to our eighties, brings new insights and new opportunities for development.

My father laid great stress on observing and adapting to the rhythms of human life: he believed that failure to do this was a prime cause of neurosis. He applied this first to the rhythm of the body, the beating of the heart, the need for sleep, the rise and fall in our appetites for food and for sex; then to the senses, which so many people in urban societies neglected, so losing contact with the natural environment of life.

For keeping open the channels of communication, Frank added breathing and speech to the five primary senses, touch, sight, smell, taste and hearing. 'Any great development of consciousness will always depend to some measure upon the practice of deep breathing.' No less important (though often overlooked) in liberating the mind and the emotions was learning to speak clearly.

Frank believed that both the emotions and the mind were rooted in the body. The emotions arose from the physical feeling of hunger, leading to the desire for food and for sexual intercourse. But more than hunger and desire were involved: corresponding to the powerful emotion of frustration, there was also the no less profound emotion of satisfaction. One of the most mysterious but also distinctive characteristics of human life was the way in which the purely physical desire for sex had become surrounded by a wealth of emotions. Some of them, such as love, self-sacrifice and grief, were among the deepest feelings of which human beings were capable; others, such as the response to beauty, found expression in Mozart's music, the poetry of Shakespeare and Goethe, the paintings of Botticelli and Renoir, and a wealth of other artistic creations besides.

Just as the emotions emerged from the physical body, so he believed the mind emerged from the emotions – in this case from curiosity, the desire to know. The mind, he maintained, could never be dissociated from the emotions. When a man dedicated his life to the single-minded pursuit of a solution to some scientific or philosophical problem, he might be able to detach himself from certain emotions, such as ambition, but it was still emotion that provided the driving force, the intellectual passion for discovering the truth, the origin of which was the emotion of curiosity.

Like the physical body, both the emotions and the mind are governed by a rhythm which prevents them from being kept at full stretch all the time. Artists, performers and intellectuals who draw heavily on their emotional and mental resources have learned the need for a pause in which these must be allowed to lie fallow and they can recharge their energies. Similarly, faced with a problem which appeared insoluble, a writer, a musician or a scientist who broke off and left his unconscious to come up with an answer often found that the problem solved itself.

Frank was no less certain that there was a rhythm of the spirit to be observed and respected in the inner life. He urged his listeners not to fall into the same trap as he himself had when he had attempted to storm the spiritual heights:

When I was fairly young I fell in love with the idea of the spiritual life. I concentrated all my energies on trying to develop the inner life. I undertook deep breathing, meditation and fasting; I could hardly find time to do my work. I investigated every system; I belonged to every conceivable school of thought. And what was the result? It ended up in an appalling sense of strain, a reaching after some unattainable object which I could never make clear to my mind and feeling – and a foolish contempt for ordinary outer things . . .

When you speak about the inner life, don't put on a special voice and conjure up a sanctimonious look in your eyes. Don't strain after invisible powers. Remember that relaxation, which is the beginning of wisdom, is not to be learned by effort. Think of relaxation not as a mental gymnastic, but as an art, and realize that at bottom all art is play. Don't believe that the universe is filled with an intense moral purpose. Hindu teaching comes much nearer the truth when it describes the Creation as 'the play of Brahma, the play of God'.

II

The development of the self, my father believed, depended not only upon heredity and environment, but upon the attitude which individual men and women adopted towards it. Self-consciousness and the confidence it brought had been the source of all mankind's achievements, but also of a self-absorption and fear of the future which paralysed people's energies.

Was there any way of overcoming this anxiety? My father's answer was, Yes, if you can find a way of breaking the inner circle of your own thoughts and emotions, the obsession with yourself, so renewing your energies by directing them outward. To do so meant overcoming strong forces of resistance to change – inertia and fear of the unknown. But he suggested two ways in which bridges could be built to a wider contact with life: culture and friendship.

How can one make contact with that other world of culture? It could be through music or art, but for Frank the obvious answer was through literature, and he spent a whole lecture in coaching his audience in how to read. You could read to acquire information, but that was not the purpose in reading the imaginative literature he had in mind – a poem, a short story, a passage from a novel (Emily Brontë's *Wuthering Heights* or Tolstoy's *War and Peace*) or a passage from the Bible. First, get your mind into a quiet state; the best way to do that and to concentrate is by deep breathing. Then read your passage or poem very slowly; don't be in a hurry. Read it a second time, and pause to see what impression it has made on you, what emotional reaction it has created – and what produced the impression: was it, for instance, something to do with the vowels?

The third time you read it, begin to look for a pattern, and through the pattern come into touch with the writer's thought:

Become aware of something that begins to stand independent of the words and sentences in which it is expressed, something that has about it emotion, pattern and *power*. That is the word I wanted to come to: the *power* to change your emotion, your thoughts, even to have a physical effect on your nerves.

With music and painting the same process has to be followed: learning to listen in the first case, learning to look at and see a picture in the second. Frank's final word of advice was to carry out the exercises he had suggested very slowly and not be discouraged if it took time to achieve the effects he had described. For, if one persisted, there would come the revelation that there is a universe of mind, imagination and emotion – a universe to which you have access and in which you can participate as much as in the universe of matter. 'Once you have made that discovery the world will never appear the same to you again.'

The second way of breaking out of the isolation of self was friendship. 'With culture you begin to establish a relation with the past and the present; with friendship you enter into the most spiritual relationship that mankind knows.'

Frank never failed to recognize that the oldest and most powerful of all relationships is that between man and woman. Sexual feeling and intercourse remain the strongest of all human impulses after self-preservation, capable of producing both the most creative and the most destructive effects in individual lives and families. But the primary purpose of reproduction by no means exhausts the sexual energies; the surplus gives emotional warmth, urgency and meaning not only to human companionship, but to music, drama and the other arts, as well as to many of the other human activities which build up the structure of society.

Psychologists recognize that every man has in his nature feminine elements and every woman masculine, the balance between them varying widely between individuals. Frank saw man and woman as a twofold manifestation of a fundamental human unity. This seemed to him one of the great mysteries, providing endless fascination in exploring the overlap and the difference between the feminine and masculine experience of life.

So far, however, the relations between men and women had not been based on equality. The distinctive role of women had been defined by their sexual and reproductive functions, from sex object for the satisfaction of men's sexual desires (the Victorian moral code refused to recognize that women had any sexual needs of their own) to marriage and the birth and rearing of children. A woman's world did not extend beyond the home.

The twentieth century had seen women rebel against this restrictive typecasting and claim an equal right with men in deciding on their role for themselves. Many women might still prefer marriage and children, combining it with a job, but the choice should be theirs, not something into which they were forced by social pressure. Frank was convinced that even when women made careers in occupations traditionally reserved for men – business, public administration or law – they would bring to them a distinctive approach, as they had already begun to do in medicine. The differences to which we owe so much of the interest and quality of life would remain, but on a much more equal footing. 'I believe', he wrote, 'that probably the greater determining factor of the future is going to lie in the released personality of woman and the full achievement of womanhood.'

III

Even in the earliest examples of Frank's new departure, it is evident that his interest in psychology concerned more than a way of helping people to overcome their personal difficulties. His readiness to do that was not in doubt, but he had come to believe that there was something much bigger at stake. The more he became absorbed in the development of a spiritual consciousness which could take the place of a failing religious orthodoxy, the more he became convinced (as Jung had been) that psychology was better fitted to open the way to such a revolution than any other approach.

His starting point, which he explored in a number of talks in the 1940s, was the relationship between the conscious and unconscious minds. He began a talk on 'The Structure of the Mind' by making clear that, while he would make use of the findings of psychology as a science, he would not be limited by them, any more than Jung was.

I want you to get clearly in your minds that before there is any manifestation of the mind in sense, in thought or in image, the mind exists independently of those things. Mind is reality in itself; it expresses itself through physical manifestations, through thought, through image, and through all the processes of evolution, but nevertheless it is a reality in itself. There is a universal mind before there is any manifestation of mind in physical cell, or in matter, in thought, or in image, and it is this universal mind that initiates all the processes by which mind comes into manifestation in an individualized way. As a basis of our talks we suggest that there is a universal mind that exists before any manifestation takes place.

Frank remarked that in modern times there was more talk about the unconscious mind, but the development of the conscious mind was equally remarkable. It had developed very slowly, over millions of years, out of man's instincts and senses. Thought and imagination, which were its most important characteristics, were neither of them physical, but had developed in the brain a physical instrument of incredible complexity, capable of transferring the sense impressions it receives into a series of images and eventually into thought able to create what we call the consciousness of an inner life.

My father suggested three characteristics of the conscious mind on which to concentrate.

Our consciousness depends upon memory, and memory is divided into two unequal parts: involuntary and voluntary. The former we can't control. All the impressions we receive are built into the unconscious mind, but we cannot be sure which we shall recall. The involuntary memory forms the raw material out of which the second, conscious, memory is built up. [As a way of developing it, my father suggested that it is almost a necessary condition of learning any subject that you should form an interest in it.] The sharpest impressions are made when only one sense – hearing or seeing – is used. If you are listening – listen; if you are seeing – see.

Finally, never try to remember immediately after receiving an impression. The great secret of memory is relaxation; it is strengthened by a quiescent period.

It is of course a fact that for thousands of years artists and writers have made great use of the unconscious, drawing upon it for the creative manifestations of painting, music, art and religion. But it was not until the end of the nineteenth and the beginning of the twentieth century that men and women were able to think consciously about the unconscious and its significance. Above all, it was only then that they were able to make the distinction between the conscious mind and the unconscious depths out of which the great creative impulses and powers – and sometimes also the great destructive elements – emerged.

The unconscious mind is so called because it is not under our control. We cannot by an act of the will just dip into it and take what we want. It is working all the time without our being aware of it, absorbing elements in our experience to which we have not paid any attention, and retaining other elements which we discard as we develop – for example, our very vivid experiences from childhood.

Another function of the unconscious mind is that it tries to protect your consciousness from shock, burying unpleasant experiences out of sight. It takes every experience which you have had and have forgotten, drawing on the collective unconscious and the vast past which has been handed down through the human race. It is all the time seeking to make a unity, relating the crude experiences of the moment to echoes of past experiences which give those experiences significance and meaning.

You must set great value upon your consciousness. It will not, however, be much use if it does not keep a close relationship to the unconscious. The situation can arise where a man or woman becomes so intent upon some purpose that they simply use their psychic energy to achieve that end and become cut off from the richness of the unconscious. Then, somewhere about mid-life, a devastating awareness descends on them: the mind no longer seems to function as it used to do, and the appetite for life, for thinking, for action, begins to wane.

My father was anxious not to have his listeners go away feeling that the unconscious was a menace. On the contrary, the thinking powers of man are refreshed and renewed in it whenever he draws on it.

But beware of isolation, of directing all your energies to some great end. You can keep in touch with the unconscious mind in a thousand different ways – by poetry, drama, literature, music, art, religion. There must be time for silence in your life, there must be contact with the arts and all the other products of the unconscious.

If you can maintain that relationship of consciousness with the unconscious, so that for part of every day you are immersed in that life-giving stream, you will gradually bring about the integration of these two great powers in your mind and learn to think through your experiences.

18

'The world is too much with us; late and soon, Getting and spending, we lay waste our powers'

I

My father believed that for a long time the Western world had been in a state of crisis of which the Second World War was the culmination. While Western civilization had survived the succession of military and political, economic and social threats with which it had been plagued, underlying these was a psychological and spiritual crisis of which the others had been an expression.

From the first half of the nineteenth century, the growth of industry and commerce, the rapid increase in population, especially urban population,* and a more hectic and competitive pace of living had led men and women to direct their energies increasingly outward, at the expense of their inner lives, the impoverishment of their emotional natures and the neglect of their spiritual needs.

As early as 1807, in one of the most famous of his sonnets, Wordsworth captured what R. H. Tawney later called 'the sickness of the acquisitive society':

> The world is too much with us; late and soon,
> Getting and spending, we lay waste our powers:
> Little we see in Nature that is ours;
> We have given our hearts away, a sordid boon!
> This sea that bares her bosom to the moon;

---

* He did not forget that in the first half of the nineteenth century Bradford had been the fastest-growing town in Britain.

The winds that will be howling at all hours,
And are up-gather'd now like sleeping flowers;
For this, for everlasting, we are out of tune;
It moves us not . . .

There is no need to repeat what has been said a thousand times since about the mixture of materialism and trivialization which has characterized so much of modern Western civilization. The interest lies in asking, What had my father to say that was distinctive for those who turned to him for guidance in the most terrible decade of the twentieth century, between Hitler's occupation of Prague in March 1939 and Stalin's blockade of Berlin in 1948–9?

To begin with, he argued that the origin of the crisis lay in the surrender of self-consciousness to egoism, leading it to become so absorbed in the manipulation of the external world that it lost touch with the unconscious, the source of all psychic energy. Frank identified four ways in which this could happen and result in weakening the power of the conscious mind. The first was idealiz-ation, the refusal to acknowledge the dark side of life – cruelty, evil and tragedy. The second was rationalization, the refusal to admit the irrational forces in our lives – emotion, fear and hope against all the odds. The third was materialism, reducing life to a physical process, excluding any imaginative or spiritual dimension. The last, a product of materialism, was scepticism, living on the surface, with a growing disbelief in anything, and an inner empti-ness. Such communication as got through expressed itself in the apocalyptic visions, despair and anxiety characteristic of much contemporary art, from Eliot's poem *The Waste Land* to the paintings of Francis Bacon.

This led, on the one hand, to the drying up of the inner life and, on the other, to the frustration of the energies of the unconscious, denied their natural expression at the conscious level. As a result, these energies simmering underneath burst out in a terrifying uprush of destructive power. This was what had happened in the First World War and, on an even larger scale, in the Second. If ever there had been a human manifestation of the destructive power of the unconscious, it was in Adolf Hitler.

Frank pointed out that, in externalizing his energies, man had made great use of his intellectual powers. As a result, the intellect had come to occupy a dominant position, no longer balanced by but at the expense of our other faculties, the senses, the emotions, intuition and imagination. This had had the effect of narrowing down man's contact with reality to what satisfied intellectual criteria, so devaluing and shutting out a great area of human experience – most important of all the faculty of imagination, which had the power to create and open up new, untried, possibilities in the future.

Remembering what had happened after the First World War, Frank believed that, whatever merit there might be in particular proposals for reform, the hopes which, after the Second World War, many placed on planning and collective action to produce a better and more equal society would end in disillusionment. The roots of the crisis lay deeper than the social and economic arrangements of our society, and were not susceptible to political action, whether revolutionary or reformist. Even if we could deal with the crisis materially and socially, we should still be left with the mystery of death and the meaning of life.

At that deeper psychological and spiritual level, change could not be produced by mass conversions any more than by collective action. Many were dissatisfied with their lot but were gripped by fear of change and clung to the defences – possessions, position, routine – which they had built up to protect themselves against it, shutting their eyes to anything that might disturb or force them to look at themselves from the outside. They took refuge from inner conflicts and external demands in a self-induced unconsciousness. Like the demons in the Gospels, they cried out, 'What have we to do with thee . . . ? art thou come hither to torment us . . . ?' (Matthew 8:29).

II

But why should we assume, Frank asked, that the evolutionary process had ended? The development which had led from the simplest level of consciousness, at the beginning of evolution many millions of years before, to the complexity of human self-consciousness, and the freedom that gave, was a marvellous achievement. What reason was there for supposing that it was not continuing?

One strong argument for expecting it to go on was the fact that, while self-consciousness had given man extraordinary powers, the use he made of them was frequently self-defeating. Self-consciousness could all too easily become a burden, creating anxiety, producing contradictions and frustration, in too many cases manifesting itself in evil and leading to tragedy. On the other hand, it could also provide experience of perfection in the arts, of compassion in the service of others, of love in personal relations. The first of these pointed to the need, the second to the possibility of a further advance to a form of higher consciousness that would overcome the frustration from which human beings suffered and represent as great an advance from self-consciousness as that had from community consciousness.

My father could see no reason why human development should have halted at its present unsatisfactory level. He laid particular stress on the frustration which seemed to be inseparable from self-consciousness, seeing in it the dynamic element, unique to man, which, as in earlier stages of his evolution, was capable of driving him to seek for a way of overcoming his limitations.

Hope lay, as it had always lain, in individuals, not in the masses – in individuals driven by frustration to rebel and break out of the prisons which man had created for himself. This was how the sensibility of an age had been changed by Christianity. What had begun as an experience of a handful of people in a remote corner of the Roman Empire had generated the incredible driving power which, in the name of Christ, had built churches in every village and town in Europe and the New World. This process had been repeated in the Renaissance and again in the romantic movement, starting with individuals and once more producing a profound change in the way men and women saw and experienced life. My father's deepest conviction was that the time had come for another such renewal, even if it took several generations to complete it.

Trying to imagine what might be the characteristics of a further stage of consciousness beyond our present self-consciousness, Frank came up with four ideas which, as he freely acknowledged, he took from the mystics, from the poets, and from writers as diverse as Plotinus and Böhme, Nietzsche and Dostoevsky. They were:

overcoming the divisions within ourselves which so frequently defeat our purposes;
overcoming the separateness of the self;
reconciling the unconscious with the conscious mind;
recognizing the need to integrate evil and the shadow side of life.

All four are variations on the single theme of unity.

At this stage in our development we cannot hope to grasp the whole scheme of which we are a part.

We have to return the intellect to its true ground as the instrument, not the master, of consciousness, and begin not with systems and the abstractions of philosophical thought, but with concrete experience. And the key to that lies in liberating the imagination, the creative not the analytical function of the mind, which has the power to open our eyes to the extraordinary universe in which we live and to re-create our vision of reality. For, as Blake wrote, 'If the doors of perception were cleansed every thing would appear to man as it is, infinite.'*

On this view the self becomes not an end in itself, still less something to be denied or suppressed, but a means, an instrument, that will enable you to break out of the closed circle of cause and effect and cross the threshold to that condition of 'at-one-ment' – of 'being at one' with others, with nature, with God – which has been the distinctive experience of the mystics in every age and civilization.

To begin with, the experience will be only momentary or, at best, intermittent.

* *The Marriage of Heaven and Hell* (c. 1790–93), Plate 14.

Think of yourself [Frank said] as a pilgrim or explorer. You are ascending a mountain track, and at the present moment the track is running up a deep gully. The only thing that presses on your consciousness at the moment is the forbidding rocks, but you are a pilgrim, you know that you must go on. In another hour's climbing you will come to a spur where just for a moment you emerge out of the ravine and can see beyond peak upon peak lifting their crests into the sunlight. The thought, the shattering thought that I want to leave you with, is that you are the mountain track, the mountain and the peaks beyond – you are all those and yourself. To bring this home to you more vividly I will read part of one of my favourite poems, by Ralph Waldo Emerson. It is called 'Brahma', the Hindu word for the divine reality, of which the entire universe of matter and mind is a manifestation, and Brahmin is the Hindu word for priest.

Brahma (1867)

If the red slayer thinks he slays,
　　Or if the slain thinks he is slain,
They know not well the subtle ways
　　I keep, and pass, and turn again.

Far or forgot to me is near;
　　Shadow and sunlight are the same;
The vanished gods to me appear;
　　And one to me are shame and fame.

They reckon ill who leave me out;
　　When me they fly, I am the wings;
I am the doubter and the doubt,
　　And I the hymn the Brahmin sings.

III

My father was convinced that, looked at from a psychological, not from a theological or intellectual, point of view, religion still had an indispensable role to play. No psychologist, for example, could

ignore the enormous contribution religion had made to culture.
Without the works it had inspired, architecture, music, painting,
drama and literature would be immeasurably the poorer. Its importance lay in keeping alive, in face of a shallow worldly-wise scepticism, the sense of mystery and awe, the wonder at life, the instinct
for order without which the arts and culture wither. And it did
this not by preaching, by theological argument and dogma, but by
transmitting through the personal and collective unconscious those
primal images – the myth of chaos and creation, the eating of the
fruit of the tree of the knowledge of good and evil, the expulsion
from paradise, sacrifice, death and resurrection – which revealed
heights and depths that the intellect could not express.

None of these images was literally true: there never was a Garden
of Eden, an Adam and Eve, a tree of the knowledge of good and
evil, or a serpent that could talk. But all of them presented profound
truths about human life. Hell and the Hindu law of karma might
be concepts that rational thought could not accept, but you had
only to visit a mental hospital to find that they described conditions
all too familiar to a psychiatrist. The scriptures of all the great
religions presented a version of the creation myth: that there was
chaos and that some great power came and built up the universe
out of that chaos. Scientifically, this might not make sense, but
psychologically it was profoundly true: the dark chaotic elements
are the creative powers.

Many people, Frank suggested, felt a secret guilt or resentment
because they could no longer accept what the Churches taught.
But their revolt was a sign of their growth, their doubt a religious
experience.

This was a familiar story in the history of religion. In the case
of Hinduism, the revolt that produced a religious impulse for
renewal was by Buddha; in the case of the Hebrew religion it was
by Jesus; in the case of Roman Catholicism it was by Luther. In
each case the revolt was creative not destructive, and what was
living – the primal images – was carried forward.

The trouble was that many who could grasp the need for change
intellectually found it far more difficult to accept it emotionally
and integrate it into their inner life. 'Although our thought can

change like the minute hand of a clock, our emotions, like the hour hand, change much more slowly.'

To accept change meant not merely living physically in the twentieth century, but being prepared to accept modern experience and modern knowledge – in particular the findings of science and the social sciences, the rewriting of history. But 'the modern' appeared to call in question everything that had hitherto been generally accepted. The experimentalism of modern art (Picasso, Henry Moore), of modern music (Stravinsky, Schoenberg) and of modern literature (James Joyce, Strindberg), like Freud's exploration of the unconscious, encountered a passionate hostility. Deeply disturbing was the feeling that nothing was any longer secure – not only the traditional forms of art and religion, but morality; not just the structure of society, but even that of matter and the universe.

At first we resisted this questioning of everything, and then began to admit that there was no resisting it, and realized that this was our experience. We felt ourselves shaken and naked.

What did those who were wise say in this crisis? 'Well, even if I am disillusioned and suffering, the central core of "I am" still exists.' And they went on to say, 'There is something real in all this: I am still alive and awake and aware.' This is more than can be said for those who refused the experience and sought to escape it. It proved to be a judgement between the quick and the dead. It is only those who have endured the disillusionment and suffering, and said, 'Something is trying to reach me in this, and I am trying to reach something beyond all this experience' – it is only those who are really alive.

We begin to realize that all the wealth of the past – the living creative energies which were mediated to us through the traditions which have been destroyed – still lives in us. But we want these energies still to be expressed in the old forms. We turn this way and that in our efforts to revive them – but such revivals tend to be synthetic and no longer have any foundation in reality.

We have to learn to wait. *Something* sustains us in life and consciousness; we are never cut off from reality – our problem is to apprehend it. It is always working upon us, and close at hand. So when we have in some measure recovered from the shock and bewilderment – and if you have not felt these, you have not had the modern experience, you have shut it out – then we begin to realize what the wisest teachers of the past, such as the men of the early Christian age and the men of the Renaissance, who lived through similar experiences, tell us – that what matters is to have come through and not despaired.

The fact we have to accept is that it is not we in our generation, or the wickedness of man, that have destroyed the old forms, but reality, in order that men and women should not be imprisoned in them but be delivered by a new birth. Then we can stand outside them and read them and their meaning in a deeper and more universal way. If we can rise to this vision, we can walk without fear. Reality will not let us down nor deny anything that is precious within us; reality will in the end answer all the deepest craving of our being.

IV

In all his discussions of the further development of consciousness, my father came back to the same two simple pieces of advice: 'Do not try to force yourself. Practise detachment; learn to be patient and to trust life. Do not judge or condemn. Learn the law of generosity, to give and to forgive – including forgiving yourself.' For most people, the most difficult application of forgiveness is to evil, the shadow side of life, which my father believed had in the end to be integrated with the light – as in Blake's *The Marriage of Heaven and Hell.*

The myth of the Fall makes clear that from the earliest times the experience of evil was seen as inseparable from the human condition. As my father said, it is all there in the opening chapters of Genesis: the temptation by Satan in the form of a serpent; the eating of the forbidden fruit of the tree of the knowledge of good and evil, bringing with it the knowledge of death; the discovery of sin and guilt (hiding from the Lord among the trees); the discovery of sex and shame; Adam and Eve's banishment from paradise, condemned to a life of labour, the first episode in which was Cain's murder of his brother Abel:

And when the Lord saw that man had done much evil on earth and that his thoughts and inclinations were always evil, he was sorry that he had made man . . . and said: 'I will wipe them off the face of the earth.' (Genesis 6:5–7)*

Only Noah was spared, although the hopes of a better beginning after the Flood were soon shown to be vain. To quote a remark of my father's in a 1944 lecture:

So many people think this disintegrated age is a very wicked one. But all ages are wicked. There has never been an age when humanity has escaped from the shadow of evil; it cannot. As T. S. Eliot wrote:

> Between the motion
> And the act
> Falls the Shadow†

The first point to be clear about, Frank continued, is the reality of evil. We resist this. We are reluctant to accept that we live in a world in which everything we experience is linked with its opposite: love–hate, pleasure–pain, life–death, happiness–despair.

Jakob Böhme, the German shoemaker-mystic, put what I am trying to say in a single sentence: 'All things consist in yea and nay.' You think that over. Those are the two answering depths, without which there would be no life, no universe, no history, no anything.

The shadow [Frank continued] may appear menacing and destructive, but is actually creative. It is the darkness of chaos out of which Creation emerges . . . The shadow power of things is the depth that reveals the light; it is the inertia that makes manifest the energy; it is the darkness in which the light alone can shine.

*

* Genesis 6:5–7: 'And the Lord saw that the wickedness of man was great in the earth, and that every imagination of the thoughts of his heart was only evil continually. And it repented the Lord that he had made man on the earth, and it grieved him at his heart. And the Lord said, I will destroy man whom I have created from the face of the ground . . .'
† The Hollow Men (1925), in T. S. Eliot, The Complete Poems and Plays (Faber, London, 1969), p. 85.

It was not for nothing that Satan (otherwise Lucifer or the Devil) played so prominent a part in Christian mythology. The Book of Job describes Satan explicitly as appearing in heaven among 'the sons of God' (Job 1:6). In the Gospels, when Jesus returns from his baptism in the Jordan, 'for forty days [he] was led by the Spirit up and down the wilderness and tempted by the devil' (Luke 4:2). It was necessary for Jesus to confront the dark forces of the unconscious before he could begin his ministry; he would not have possessed the creative powers he displayed if he had not first been subjected to this ordeal.

But this was not the end of Satan's role. 'Having come to the end of all his temptations,' the Gospel adds, 'the devil departed, *biding his time*' (Luke 4:13). That time came when Satan was called upon to play his part in the climax as well as the beginning of Jesus' ministry:

The devil had already put it into the mind of Judas son of Simon Iscariot to betray him. (John 13:2)

At the Last Supper in the upper room, Jesus told his disciples:

'In truth, in very truth I tell you, one of you is going to betray me.' The disciples looked at one another in bewilderment: whom could he be speaking of? . . . Jesus replied, 'It is the man to whom I give this piece of bread when I have dipped it in the dish.' Then, after dipping it in the dish, he took it out and gave it to Judas son of Simon Iscariot. As soon as Judas had received it Satan entered him. Jesus said to him, 'Do quickly what you have to do.' No one at the table understood what he meant by this . . . Judas, then, received the bread and went out. It was night. (John 13:21–30)

The Devil plays no less a part in the other monotheistic religions – Judaism, Zoroastranism and Islam. He is the fallen Angel of Light (Lucifer) who was driven out of heaven for the sin of pride, for the sin of loving himself more than God – that love of self, that egoistic will which is the source of so much evil in the world.

But the Prince of Darkness is at the same time the *necessary* opponent, the *necessary* shadow of God. In Frank's own words:

The shadow is the fourth figure in the pattern of the Deity – Father, Mother, Son and Satan. The shadow creates the darkness against which all the glory of light can be manifested. You could have no conception of light without darkness. Wherever there is the shadow, there is the light that casts it. They are the two sides of the same manifestation.

So Isaiah writes, 'I am the Lord and there is none else. I form the light, and create the darkness: I make peace, and create evil: I the Lord do all these things' (Isaiah 45:6–7).

From this Frank argued that not only do we have to accept evil as inescapable in this world – as shown by history with all its cruelties and failures – but, if we are ever to achieve that unity which all the mystics have seen as the ultimate consciousness, we have also to accept as necessary the reintegration of the shadow, of the dark forces, with the light, and the reconciliation of Satan with God. That is where the great law of Jesus comes into operation: the law of forgiveness. Or, as Blake wrote, 'The spirit of Jesus is the continual forgiveness of sin.'*

* *Jerusalem* (1804–20), Plate 3.

19

Birth, Death and Immortality

I

As my father freely admitted, to discuss such possibilities was going well beyond what most psychologists – always with the exception of Jung – would regard as admissible. Anxious to secure recognition of their subject as a scientific discipline, most psychologists – and most modern philosophers too – regarded the existence of the soul as an illusion, a frustrated wish-fulfilment or, at best, an unproven and misleading hypothesis. You were born and therefore were going to die, both physiological facts, no more; consciousness was an epiphenomenon, a secondary by-product of brain activity which ceased with death.

Frank refused to accept this. Following the Platonic tradition, he regarded the psyche or soul – thought, feeling and imagination – as being as real as the body, and its function as central to the study of psychology. He made no claim to provide scientifically verifiable answers to such questions as the meaning of life and what might lie beyond death. But he did not therefore believe that such questions could be ignored. He regarded them as legitimate matters for discussion, and the beliefs which men and women – including the greatest artists, poets and thinkers – had drawn from their experience over the centuries were testimony to be taken seriously, not brushed aside.

My father's primary interest, as I have said, was in opening his listeners' minds to the possibility *in this life* of breaking out from a self-centred individualistic consciousness and reaching out to one which was universally centred. He likened such a move to the revolution which replaced the Ptolemaic system, with the Earth as the centre and the Sun revolving around it, with the Copernican system, in which it was the Sun, not the Earth, which was the centre, and the Earth, not the Sun, which revolved around it. He believed that there were men and women who had already taken this further step in the development of consciousness, that it was potentially within the reach of any man and woman, and that this might in time lead to a general shift in consciousness, comparable with that which followed Copernicus' path-breaking discovery – although this was by no means certain, and in any case might take a hundred or two hundred years to accomplish.

But what was the relationship between life in this world and that unseen world which, as he and so many others before him believed, lay beyond death?

Like Plato and Wordsworth, Frank was convinced of the pre-existence of the soul:

> Our birth is but a sleep and a forgetting:
> The Soul that rises with us, our life's Star,
>   Hath had elsewhere its setting,
>   And cometh from afar.*

He was no less convinced that the soul and consciousness continued to exist in some form after death – a belief never more movingly stated than in the last lines, which he loved to quote, written by Emily Brontë not long before her death in December 1848 at the age of thirty:

> O God within my breast,
> Almighty! ever-present Deity!
>   Life – that in me has rest,
> As I – undying Life – have power in Thee!
>
> Vain are the thousand creeds
> That move men's hearts: unutterably vain;
>   Worthless as withered weeds,
> Or idlest froth amid the boundless main,

---

* William Wordsworth, 'Ode, Intimations of Immortality', v (1807).

To waken doubt in one
Holding so fast by thine infinity;
So surely anchor'd on
The steadfast rock of immortality.*

Beyond avowing a belief that was as firm as Wordsworth's or Emily Brontë's, however, my father was careful to avoid being drawn into speculating on what might be the character of life beyond death or the nature of the ultimate reality. I believe there were two reasons for this. One was the objective he had set himself in his psychology lectures: of reaching out to an audience alienated by orthodox religious views and likely to be suspicious of what they might take to be their reintroduction by the back door. The other was the reticence he recommended and practised in speaking about personal experience. In no more than two or three of the 115 lectures he delivered between 1939 and 1951 did he depart from this rule and reveal his private thoughts about either question. What he had to say, however, has an importance for understanding his beliefs out of proportion to the number of times on which he shared these with his listeners.

One such occasion was the lecture 'Birth, Death and Immortality', which he delivered in December 1950. My father described birth as 'the soul's acceptance of the instrument of a body in order to make contact with the exterior world, the objective aspects of reality'. He thought there was also another reason for this acceptance: in order that the soul might play its part in the transformation of matter. But the soul was both blind and dumb until transformed by the power of the human psyche working upon it, for example through the arts, such as music, and through the creation of human thought and speech.

The personality or psyche that came into manifestation was not a whole, but was a branch or leaf of something greater. Our centre remained elsewhere; the real self was outside time and space, and the life of the psyche as we knew it was something put forth into

* 'Last Lines' (1848).

time. The Fourth Gospel expresses the thought in a single sentence: 'I am the vine, ye are the branches' (John 15:5).

What did my father mean by the 'real self'? In two other lectures written the same year (1950), he described it as 'the Hidden Witness, the witness of all our actions, our thoughts and emotions, our vanity and pride, but in itself never visible. Made in the image of the divine pattern, it is the judge and assessor of our temporal manifestations.' The real self itself was never visible, but like 'the Way', of which it was a part – the Way of the Chinese Tao, of Buddha, of the Christian gospel – it was still active even when you had lost all consciousness of it and were wholly preoccupied with the false self which you presented to the world. In the words of W. H. Auden and Christopher Isherwood:

> Nothing is done, nothing is said,
> But don't make the mistake of believing us dead.*

The real self and the Way were what all literature and art sought to explore in the language of myth, image and symbol.

Frank made a striking juxtaposition of two quotations. The first was from St Augustine: 'Because men have become exiles, even from themselves, there has been given also a written law, "because thou wast a deserter from thy heart".' The written law of morality was in effect a substitute for the real self. The other quotation was from the parable of the prodigal son, who had left home and lived in exile: 'When he came to *himself* [i.e. his real self], he said . . . I will arise and go to my father' (Luke 15:17–18).

Frank was drawn to the ancient idea of reincarnation, or the transmigration of souls, which appears in Hinduism and Buddhism and was adopted by Pythagoras and Plato. According to Aldous Huxley, in his anthology of mystical writings *The Perennial Philosophy* (1946), the term 'immortal' should be reserved for that

---

* *The Dog Beneath the Skin* (1935) *Plays and Other Dramatic Writings, 1928–1938* by W. H. Auden, ed. Edward Mendelson (Faber and Faber Ltd, London, 1989), p. 194.

minority of souls who have completed this pilgrimage and reached the final state of liberation from time and space in the Eternal Now. The term to be applied to those who had not was 'survival', whether they had achieved a stage of partial deliverance or, with the majority, were compelled to continue 'the weary cycle of birth and death' until they had. Frank thought this could take many lives, possibly in worlds other than the earth.

Following this line of thought, my father saw death as the withdrawal of the branch psyche from a particular incarnation in the exterior world. As long as we believe that the whole psyche or soul is involved in physical incarnation, death must appear as extinction and therefore as a tragic waste – think of the waste of a Mozart or a Schubert dying young, with so much left unrealized. But if we think of death as only the withdrawal of the branch into the real self that endured, then it is not wasted, because all that has been gathered and achieved is preserved.

There still remains, however, the problem of separation. Frank believed that a shared life is essential to our happiness. All the fruitfulness of a man's life is drawn from the experience of living within a community. We have to realize that we live most fruitfully in unity – in the unity, for instance, of the marriage of man and woman. Divorce (he remarked in passing) is not immoral: if certain conditions cannot be fulfilled, divorce can be a very moral act. The idea that marriage is for all eternity is ridiculous, unless there is something in that relationship that is eternal, something that belongs to the real self.

The sorrow and loss we feel when the separation of death takes place is really an indication of our dependence on one another. When it is a great love, the sorrow is real enough, but it does not extend into the unseen dimensions; there, we always come together again. As long as we think of ourselves as permanent separate units, we cannot visualize that. The truth is that the phenomenal self we know in this world is not itself immortal, but is a temporary expression of the real self. That will be revealed, however, only when the phenomenal self becomes a luminous glass through which the real self can be discerned. 'How often', my father added, 'have I had to deal with the idea that death is a going away into space.

It is not. The mysterious happening which we call death is a withdrawal, a passing within. Just as birth is not the beginning of the self, so death is not the end.'

II

The other question, 'What is the nature of the ultimate reality?', Frank took up in a lecture, 'Exploration of Spiritual Reality', which he gave in June 1950. As a description of spiritual reality he quoted again from Emily Brontë's 'Last Lines':

> With wide embracing love
> Thy spirit animates eternal years,
> Pervades and broods above,
> Changes, sustains, dissolves, creates, and rears.

For his starting point he took a theme developed in other lectures: the Kingdom of the Imagination. While this could always be enjoyed for its own sake, it could never be an end in itself but was a bridge linking a world which revelled in expressing itself in images and forms to one which was beyond expression in any of these.

All great music is a vast speaking of something beyond: like all great works of art, it awakens in us questions and desires for that which is veiled behind and beyond it . . . The human imagination, at its highest, is a very close replica of the imagination that creates the universe.

Frank delighted in bringing together John Bunyan, the seventeenth-century tinker imprisoned in Bedford jail, and Dante Alighieri, the medieval patrician exiled from Florence. Both were masters of the inner life; both saw the progress of the soul as a pilgrimage, ending in Bunyan's vision of the Holy City and Dante's vision of the Eternal Light.

The ultimate reality – which some call God – has also been variously described as universal mind, the seat of the purpose which encompasses the totality of all things in the universe; as the Eternal

Now existing outside of time and space; as the unity which binds together all the divisions and resolves all the conflicts – nirvana in the Buddhist version, paradise in the Christian.

Following Blake, who declared 'Energy is Eternal Delight',* Frank was particularly attracted to the concept of the universal mind as energy – the same force which manifested itself on the physical, psychic and spiritual planes.

None of these descriptions, however, made any sense except to those who were already searching for the Way. In introducing *The Perennial Philosophy*, Aldous Huxley wrote:

The nature of this one Reality is such that it cannot be directly apprehended except by those who have chosen to fulfil certain conditions, making themselves loving, pure in heart, and poor in spirit ... in a state of detachment, charity and humility. Why should this be so? We do not know. It is just one of those facts which we have to accept, whether we like them or not and however implausible they may seem. Nothing in our everyday experience gives us much reason for supposing that water is made up of hydrogen and oxygen ... Similarly nothing in our everyday experience gives us much reason for supposing that the mind of the average sensual man has, as one of its constituents, something resembling, or identical with, the Reality substantial to the manifold world; and yet, when that mind is subjected to certain rather drastic treatments, the divine element, of which it is in part at least composed, becomes manifest, not only to the mind itself, but also, by its reflection in external behaviour, to other minds.

My father said the same thing:

There is no man or woman who can give you a complete description or definition of reality ... The two greatest teachers who ever lived – Jesus and Buddha – never made any such claim ... But we *can* say certain things about the right approach to reality.

Like all the great teachers of the past, Frank saw the principal obstacle, the dominant evil of the human mind, in egoism – Huxley's

---

* *The Marriage of Heaven and Hell* (c. 1790–93), Plate 4.

'self-will, self-interest, self-centred thinking, wishing and imagining'.

As long as you are in that darkness [Frank continued], as long as you think of things in the narrow way in which we all tend to do because of our ego, we are beset by fear, we think of the universe as hostile. But when we begin to think about it as universal mind, when we begin to think of ourselves as *part* of that universal mind, we begin to liberate ourselves from our obsession and free ourselves from fear. You know, most of our afflictions and sorrows are in the apprehension rather than in the actual experience – the apprehension of the long years in which they may have to be borne. But when the mind is emancipated from that apprehension and we can feel that we live, move and have our being in the universal mind, fear begins to be replaced by an interest in life.

The number of people who at any one time have committed themselves in this life to the search for the Kingdom of God, or whatever other name we give to ultimate reality, has always been small. As Jesus said more than once, it is a secret kingdom: 'The kingdom of heaven is like unto a treasure hid in a field . . . like unto leaven hidden in three measures of meal . . . like a pearl of great price for which a man sells all he has to possess it' (Matthew 13:33–46).*

At the same time Jesus (whom my father regarded as the greatest of teachers, a spiritual genius, but, as we saw earlier, as a man not a God, the natural son of ordinary people, Joseph and Mary) taught that the finding of the Kingdom – the achievement of Godhood by humanity – was open to all men and women.

Jesus believed that about you and everybody, but then the religious took fright and said that it was not for you and me but for him alone and that

---

* Matthew 13:33–46: 'The kingdom of God is like unto leaven, which a woman took, and hid in three measures of meal, till it was all leavened . . . The kingdom of heaven is like unto a treasure hidden in the field, which a man found, and hid; and in his joy he goeth and selleth all that he hath, and buyeth that field. Again, the kingdom of heaven is like unto a man that is a merchant seeking goodly pearls: and having found one pearl of great price, he went and sold all that he had, and bought it.'

he was different, the 'only begotten Son' of God (John 3:16). Nonetheless, the fact remains that he saw the end of humanity as the achievement of Godhood and believed that you or any other human being could become a partaker of the divine nature. *How* that is to be achieved, no man knows, but Jesus summed it up in the single sentence 'He that saveth himself shall lose himself, and he that loseth himself shall save himself' (Matthew 10:39).*

Many mystics, drawing on their own brief moments of vision, have sought to express what they conceived to be the final state of union with reality. One attempt which appealed strongly to my father as well as to Aldous Huxley was the work of Thomas Traherne, a seventeenth-century mystic whose writings were recovered only at the beginning of the twentieth century.

This is what I mean [Frank told his audience] by the experience of reality, written by Traherne:

> You never enjoy the world aright till the sea itself floweth in your veins, till you are clothed with the heavens and crowned with the stars, and perceive yourself to be the sole heir of the whole world, and more than sole, because men are in it and are every one sole heirs as well with you. Till you can sing and rejoice and delight in God as misers do in gold and as kings do in sceptres, you never enjoy the world.

The man who wrote that felt himself to be 'sole heir of the whole world', and when he used the word 'God' he was thinking of the summation of the totality of things. Until you have that oneness of reality you don't know reality. Reality is not an intellectual thing, it is an experience; you are one with the thing itself; it is *one* and you are part of it!

If Traherne did have that experience, however, it is quite clear that his representation of it has left out the experience of the dark side as well – of pain, sorrow, struggle. The mystic knows about the dark night of the soul, the Gethsemanes, and the Calvaries, but you will notice that those words of Traherne's were written in a mood of ecstasy. When he gets to that, the

---

* See note on page 114.

ecstasy is such that the dark side is overwhelmed and the darker aspects swallowed up in a unity like a great symphony. As St Paul wrote in the Epistle to the Hebrews (12:2), 'Who for the joy that was set before him endured . . .'

The word my father used to describe Traherne's experience, 'ecstasy', is a term borrowed from the ancient Greek and means literally 'standing outside oneself'. It was, Frank said, 'a direct transcript of an experience of reality'. However, the only reference to a personal experience of ecstasy which I have come across in all my father's sermons and lectures is no more than a single sentence: 'Wandering alone amid the beauties of the Lake District after an illness, I once lived in ecstasy for three days; it was almost intolerable, every object shone with another light, every sound had about it an unbearable significance of joy and beauty.' Otherwise he remained silent about the source of the certainty which sustained him.

PART VI

THE ROLE OF LITERATURE

20

The Greeks and the Birth
of Literature

I

The wealth of human experience on which my father had based
his lectures and sermons had been drawn from religion and from
mysticism, evolution and psychology. An alternative was available,
however, in the lectures which my father undertook to give on
literary subjects outside any religious framework, for the Bradford
Evening Institute. He was given wide freedom in his choice of
subjects, and used it well for twenty-five years, from 1930 to 1955.
Unfortunately his notes have survived only for 1948 to 1955, but
these are sufficient to give an idea of the range of his interests.
Those I have chosen are the ancient world (the Greeks, the Jews
and the Romans), Shakespeare, the novel in the nineteenth century,
and a retrospect at the end of the first half of the twentieth.

For many modern men and women the treasures of the past, the
great scriptures, the story of Buddha and the Gospels no longer have
meaning on the basis of literal, historical fact or even philosophical
truth. But they can be approached from the standpoint of literature
as art.

This is why I have included in our lectures not only the appreciation of
Greek literature but also the Hebrew epic narrative and the New Testament.
It is this appreciation of literature as art that enables us modern men and
women to penetrate and appreciate the most primitive and archaic periods
in art and literature. We can appreciate certain of the great simplifications
of early human feeling in relation to the elemental things like corn and
vine, bread and wine, fire and light, the sanctity of the threshold and the
lament over the passing of spring or the death of a little child, the grace of
early love between young men and women. We can enter into the thrill of

the craftsman who first strung a lyre or a harp, of the sculptor who out of the rough rock fashioned the image of hero or god, or of the cave painter (more than 32,000 years ago) who captured with amazing skill the animals painted in living colours.

Matthew Arnold, in the nineteenth century, wrote that the two great creative streams in English culture flowed from the genius of the Greeks and from that of the ancient Hebrews. Both have formed part of the lingua franca of Western culture – in music, painting and architecture as well as literature – for twenty-five centuries. But today both a classical education and the reading of the Bible have suffered an eclipse.

As the two cultures reach us, they are apparently a unity, highly stylized and at first sight complete. But the work of biblical and classical scholars has made it clear that the unity has been imposed upon them; that they are a gathering together of many fragments of legend, tradition, tribal memories, scraps of law and poetry reaching back to an earlier period, with the memory of wandering and fighting, migration, primitive fears and barbaric customs, among them human sacrifice.

Both literatures also drew upon the mythologies of older peoples, for example the Babylonian and the Egyptian and the creation myth recorded in Genesis. I am anxious to mention this thread of continuity with the oldest traditions of mankind, going back to the Bronze Age (to the Old Stone Age in the case of the cave-painters) and reappearing again and again, not least in modern literature.

It was St Paul who wrote, 'The Jews require a sign, and the Greeks seek after wisdom' (1 Corinthians 1:22). After God had answered the protest of Job, the Jews bowed their heads and accepted Yahweh, the eternal and inscrutable – but nothing else. In both ancient and modern times they have been great rebels.

The Greeks also felt the mystery, the awe and even the terror of the unknown, but, where the Jew submitted to it, the Greek responded with the bold answer 'It is something like myself.' He peopled the heavens with living creatures, gods and goddesses, and projected something of himself on to them. From this developed one of the richest of all mythologies. Man is no longer confronted by blind forces, but by beings whom he endows with his own passions and inconsistencies, his own virtues and vices.

The Greeks dealt with these beings as they dealt with their fellow men and women, and were on familiar terms with them. They tried the experiment of using poetry (Homer) and, later, drama (which they created) to gain some sort of control over the unknown powers in the outer world – and within themselves. It was the first adventure of thought, the first attempt to give some rationality to man's experience of life. If a Greek felt hatred, it was Ares, the god of war, working within him; if he was inspired to write poetry, it was Apollo, the god of art.

To bring order into life and expel chaos, the Greeks created not a church but a city, the *polis*. They drew a wall around themselves and, under the protection of Athena or some other deity, devoted themselves to establishing in the *polis* a centre of order, light and beauty, which they were prepared to defend to the death against the barbarians without. To this day, the image of Athens, with the Sacred Way winding up the Acropolis to the long-lost statue of Athena enshrined in a shining white Parthenon, still exerts a fascination over the modern world's imagination.

My father began with the Homeric epics. Their origin is obscure and has been much debated by scholars. It is generally agreed that there was a poet called Homer who lived during the eighth century, i.e. before 700 BC, probably in Asia Minor, and that he played a leading part in shaping and writing down what had begun as a series of oral poems, sung to the accompaniment of the cithara or lyre. There is also general agreement that the *Iliad*, the story of the Trojan War, and the *Odyssey*, the adventures of Odysseus following the war, are each the product of one poet's work – possibly the same poet – with the *Odyssey* slightly later than the *Iliad*.

Whoever was the author or authors, the poems are an extraordinary feat, each running to twenty-four books, with the first complete version established at some time in the sixth century for the four-yearly festival, the Great Panathenaea, held in Athens. The Homeric poems held a unique place in Greek life as something more than works of literature, as a symbol of Hellenic unity and heroism and the foundation of moral and even practical education.

The two great primitive motifs of the Homeric poems were heroic fighting, and undying fame, the Homeric view of immortality. The wandering, fighting men were far from home and without gods, but there remained with them two divine emotions: *aidos* (shame) and *nemesis* (we still use this Greek word for retributive justice).

Let us speak first about *nemesis*. You have committed an act which no one may have seen but which makes you feel shame. The earth, the sun, the water, the air full of eyes, these are no longer friendly. *Nemesis* comes to mean the haunting, impalpable blame of the earth and sun, air and water, the gods and the dead.

Now we come to *aidos*. Some people make you feel uncomfortable and ashamed. Strangers, suppliants, old people, children and the blind, the disinherited, the injured, the helpless and especially the dead and the orphaned. These are all charged with *aidos*. Wrong them and they become, without any word of theirs, incarnate curses; they are charged with the wrath of the gods.

This is the beginning of a growing sense of social conscience. What the helpless ones report of you to Zeus outweighs all other judgements. This is the emotional drama of the *Iliad*, the struggle between Achilles' wrath and *aidos*. When Hector, the son of King Priam and the leader of the Trojans, kills Achilles' lover Patroclus, Achilles is filled with grief and wrath, routs the Trojans, kills Hector and, in a gesture of humiliation, drags his dead body round the walls of Troy. But Achilles, as well as wrath has *aidos* and *nemesis* in his heart and, when Priam comes to beg the body of Hector, he yields to the gods' insistence and surrenders it for a proper burial.

II

One of the great inventions of the Athenians was the drama, represented by the three great tragedians of the fifth century BC, twenty-five centuries ago, Aeschylus, Sophocles, Euripides, and by the no less great comedian Aristophanes. It was Aeschylus who lifted the art from its origins as choral and largely static recitative to fully developed drama, the presentation of action. He was born of a noble Athenian family and served as a soldier in two of the most famous battles against the Persians: Marathon and Salamis.

Of eighty known titles, there are only seven complete plays of Aeschylus left. It was the trilogy known as *Oresteia*, based on Homer, which attracted Frank. Orestes was the son of Agamemnon, King of Mycenae, and his wife Clytemnestra. When Agamemnon returned from the Trojan War he found that his wife had taken a lover, Aegisthus, who murdered him. On reaching manhood, Orestes avenged his father by killing both his mother and her lover. His conduct was regarded as exemplary, but he was haunted by the Furies for the crime of matricide. Orestes had acted in accordance with the law of vengeance. Having posed as a stranger with tidings of his own death, after killing his mother he sought refuge from the Furies at Delphi. He was finally delivered by Apollo, who prompted him to go to Athens and plead his case before the court of the Areopagus. The jury divided equally, and Pallas Athena, the patron goddess of Athens, gave her deciding vote for acquittal.

The fascination of the play lies not only in a dramatic splendour of the first order, but in the attempt of a deep and powerful mind to think out the problems of life in relation to evil, punishment and forgiveness. To the Greeks, the moral law between men and the physical law in nature were two aspects of one reality. 'Nothing too much' is the rule of both . . .

Deeply troubled by the factions which divided his native city and threatened civil war, Aeschylus offers a resolution of the tension, replacing strife with harmony, bloodshed with peace, revolution with the rule of law. To crown it, Aeschylus placates the Furies, the nameless gods, old divinities who have lost their place, transferring them to Athena's city, where they will again enjoy worship as the Eumenides, 'the well-wishers'.

My father illustrated the continuity by pointing to the later history of the Orestes story. Both Sophocles and Euripides made use of it. After that there was a long period of neglect, followed, however, by a second flowering in Voltaire's *Oreste*, Goethe's *Iphigenie auf Tauris*, Eugene O'Neill's *Mourning Becomes Electra* and, in opera, in Gluck's *Iphigénie en Tauride* and Richard Strauss's *Elektra*.

The great service the Greeks rendered to mankind was to lift man from enslavement to the blind forces of fear to the vision of a ruler whose will was righteousness. This was the theme of another trilogy of Aeschylus, only the second episode of which, *Prometheus Bound* (*c.* 465 BC), has survived. When war broke out in heaven between the Olympian gods and the Titans, Prometheus, a Titan son of Themis, who was taught by her that the victory could only be won by thought, not violence, took the side of the gods and persuaded Zeus to apportion their various functions and honours. But Zeus had no use for men and proposed to destroy the human race and create another in its place. Prometheus was the only one who spoke against him, and when Zeus mistreated mankind he stole the secret of fire from the gods and gave it to man. In retaliation Zeus chained Prometheus to a mountain peak in the Caucasus where every day the eagle, the winged hound of Zeus, came to tear his liver.

Prometheus remained defiant, but in Aeschylus' version both he and Zeus were taught by suffering and experience to learn from their mistakes. As a result, Zeus was reconciled with Prometheus and became the protector of supplicants, one who forgave because he also craved forgiveness. Zeus, who began as a warrior god, 'built a road to thought' and established 'learning by suffering' to be an abiding law.

Aeschylus' two successors, Sophocles and Euripides, carried still further this focusing on human experience and human tragedy, Sophocles in *Antigone*, for example, and Euripides in *The Trojan Women*. My father's insistence on the Greeks (Athens in particular) as the founders of the European humanist tradition is given added support by the Greek invention of history (Herodotus and Thucydides) and of philosophy (the Ionic philosophers, followed by Socrates, Plato and Aristotle). The Greek contribution is the effective beginning of serious study in both disciplines.

21

The Jews and their Identity

The Hebrew epic narrative begins with the magnificent myth of the Creation, the expulsion of Adam and Eve from the Garden of Eden, the Flood, God's covenant with Noah, and the Tower of Babel – all in the first eleven chapters of Genesis.

There is no other figure in the Old Testament to compare with Moses; as the Scripture itself says, 'There hath not arisen a prophet since in Israel like unto Moses, whom the Lord knew face to face' (Deuteronomy 34:10). A mountain of a man, he wins our admiration by the patience he shows in coming between and bearing the brunt of his people's complaints on the one hand and the Lord's anger with them on the other. He is indispensable to both but, after all he has done to lead the Israelites out of the wilderness and to interpret a capricious Lord's demands, he fails to satisfy him and is condemned not to enter the Promised Land, but only to see it from afar.

The other, very different, figure who attracted my father was Jacob:

Like Odysseus, he was a man of many wiles and infinite resource, combining outward vacillation with an inner core of tenacity that never let go. He cheated his brother, Esau, out of his birthright and cheated Laban out of his flocks, but he was prepared to serve fourteen years for Rachel, Laban's daughter, whom he loved, and he had a special feeling for his son Joseph, whom he chose to succeed him.

The two decisive episodes in Jacob's life took place at night. On the way to Haran he fell asleep and dreamed that he saw a ladder reaching from earth to heaven and on it angels going up and down. And the Lord appeared to him and blessed him and his descendants, declaring, 'I am with thee, and will keep thee whithersoever thou goest.' And when Jacob awoke, he said, 'Surely the Lord is in this place; and I knew it not.' Then he was afraid and said 'How dreadful is this place! this is none other but the house of God, and this is the gate of heaven' (Genesis 28:10–17).

The second occasion was when he crossed the ford of Jabbok. He had sent his family ahead, and a man appeared who wrestled with him until the break of day. When the man could not throw him, he dislocated Jacob's hip and said 'Let me go, for the day breaketh.' But Jacob would not let the man go unless he blessed him. The man said to Jacob, 'What is thy name?' and he answered 'Jacob.' The man then said, 'Thy name shall be called no more Jacob, but Israel: for thou hast striven with God and with men, and hast prevailed.' The man blessed him and Jacob called the place Peniel, that is 'Face of God', because, he said, 'I have seen God face to face and my life is preserved' (Genesis 32:22–30).

My father was convinced that it was not theological arguments nor history – a history as full of quarrelling and war as the *Iliad* – which had given the Old Testament its enduring appeal, but the impact of such myths and such characters as Moses and Jacob.

Perhaps we shall discover that for us moderns the appeal of poetry is stronger than the appeal of doctrine. Older generations assimilated its humanism through its divinity; we may assimilate the divinity through its humanism. Forget the doctrine and concentrate on the beauty.

The history of the Jewish people was a turbulent story, culminating in the Babylonian exile of the sixth century BC. It was during this that the historical books of the Old Testament, from Deuteronomy to Kings, and some of its finest writing were composed. There is no more splendid example than the Second (Deutero) Isaiah, so magnificently set to music by Handel more than two thousand years later:

> Comfort ye, comfort ye, my people, saith your God . . .
> The voice of him that crieth in the wilderness,
> Prepare ye the way of the Lord, make straight
> In the desert a highway for our God. (Isaiah 40:1–3)

The Persian emperors allowed the Jewish community to end their exile and rebuild the Temple in Jerusalem. But many did not return to Palestine; instead, the exile was followed by the beginning of the Jewish Diaspora (Dispersal). Six hundred years later, by the time of the Roman destruction of Jerusalem in AD 70, an estimated 5 million Jews were living in Jewish communities outside Palestine and Jews made up 40 per cent of the population of Alexandria, the biggest city of the Levant.

Scattered throughout the ancient world – and later the New World as well – the Jewish people came to depend upon their religion for their national identity, stubbornly maintained in the face of persecution and discrimination. And this religion in turn depended upon the Old Testament, which was read, prayed over and taught in their synagogues and in their families, providing them with their laws, shaping their ideals, and inspiring their worship. They became, in their own phrase, 'the People of the Book'.

II

The Jewish Diaspora had a special importance for the growth of Christianity. Scattered through the cities of the Levant and the Mediterranean world, the Jewish people had learned to make use of the Greek lingua franca as well as their own language. The New Testament was all written not in Hebrew but in Greek. As early as the third century BC a start had been made on translating the Old Testament into Greek. As a result, the Old Testament and the New Testament went into the Christian Church together, and spread to every country in Europe and later to the Americas. One example of the power they developed is the fact that the Hebrew myth of creation embodied in the Old Testament superseded the racial mythologies of Greek, Latin, German, Slavonic and all other Western peoples.

But more important than the language in which they were written was what they had to say:

Even the most impartial historian [Frank wrote] is compelled to say that the New Testament gives unmistakable evidence of the rebirth, or even new birth, of the human spirit, and this at a time when Graeco-Roman culture was entering upon the final stage that was to lead to its dissolution. It marks the end of an age and expresses the creative energies which were to produce a new dispensation in the Mediterranean world and eventually beyond the limits of that world.

The man who gave expression to this new birth was Paul, a Greek-speaking Jew, born in Asia Minor, who was also proud of his Roman citizenship. His letters – the earliest extant Christian documents – antedate the Gospels of the New Testament. More than half of the Acts of the Apostles deals with his career, and, taken together with the letters written by him or in his name, makes up one-third of the New Testament.

The central concept in Paul's thought [Frank wrote] was of a new humanity, and indeed a new Creation, by virtue of the appearance of the Second Adam, the Heavenly Man who has liberated the first from the domination of darkness. No less important was Paul's vision of a world Church, a universal religion, not limited to Jews but open to all who accepted the call of Christ. In keeping with this, although the first Christians were Jews, the New Testament was written in Greek, the language Paul used in his letters and the language of the Gospels.

During the next three hundred years, Christians were subject to periodic persecutions – the first by Nero in AD 64 – and were divided among themselves over theological issues. Nonetheless their numbers steadily grew, and in 312 Emperor Constantine the Great became a Christian; he later founded Constantinople (conceived to be a new Rome) as a Christian city. Although not foreseen at the time, this led ultimately to the permanent division of the Roman Empire into two: the eastern half, which became the Byzantine Empire, with the Orthodox Eastern Church following the Greek rite, and the western half, which became the Holy Roman Empire, with the Roman Catholic Church following the Roman rite and the Pope as its head.

The eastern half was largely a closed book to my father, as it is to most of us, but Rome caught his imagination – 'the great reservoir which collected the water of many cultures and civilizations and became the conduit by which they were brought to the West'.

In one of the bravura passages which delighted his audience, he summarized the history of Rome in a single paragraph:

Beginning with the overthrow of their Etruscan kings, c. 500 BC, the Romans established a republic which lasted for four centuries, conquered and consolidated the Latin people, subdued the Celts, fought and defeated Carthage, fought and defeated the Macedonians, subdued the Greek cities on the mainland of Europe and on the coast of Asia Minor, and reached its peak under Julius Caesar (murdered 44 BC), finally taking the form of an empire and, under a long line of emperors, conquering and governing the Mediterranean world and beyond as far as these islands. Divided into east and west, Rome saw the birth of Christianity as a universal religion, finally declining under the pressure of barbarian invasions from without, corruption and decadence from within, but even so projecting into the future the organization of the Catholic Church under the papacy which dominated the life of the Middle Ages.

The Romans themselves recognized the originality of the Greeks in the arts, in architecture, in poetry, in drama, in rhetoric and in philosophy: 'There was a perceptible decline from the springtime of the Greek genius, from its exuberant freedom and deep humanism. A certain stiffness falls upon the living breathing beauty of Greek art and poetry.' Even Virgil and Lucretius, the greatest of Roman poets, whose genius no one can deny, were all the time looking over their shoulders at their Greek predecessors, especially Homer – the *Aeneid* is a sequel to the epics of the Trojan War – and the Greek dramatists.

Where the Romans showed their genius was not in originality but in their practicality – a record in government and administration which has never been equalled. The Romans conquered, but they also consolidated, seeking to win over and incorporate the original traditions of the peoples they defeated. The same practical genius shows in their development of law – not just custom and usage, but natural law:

Certain rights and duties, certain obligations you must observe not because you are a Roman, but because you are a human being. Something more fundamental than the law of the tribe or the nation, something that arises out of nature. To feel that, to obey that and to apply it as the basis of social life and personal conduct is the greatest gift of Roman civilization to mankind.

Finally, the Latin language, corresponding to the Roman feeling for government and law – a language in which you can discipline thought, be clear and precise, and say what you mean without ambiguity. Jerome's translation of the Bible into Latin (he lived c. AD 342–420) made it the language in which men and women prayed and opened their hearts for more than a thousand years, until the Reformation. For the same thousand years it provided Europe with a language in which all educated persons, whatever their nationality, could communicate – the language of St Augustine and St Thomas Aquinas, of science and engineering, of philosophy as well as law and politics.

22

Shakespeare

I

Shakespeare's creation requires nothing less than a world to describe it. No other writer then or now has possessed his command of the English language, or so brought to life the characters with whom he filled his works – characters as diverse as Hamlet and Lear, Cordelia and Lady Macbeth, Shylock and Falstaff. His personality remains hooded, and his nature was completely identified with his imagination.

It was characteristic of Shakespeare that he was careless about his plots, not bothering to devise them himself, but taking his raw material from any source that was handy. Very soon, however, he began to work upon them in a new way, ignoring the old unities of the classical drama, and giving depth and character to what were at first stock characters.

His characters are not mere actors in time but creations endowed with their own independent life. Thus Hamlet is an immortal figure, moving amid the setting and furniture of a crude melodrama: ghosts, open graves, adulteries, poison and fights. The same is true of Shylock and Falstaff. Julius Caesar is another striking example: murdered early in the play, he dominates it to the end. These characters make hay of history, of plots and settings; they are the play itself, which Shakespeare fills with the atmosphere, power and content of his own deep poetic vision.

Frank did not regard Shakespeare as a mystic, but he was struck by the difference between Greek and Shakespearean tragedy. For the Greeks, tragedy was a conflict with a fate that was inevitable; there was no getting out from under. For Shakespeare, tragedy arose entirely from the awakening of an inner conflict, the result of some fault in the character of the protagonists – Lear's doting fondness, Othello's trusting nature, Macbeth's ambition.

Even so, tragedy is never thought of as complete spiritual disaster: Lear dies restored by Cordelia's love; Othello recovers his faith in Desdemona; Macbeth dies delivered from the evil spell woven by the witches; Hamlet is cured of his indecision – 'If it be now, 'tis not to come; if it be not to come, it will be now; if it be not now, yet it will come: the readiness is all . . . Let be' (V.ii.233). There is sorrow, storm, upheaval, but no absolute tragedy. Shakespeare has absorbed the great Christian feeling that the world's sorrow is caused by suffering. In the end the redemptive forces triumph even in death.

Shakespeare's own creative life followed the same pattern. *The Winter's Tale* and above all *The Tempest* replace the dark passions of the tragedies 'with a kind of agony of hope, the thought of reconciliation and forgiveness', perfectly expressed by Prospero in a speech full of allegory:

> . . . these our actors,
> As I foretold you, were all spirits and
> Are melted into air, into thin air:
> And, like the baseless fabric of this vision,
> The cloud-capp'd towers, the gorgeous palaces,
> The solemn temples, the great globe itself,
> Yea, all which it inherit, shall dissolve
> And, like this insubstantial pageant faded,
> Leave not a rack behind. We are such stuff
> As dreams are made on; and our little life
> Is rounded with a sleep.
>
> (*The Tempest*, IV.i.148–58)

II

In his early plays Shakespeare is intoxicated with the magic of mere words. In his middle period he manages to maintain a clear balance between word and thought; then, in the great tragedies, the demands his thought and emotion make on words become so great that there is at times a sense of incoherence which, paradoxically, is powerfully suggestive, as in *Macbeth* and *King Lear*. Finally, in *The Tempest* he achieves an unrivalled economy and mastery of language, with line after line conveying an unearthly beauty and peace.

It was the histories, beginning with the key play of *Richard II*, that convinced my father of the organic character of Shakespeare's mind. The murder of the king involved the whole realm in chaos; the underlying order of life and nature, inherited from the Middle Ages, was destroyed, evil had been done, and atonement must be made. It was Richard III who marked the culmination and end of the cycle of chaos and disorder.

The essence of the comedies is the differentiation of character in the events and people of everyday life. Shakespeare had a genuine appreciation of homespun ordinary characters with their oddities, their grossness and their slyness, especially in country life – with no better example than the world of Bottom and the rude mechanicals. In contrast is his use of wit, 'a kind of intellectual exuberance, playing with words and ideas so that they sparkle and shine like shallow waters rippling under sunlight'. This is matched by his sense of intellectual irony; the comic element serves to deepen the intense seriousness of life.

Falstaff is the greatest of comic creations. He can make everything seem comic; he is utterly amoral, defies convention, and exploits an element of picaresque truth in his jeers and jibes. Fundamentally he is a fraud. Posing as wicked, when he is dying he betrays his innocence – 'a' babbled of green fields' (*Henry V*, II.iii.17). He lived a double life, but he had never inwardly been far away from the green pastures of childhood.

*

Taking each of the four great tragedies in turn, my father found in *Hamlet* the projection of Shakespeare's obsession with death:

Hamlet is touched with the consciousness of death from the appearance of his father's ghost. This contact with the frozen realm infects him, and he stalks through the play a terrible dealer of death, whose victims include Polonius, Ophelia, Rosencrantz and Guildenstern, the Queen, the King, Laertes and finally himself.

Macbeth represents the invasion of supernatural evil, an impalpable presence in the air, in the earth, yet at the last moment of the play the evil spell cast by the witches is broken:

> And be these juggling fiends no more believed,
> That palter with us in a double sense;
> That keep the word of promise to our ear,
> And break it to our hope . . .
> . . . Lay on, Macduff;
> And damn'd be he that first cries 'Hold, enough!'
> (V.viii.19–34)

Lear represents purgatory, remote in time, a grotesque, cold, alien world, where every natural symbol is distorted and the putting out of Gloucester's eyes is matched with Lear's madness. In the mad scenes Shakespeare pushes language to the limit. When Cordelia wakes him, Lear replies:

> You do me wrong to take me out o' the grave:
> Thou art a soul in bliss; but I am bound
> Upon a wheel of fire, that mine own tears
> Do scald like molten lead.   (IV.vii.45–8)

In *Antony and Cleopatra* the realm of Cleopatra first appears as an earthly paradise remote from all the stress and strain, all the ambition of the Roman world. When the might of the world invades it, the careless confidence with which Antony and Cleopatra treat it leads to disaster and misunderstanding, yet their love for each other rises above defeat, celebrated in some of Shakespeare's most memorable lines.

ANTONY: I am dying, Egypt, dying; only
    I here importune death awhile, until
    Of many thousand kisses the poor last
    I lay upon thy lips.   (IV.xv.18–21)

Cleopatra is resolute in her determination to follow him:

CLEOPATRA: Give me my robe, put on my crown; I have
    Immortal longings in me . . .
    . . . Methinks I hear
    Antony call . . .
    . . . Husband I come:
    Now to that name my courage prove my title!
    I am fire and air; my other elements
    I give to baser life . . .
CHARMIAN: . . . So, fare thee well.
    Now boast thee, death, in thy possession lies
    A lass unparallel'd . . .   (V.ii.282–315)

As Cleopatra kills herself, her woman Charmian is only a pace behind. Finally, Caesar, the victor in battle, finding Cleopatra's corpse, orders:

    . . . Take up her bed . . .
    She shall be buried by her Antony:
    No grave upon the earth shall clip in it
    A pair so famous . . .   (V.ii.356–60)

23

The Nineteenth Century
and the Novel

I

My father did not share the view of many critics of his time that novels had an ephemeral character and did not deserve to be included in the discussion of serious literature. On the contrary, he maintained that the novel was the best introduction to what people thought and felt, from the eighteenth century to his own day and the revolution launched by television.

By a striking coincidence, within the eight years 1811–19 three men and three women were born whose combined impact brought the English novel to new heights. They were Thackeray, Dickens and Trollope, Charlotte and Emily Brontë and Mary Ann Evans (known as George Eliot).

From the first appearance of *The Pickwick Papers* in serial form in 1836, when he was no more than twenty-four, it was clear that Dickens was a genius with an inexhaustible store of mental and emotional energy – a marvellous mixture of realism and fantasy, of horrors and fairy tales – who had an eye for and the power to present the strangely sinister in human life and even in the inanimate furniture of the material world.

As with Shakespeare, Dickens' plots do not matter; he often does his best when he forgets them. What matters is the atmosphere he creates. His characters are so vivid that they wander about in your imagination quite independently of the novels in which they appear. Who cares where Sam Weller or Mrs Gamp or Mr Micawber fit into the plot? They are immortal, like the gods, and have all space and time in which to wander freely.

*

The fact that the three women novelists had to disguise their sex by publishing their books under male pseudonyms reveals the depth of prejudice which they encountered. The first to appear was Charlotte Brontë's *Jane Eyre*, under the pseudonym Currer Bell in 1847.

Suddenly the air became electric. Here was something new in fiction. The stuffy Victorians suddenly realized that woman had passions and demanded the full satisfaction of her desires and dreams. Charlotte won her place as much by her personality as by her art. A plain little governess who was also a creature of fire, she lived and burned in the pages of *Jane Eyre* and *Shirley*.

While Charlotte's novel was in the first flush of its success, in December 1847 her sister Emily Brontë's *Wuthering Heights* was published and met with little critical attention.

A later generation, however, has taken my father's view of *Wuthering Heights* (originally published under the pseudonym Ellis Bell) as a masterpiece: 'The whole cycle of demonic passion is presented with consummate art; the creatures she brings to life are a race apart, not mortals but elemental powers akin to the moorlands and the storms that sweep across them.' On the strength of her one novel and a handful of poems, Emily Brontë retains a place among the greatest English writers.

Mary Ann Evans, or George Eliot, as she is still known, lived on into the late Victorian Age, dying in 1880. By then she had become a serious-minded intellectual – a masculine mind, in my father's view – who brought a new level of psychological subtlety to novel-writing:

There are two women, or perhaps a man and a woman, always at war in George Eliot. One woman wrote the early books – *Adam Bede* and *Silas Marner* as well as *The Mill on the Floss* – in which she drew on the English Midlands of her girlhood spent among country scenes and people. The other woman, or man, was the rationalist and freethinking scholar who went on to produce her later books. Among them were *Middlemarch*, one of the greatest novels in the English language, and *Daniel Deronda*, which reveals George Eliot's nostalgia for some deep religious vision to take the place of the evangelical Christianity she had rejected.

II

My father believed that there was much to be gained by placing English writers in the context of European and American literature. His own enthusiasm for Balzac, for instance, had not diminished since he had first introduced Balzac to his class twenty years earlier, in 1930. At the other end of Europe, my father believed that the three Russian novelists Turgenev (1818–83), Dostoevsky (1821–81) and Tolstoy (1828–1910) initiated a revolution in human consciousness in the second half of the nineteenth century.

They seemed not only men of great imagination and intellectual powers but to have lived, before writing, at a level of human experience which made the Western novelists seem a little complacent and tame. None of them – not even Turgenev – had the Western objection to striking an emotion on its topmost note, while the sickness in mind and body, with a touch of madness, which affected Dostoevsky's characters seemed to their author to be the norm for humanity. Of Dostoevsky it has been said that he felt ideas as others feel cold or hunger and thirst, and that his senses responded to ideas as those of others to passions.

Turgenev represents a halfway house between the French objective novel – he was an intimate of Flaubert, the Goncourts and Zola – and the Russian analytical novel.

He is the most poetical of the Russian realists, one whose character-drawing does not depend on analysis and psychology but on a subtly woven atmosphere that accompanies the character like an aura. His own masterpiece, *Fathers and Sons* (1862), provides a famous portrayal of the nihilist hero Bazarov and of the split between the two generations, the younger, radical revolutionary intelligentsia and the older generation of the liberal gentry to which Turgenev himself belonged.

It took Tolstoy almost seven years in the 1860s to write *War and Peace* – by common consent one of the greatest novels ever written, despite its elaboration at length of his determinist view of history. Its huge panorama presents the histories of five aristocratic families, portrayed against a vivid background of Russian social life in the period 1805–14 and the drama of Napoleon's invasion of Russia. Among more than sixty characters filling the stage are the unforgettable Natasha Rostov and the bumbling Pierre and proud Prince Andrei, with both of whom Tolstoy identifies himself.

It was Dostoevsky who made a greater impression on my father than any other novelist. Condemned to death for taking part in an illegal radical group, at the last moment he had his sentence changed to four years' hard labour in Siberia, followed by four more years as a soldier in the ranks. The experience not only left him liable to epileptic fits, but converted him from radicalism to respect for the established order, including the Russian Orthodox Church, and a belief in the messianic mission of the Russian people. Between 1864 and 1865 misfortunes overwhelmed him: his wife and brother died, and he had to flee abroad to escape imprisonment for debt, contracted an inveterate passion for gambling, and was reduced to pawning his clothes to pay his hotel bill.

It was in these circumstances that he wrote the first of his four masterpieces, *Crime and Punishment* (1866), a novel which achieved immediate success. It did not, however, relieve his desperate circumstances. For four years he lived in abject poverty abroad, experiencing epileptic seizures, incessant gambling, bankruptcy and the death of his first-born. Only his second wife's devotion and belief in his genius kept him going while he completed *The Idiot* (1868–9) and *The Possessed* (1872). By the time he came to write his greatest work, *The Brothers Karamazov* (1879–80), he had become nationally recognized as a major author, living quietly in a small town while his wife took down the text in shorthand. Only a few months after completing the manuscript, he died early in 1881 while still short of sixty.

Dostoevsky's realism combines power of imagination and language with an intense psychological analysis of his characters, from

Raskolnikov's justification of murder in *Crime and Punishment* to the reaction of the four brothers to the killing of their father in *The Brothers Karamazov*. What Dostoevsky is capable of at the height of his powers is shown in the famous 'Legend of the Grand Inquisitor' in the latter.

'Man does not belong to the objective world order; you cannot confine him to the surface of things.' With Dostoevsky man plunges into the spiritual world, and it is like a descent into hell, where man will find not only Satan and his kingdom but also God and heaven too. Because man is a spiritual being he is free to choose between good and evil, but evil (always present in Dostoevsky's mind) can all too easily destroy his freedom. 'There is a deep apocalyptic element in Dostoevsky's writing, and his prophetic vision of Western man has been tragically fulfilled in the twentieth century – one reason why he has continued to be read throughout it.'

Looking for a playwright to round off his discussion of realism in the novel, my father might well have chosen the Russian Anton Chekhov. Instead he turned to the Norwegian Henrik Ibsen, whose run of twenty successful plays began with two outstanding poetic dramas, *Brand* and *Peer Gynt*, then brought realism into the theatre with *Pillars of Society*, *A Doll's House*, *Ghosts*, *An Enemy of the People*, *The Wild Duck* and *Rosmersholm* (1877–1886) – all the subject of protest and controversy, not least in Britain.

Living a lonely life abroad in Europe for nearly thirty years, Ibsen did not need long or continuous contact with society. A chance word, a chance meeting, a sudden recollection were enough to fertilize that powerful imagination which then, feeding on itself and nourishing the germ, gave birth every two years to a play, bringing into the world entirely new characters owing everything to the mind and spirit of the dramatist.

III

My father concluded with the English novelist Thomas Hardy, whom he described as 'the last and greatest classicist in form, yet at the same time one of the forerunners of the modern spirit in content of idea and vision'.

As an example of Hardy's art at its best, Frank chose *The Return of the Native* (1878). The duration is a year and a day; the place is Egdon Heath; the action the Heath's silent power to attract, to repel and to destroy – a power described in the opening pages – 'A Face on Which Time Makes but Little Impression' – which Frank read to his class:

A Saturday afternoon in November was approaching the time of twilight, and the vast tract of unenclosed wild known as Egdon Heath embrowned itself moment by moment. Overhead the hollow stretch of whitish cloud shutting out the sky was as a tent which had the whole heath for its floor.

The heaven being spread with this pallid screen and the earth with the darkest vegetation, their meeting-line at the horizon was clearly marked. In such contrast the heath wore the appearance of an instalment of night which had taken up its place before its astronomical hour was come: darkness had to a great extent arrived hereon, while day stood distinct in the sky. Looking upwards, a furze-cutter would have been inclined to continue work; looking down, he would have decided to finish his faggot and go home. The distant rims of the world and of the firmament seemed to be a division in time no less than a division in matter. The face of the heath by its mere complexion added half an hour to evening; it could in like manner retard the dawn, sadden noon, anticipate the frowning of storms scarcely generated, and intensify the opacity of a moonless midnight to a cause of shaking and dread . . .

The sombre stretch of rounds and hollows seemed to rise and meet the evening gloom in pure sympathy, the heath exhaling darkness as rapidly as the heavens precipitated it. And so the obscurity in the air and the obscurity in the land closed together in a black fraternization towards which each advanced half-way.

Where Hardy scores is by making us aware that the contemporary world and its fashions pass away, but that the creative principle of life in men and women – and in nature – remains constant.

Beauty is not a utilitarian value, it is the completely irrational mystery and gleam of eternity which upsets all our temporal values. It is only caught at rare moments by mortals in their highest consciousness. Hardy catches more of these elusive moments than almost any other novelist because he is a poet. He snatches them out of this dissolving world of passion and change, and presents us with an immortal country of the mind and the emotions.

All Hardy's great novels are full of that elusive beauty – besides *The Return of the Native*, *The Mayor of Casterbridge* (which opens with a man selling his wife and child at a fair), *Far From the Madding Crowd*, *Tess of the D'Urbervilles*, *The Woodlanders*. What makes them great? It is not easy to say. You could hardly call Hardy a stylist; he can be slow, clumsy and almost dull. But his style rises with his theme, and at the great moments there is a cumulative power which is overwhelming – yet, if you try to analyse the effect, it vanishes under your hand.

PART VII

MODERN MAN IN SEARCH
OF A FAITH

24

The Crisis of the Twentieth Century

Looking back at the end of the first half of the twentieth century, Frank found the experience of anxiety and frustration to be the dominant theme in literature. This arose from the actual experience of our age: in the shock of the First World War and the tragic disillusionment that followed it; the era of Hitler and Stalin; the Second World War and its 45–50 million dead; the division of Europe; and the threat of a Third World War even more devastating. It was hardly to be wondered at that all this destruction and fear should find expression in literature.

He saw one reflection of this in existentialism, which had a great attraction in Europe after the Second World War among such very different writers as Martin Heidegger, Karl Jaspers, Jean-Paul Sartre (who was an atheist) and Gabriel Marcel (who was a Roman Catholic). All acknowledged the influence of the nineteenth-century Danish philosopher and religious thinker Søren Kierkegaard (1813–55).

What is existentialism? It assumes that man is essentially lonely, that the deepest reality he knows is his own subjective thoughts, moods and emotions; and that these are fundamentally contradictory, paradoxical and always tend towards disillusionment and despair. Yet there is an element of tenacity in man by which he struggles and survives, even after he has abandoned hope. The only fact he really knows is that he exists, that he feels and that he is lonely. From the religious point of view he may find deliverance by a desperate act of faith. But when that is lacking, he must be content with the basic fact of his existence (hence 'existentialism') and of his loneliness and will to endure. This was the true human situation,

Kierkegaard believed, which he explored in such books as *Either/Or* (1843) and *Concluding Unscientific Postscript* (1846).

Kierkegaard remained largely unknown outside Denmark for a hundred years. But the travails of the mid twentieth century created a situation in which feelings of loneliness and guilt became inescapable and made him appear as a genius.

Literature which gave expression to these feelings (for example, Albert Camus's *The Plague*, Elias Canetti's *Auto da Fé* and Sartre's monumental *Being and Nothingness*) attracted great attention. My father asked:

Why are such books written? By an imperative impulse. We live in anarchic times, in apocalyptic days. The anarchic element is there all right, and you can hear the thunder of the sea of non-being which no man can re-enter and live. Strange passions erupt in human society and in the human psyche, and it is inevitable that these things should be reflected in the great mirror of art. All the glory and all the sorrow, all the bewilderment and all the pain as well as all the insatiable hopes and desires of the modern soul and modern society are reflected in the modern novel.

II

The greatest contribution we can make to the revival of both the conscious mind and the unconscious is to restore the imagination to its sovereign position. Again:

We have to return the intellect to its true ground as the instrument, not the master, of consciousness, and begin not with systems and the abstractions of philosophical thought, but with concrete experience. And the key to that lies in liberating the imagination, the creative not the analytical function of the mind, which has the power to open our eyes to the extraordinary universe in which we live and to re-create our vision of reality. For, as Blake wrote, 'If the doors of perception were cleansed every thing would appear to man as it is, infinite.'*

* *The Marriage of Heaven and Hell* (*c.* 1790–93), Plate 14.

The poets – Blake, Coleridge, Wordsworth, Yeats – had never ceased to protest at our neglect of the imagination, our mistaking it for fantasy, our failure to grasp its power to draw on the energies of the unconscious and reconcile the unconscious with the conscious mind. It is the poets', the artists', the composers', the architects' images – always concrete, not abstract – which reawaken our own imaginations to the marvel of life and what we might make of it.

No one has ever exercised the imagination without bringing his or her will into it. Jakob Böhme wrote that 'the universe was created by will and imagination'. Imagination integrates all our powers, quickens our senses and stimulates our intellect, integrating not just the conscious but the unconscious powers of the mind. It is as deeply involved in science or philosophy as in writing poetry or music. Newton and Einstein achieved their objectives by imagination as surely as did Dante and Shakespeare.

The unconscious mind always speaks in the language of images and symbols. These are the raw stuff of imagination, and they draw upon inexhaustible memories; they speak of that which is universal. The creations of imagination live and go on living because they speak from the depths, and this is why, when you listen to music, look at a painting or read a passage, it immediately holds you and quickens you. Imagination is as mysterious and definite and real as the fact of light playing upon the sensitive pigment of the skin. Because of some blind desire of creatures for sight, gradually that mysterious organ the physical eye was built – for that is how sight came. Just as definite and real is the impact upon mankind of the great images, not only when you understand them, but sometimes when you don't.

Is the Kingdom of Imagination an end in itself? Surely not! The music of Beethoven is not an end; it speaks of something beyond. The great forms of art are not ends, but awaken within us questionings and urges, desires for that which is veiled beyond them. We may regard the Kingdom of Imagination as a bridge, a kingdom which links up in some mysterious way with that which is beyond expression in any visible form. We know that the tantalizing part about the imagination is that while it satisfies to a certain extent it does not do so completely, because it is expressing something which is beyond expression. Keats put it in that marvellous phrase 'Imagination teases our thought with the image of Eternity.' It cannot be expressed. The great images are never explicit; they point to what lies beyond.

Closely allied with the imagination is the life of the senses, and unity of energy.

The perception of the eye, the keenness of hearing, of taste, and of touch – all that intensification of the life of the senses is built up by the life of the mind. The trouble with most people is that they never bother about their sense life, yet this is one of the greatest gifts given us. It is only the life of the mind that can quicken the senses, but it is also the life of the senses that has quickened the mind. Take the case of your hand, with its fingers and thumb. What the mind first gained by the liberation of the fingers and thumb was a tremendous step forward, not merely for the hand but also for the mind; the hand has taught the mind as much as the mind has taught the hand.

Behind the multiplicity of things, Frank saw the unity of psychic energy. Everything we meet – whether in cells, plants or human beings, the development of roots, leaves and flowers, the movement of the intellect and emotions – everything is a manifestation of energy, which manifests itself at different levels – material, emotional, intellectual, spiritual – but is always one psychic energy.

We are conscious of it only in the millionfold phenomena which we encounter, but behind all these, and the many more of which we know nothing, there is a vast sea, a unity of psychic energy. The single unit of energy represented by yourself, by the plant in your garden, by your cat, emerges out of this unfathomable ocean of psychic energy.

You may look at it in this manner. The division of the earth's continents from each other by oceans is only a surface appearance; underneath the depths of the ocean, the great land masses still run, constituting a unity, one globe, one world. The unit of life – which you yourself represent – may be compared with a single sponge growing in the ocean. It draws its nutriment out of the seabed, yet it has an independent structure of its own within the overall unity of the ocean and of the world. In the same way the self is saturated through and through with the vast unity of life energy. We are never outside it, yet within it we reveal a special structure of individual character. Although you sit here tonight as a separate individual, the life energy links you with every other living creature on this planet; you are unconscious of it, but the links are there.

Anyone who can grasp this will see him- or herself in a quite different light, and no longer feel lost in a universe of which, as he or she discovers, each of us forms an integral part.

25

Psychology and Evolution

I

The 1950s brought my father two marks of recognition in the Unitarian community at large. The first was an invitation from Manchester College, the Unitarian theological college in Oxford, to deliver the Tate Lectures, on 'The Art of Preaching'. The second was at the annual meeting of the General Assembly of the Liberal and Free Christian Churches, this time held in Liverpool, with its strong Unitarian traditions, where Frank was elected as President of the Assembly for the year 1955–6 – a simple form of recognition which gave great pleasure to his friends.

The twelve Tate Lectures were addressed to a small group of students of varying ages who had committed themselves to entering the Unitarian ministry. Frank left them in no doubt of what they were undertaking:

The vast mass of men and women are not interested. The type of religion which gains the most adherents, sacramental and ritualistic in character, allows preaching a very subordinate position, while the more educated members of the community regard it as an anachronism, a sort of vestigial remnant from an earlier and cruder state of society . . .

What answers had Frank himself got? He could see nothing in the discussion from the pulpit of moral and social problems which would meet the spiritual needs of the age. He found the justification for preaching in an irresistible urge to speak of the things of the soul, the things of the spirit, the things of God.

Remember [he reminded his listeners] that the great end of religion is the liberation of emotion. I do not mean emotion separated from thought or action, but integrated into the whole of life and experience. Never forget there is a passion of the mind, one of the deepest and most enduring passions of which we are capable. As the Gospels say, 'Thou shalt love the Lord thy God with all thy heart . . . and *with all thy mind*' (Matthew 22:37 and Mark 12:30).

The instrument we could all use towards the development of liberation was the imagination. One of the ways of cultivating this was by the use of concrete images rather than abstract language, as was done nowhere with greater effect than in the Old Testament and the sayings of Jesus. The argument for this approach was strengthened by the confusion of religious orthodoxy in the face of the findings of modern biblical scholarship. Roman Catholic theology rejected these findings, and, while orthodox Protestant theology had gradually given ground in the case of the Old Testament, it made no real concession in the case of the New Testament, continuing to insist on the literal acceptance of the Virgin Birth, miracles, the Resurrection and the Ascension.

My father argued that the root of the trouble was the failure to understand the nature of myth and poetry, which was neither literal fact on the one hand nor fantasy on the other, but *psychological and spiritual fact*, by no means limited to Christianity (another stumbling block), but to be found, as Jung had discovered, in other religions and mythologies, as different aspects of the Ancient Wisdom.

From the 1930s to the mid-1950s my father's teaching had followed a threefold pattern: sermons, talks on psychology, talks on books. The year 1955, however, saw his sixty-eighth birthday and the last of his book talks. Thereafter Frank left it to his talks on psychology (which he kept up unbroken from 1943 to 1962) to maintain a balance with his sermons.

My father did not question that in a case of neurosis it was necessary to call in a qualified psychiatrist. But he believed that there was a wide range of personal problems in which ordinary men and women could acquire sufficient understanding of psychology to help themselves. How seriously he took this is shown by the fact that in 1957–8, the two years for which we have notes, the best part of eighty-two lectures was devoted to the theme 'Talks on Personal Problems'.

Whatever the problem may be, its emergence is a sign of life. It at least indicates that the consciousness of yourself as a person has begun to take shape. Resistance is always the medium of intensified consciousness, and, to begin with, is difficult to bear. Talking in this way we can see what the situation demands and what resources we can draw on. The important factor is yourself, not abstract theories or even experimental methods.

My father began by pointing to the extraordinary achievement of life in creating the human race:

It tried all kinds of adjustment to the environment and to the development of the body; it built the brain so as to carry the light of consciousness; it gradually prepared for the mystery of self-consciousness. And then the trouble began, because the problems were handed down to the self. They came upon us very slowly, both in the race and in the individual, until today we are in a state of bewilderment.

At a time when there is more freedom than ever before, there has never been more frustration. But frustration often does not deserve the poor reputation it bears. For many of the finest things we possess were actually born out of frustration: speech, for example, and the growth of the human brain, our deepest emotions, most of our inventions, the greatest things in music, art and literature, our deepest mental life, our deepest self-consciousness. Because we could not find an immediate and shallow satisfaction, men and women had to search for ways to help themselves. As a result, our inner lives grew and deepened, the creative energies and capacities were developed. These are facts we should remember when we complain about frustration.

My father recognized that many people were bewildered by all the talk they heard about the unconscious mind.

Let me clarify the position. The *conscious mind* in you and me is focused around the awareness of self. This self is made up of many elements; in part, we are the product of evolution, of heredity, of environment, and in part we are self-made men and women. Our greatest attainment in the making of this consciousness of ourselves has been the creation of language. We turn everything into words and into thought, even our perceptions and emotions; and the more educated we become in the use of words and thought, the deeper is the consciousness of ourselves.

In contrast, it is the realm of the *subconscious* which is most quickly affected by what the self thinks and feels and does. This is the realm which is treated by the psychiatrist, because it is most accessible to his or her techniques. All man's personal difficulties arise from the subconscious, in the form of emotion, fixations and complexes.

The first, emotion, is the great source of power and energy, our outgoing towards life and the world. It takes many forms: when frustrated or repressed, the form of resentment, anger and hatred; when released, it is the source of energy and creative activity. It is an illusion that emotion and the intellect are in conflict: intellectual passion is one of the strongest passions, and intellectual pride is frustrated emotion. The great problem is how to secure the transfer of our emotion from the self to some object or purpose in which self-forgetfulness is achieved.

Frank underlined that there was nothing abnormal about seeking of help of the psychiatrist, provided men and women would face up to the need to make decisions – a responsibility they were reluctant to accept. In his view, the way to persuade them was to get them to draw back from any commitment to full achievement. 'Don't worry about the goal – that will become clearer as you take the first few steps. Begin by doing what you have to do – no more.' Both concentration and relaxation were to be seen not as setting problems, but as necessary alternative stages in the fulfilment of life. Both formed part of the natural rhythm of the body, from which the mind and the emotions must learn the art of letting go. The secret was to find the centre in which, alike in concentration and relaxation, we were at rest.

II

My father's final lectures on psychology coincided with his seventy-fifth birthday and gave him the opportunity to explain why he attached so much importance to the study of psychology and evolution.

Just as psychology is one of the key words in the thought processes of our modern age, so – my father claimed – the other key word is *evolution*. It emerged into common use in the nineteenth century, just as psychology did in the twentieth.

Both ideas met with strenuous resistance from representatives of the older patterns of thought, but both are now established as necessary to the exposition and exploration of reality. Even the idea of evolution itself must be said to evolve.

Two questions remain to be further debated:
(1) The cause of evolution: is this by chance or by directed intelligence?
(2) The goal of the process: is it a material goal which, in the nature of things, can only be temporarily achieved in time and dissolved in time, or a goal emerging out of a psychic, immaterial and instinctive source beyond the limits of time and space?

In Frank's mind there was no doubt of the answer to both questions:
(1) The cause of evolution is a directing intelligence.
(2) Both source and goal are psychic, immaterial and spiritual.

Take the first idea of a guiding intelligence. The old idea was that some overruling intelligence began and continued all the time to create and control all the processes and all the events manifested in nature and history.

But this leads straight into the problem of evil. Was this overruling intelligence responsible for all the conflicts, suffering and failures involved in the process of evolution? If so, how could we ascribe to this intelligence perfect wisdom and perfect goodness? Must we not rather accept the idea that the intelligence was within the evolving matter and life, and as it evolved had to accept responsibility for mistakes, failures and suffering involved in the process of evolution?

This brings us face to face with the major question: Is matter or mind (involving soul and spirit) the basis of the universe?

If we say matter, then all the higher values of culture (including religion, art, thought) are by-products which have no permanent significance, in fact are in the nature of an illusion.

Psychology should strongly support the alternative idea: that the origin and goal of the universe are basically immaterial in nature. This conclusion opens the door to limitless evolution in which the attainments of human personality are of incalculable significance. It gives importance to history (wherein the higher evolution of humanity is achieved), to science, because it establishes the validity of human thought, and finally to the central importance of religion.

On this level religion and evolutionary thought reach a common conclusion expressed in the famous words of St Paul: 'For we know that the whole creation groaneth and travaileth until now in the pangs of birth in the hope that they shall be delivered into the glorious freedom of the Son of God' (Romans 8:20–22).*

Or, in the words of Browning, 'Man partly is and wholly hopes to be.'†

And in that wholeness the vast adventure of creation and evolution will be achieved.

Up to this point Frank had directed our attention outward, watching the process of evolution, trying to grasp the psychic or hidden side of matter and nature, until at last we are brought face to face with mind. With this we enter a new dimension, in which all things are

---

* Romans 8:20–22: 'For the creation was subjected to vanity not of its own will, but by reason of him who subjected it, in hope that the creation itself also shall be delivered from the bondage of corruption into the liberty of the glory of the children of God. For we know that the whole creation groaneth and travaileth in pain together until now' (Revised Version); '. . . Up to the present, we know, the whole created universe groans in all its parts as if in the pangs of childbirth' (New English Bible).
† 'A Death in the Desert' (1864), l. 588.

transformed into memory – especially unconscious memory – and then into ideas and emotions. Indeed the very concepts of universe, evolution and process are projections and creations of the human mind, the phenomenon of man.

The stuff out of which humanity emerges appears at first sight to be the common stuff of nature and animal experience, the instinct of self-preservation and the struggle for survival. But man extends his power of destruction from being the weakest animal, with a longer period of weakness than any other animal, until he becomes the most rapacious and destructive of all the animals.

All this capacity and power has arisen out of man's mysterious gift of reflection. We do not act immediately, or discharge our energy in immediate action; we reflect, we invent, and only then carry out our plans. Civilization is the remarkable result of individual and collective reflection. That is the first stage of being human, the consciously purposive creation which by reflection has gained ascendancy over matter and nature.

But that is not the end of the story – far from it. The crucial time comes when we begin to reflect upon ourselves, and other emotions begin to emerge out of our minds. We become aware of the emotion of pleasure, in form and colour, and begin to look beyond our physical needs to the beauty in the living forms of plants and animals, in rocks and mountains, forests and running streams. We experience not only pleasure but also awe, wonder and even fear in our reaction to the different aspects of nature. We reach out to something beyond and greater than our selves. We begin to reflect on the mystery of reflection, and wonder what we are, whence we came, and whither we are going. We begin to wonder if there are opportunities for growth and development beyond anything we realize today.

All this universe of emotion, higher instincts and reflection, however, would have been buried and lost if it were not that the supreme importance of being human was realized in the fact that man is the bearer of the Word, the creator of language. It is the supreme mystery that patterns of sound, made by the fleeting breath of our bodies, have opened the means of expression and communication whereby the world of mind has become more real than the world of matter. I have always thought that the most profound sentence ever written was 'In the beginning was the Word, and the Word was life and the life of the Word was the light of man' (John 1:1–4).*

Gradually consciousness has grown and revealed to us the true way of life. We learn to regard the self as a seed that carries within it the promise of a richer, fuller life. The seed dies naturally, but out of the decaying seed a new life emerges, establishing a new relationship with the earth, aware of something beyond the self, transcending race and circumstances, becoming a new, creative life.

Unless we have some awareness of purpose in our lives, we tend to feel that life itself has lost its primary value. Many of course, at least for a time, find it in taking responsibility, succeeding in business, caring for a home, becoming expert in some art or craft . . .

But when all these ends and purposes are more or less achieved, men and women are not finally satisfied. Some larger purpose has been recognized, of which they have at first been unaware, an interdependence of life, a wholeness, in which alone the manifold purposes can be realized. Very slowly we become aware of the need for self-fulfilment in some end beyond all the temporary uses and purposes we have served.

This final awareness of purpose can only be achieved by an expansion of individual consciousness, which is only authoritative for the individual who experiences it. Such men and women can only say they have had the experience. These are the mystics, whose affirmations of ultimate purpose are age-long and universal. They come from many different intellectual, social and religious environments – Indian saints and yogis, Greek thinkers like Plato and Plotinus, medieval and modern saints and poets. This mysterious faculty is in all of us, but in the great majority as yet undeveloped; each of us must find his or her own way to the ultimate goal.

* John 1:1–4: 'In the beginning was the Word, and the Word was with God, and the Word was God . . . In him was life: and the life was the light of men.'

26

'The greatest mystery is the existence of order in the universe'

I

My father's preoccupation with psychology and personal problems did not lead him to neglect his lifelong interest in religion. On the contrary, his object was to show that, far from being an outmoded subject (as many people thought), from the standpoint of psychology religion was one of the greatest and most mysterious activities of the human soul. Frank summed it up in the single phrase 'In knowledge of whom standeth our eternal life, whose service is perfect freedom'.*

But what do we mean by knowledge? It is the difference between reading a map and being in a place. To know the ultimate creative mind is to become one with it as the source of our own inner life, the source of the vast outer world and the government of universal reality. A vast pilgrimage, with only a step at a time.

Frank distinguished between three types of religion: the puritan, the sacramental and the contemplative. It was the first (the puritan) which had the least appeal for him and the last (the contemplative) – the religion of the mystic and the saint – which had the greatest. Relaxation was never more difficult to practise than in the crowded, noisy modern world, but never more needed. You had to learn to forget yourself, then learn the art of non-thinking, concentrating on an image or a phrase until it fades away, leaving the deeper centres of the unconscious to stir and pour out new life.

* Book of Common Prayer, The Order for Morning Prayer, The Second Collect, for Peace.

Not surprisingly, my father recognized the imagination as the primary creative power in religion as well as in literature and the arts. It speaks to us not in the language of ideas, the language of the intellect, but in images. This is why the psychiatrist disregards what you tell him about yourself and seeks instead to know the content of your dreams, which arise from the personal subconscious.

The major religions present the images, myths and dreams of the great scriptures, especially in apocalyptic writings or dramas of creation, and the myth of the fall into self-consciousness. But from the realm of the clear light there is only one image, and that is the image of light. Light is the shadow of God.

My father saw the importance of the imagination in the links it provides to the hidden depths of the unconscious.

That is why, through the ages, the poets and prophets have fought to defend the truth-revealing value of the imagination. They all say the first step towards the cultivation of the imagination is to escape the distorting shadow – nothing else than the shadow of the self. This does not mean that the self is not important. It is the recipient of these revelations. But it must be the recipient only and not the manipulator of the communication. It must not be allowed to interfere, with its desires, wishful thinking and self-interest. It must be transformed into the eye that sees, the mind that understands and the agent that obeys.

Conventional religion has laid great stress on the Fall of Man, whereby man came to the knowledge of good and evil and so was expelled from paradise. This has always been interpreted as a fatal catastrophe. But another interpretation is possible. As God breathed into man the breath of life, man became a living soul. That living soul chose to leave the Garden of Eden and venture into a world of toil and struggle. My father argued that this was not an ignoble choice. With the birth of consciousness, man was confronted with problems which he had to solve. In a profound sense 'he fell to rise', setting out to find through the knowledge of good and evil which he now possessed a state in which it was open to him to achieve unity with the divine life.

Religion presented these ideas in the form of myths, a kind of waking dream; psychology revealed them as elements of actual human experience. As a result, we know that the Garden of Eden is not a myth but the state of infancy, which very quickly, under the urging of evolutionary forces, gives way to the stage of unconscious, instinctive life and the individual enters the creative realm of the imagination, to achieve eventually some consciousness of good and evil. Then, around the age of thirty-five, *may* come the awakening of something in the nature of spiritual awareness, in which old forces strive to hold the individual back and new forces strive to drive him forward. This is a very real battle in which we may be tempted to remain in the Garden of Eden, may fall into the depths of the unconscious, or may struggle forward towards a richer, deeper consciousness.

Here religion is of supreme value. It will present us with symbols of the higher consciousness we want to attain; it will strengthen the unconscious impulses towards it, and at the end will provide a better understanding of the experience through which we have passed.

My father took as another example of the close relationship between religion and psychology what religion calls 'revelation' and psychology describes as 'projection'. Religious people are inclined to quarrel with the use of 'projection', because they fear it will call into dispute the fact of revelation upon which they have based the whole system of religious truth. And indeed, Frank agreed, in some ways the idea of projection does mark a revolution in the conception of revelation.

Take, for instance, the image and idea of God. The older type of religion insisted that God was revealed in nature, in history, in the ancient scriptures and in the person of Jesus Christ. Christianity, in fact, was inclined to doubt the validity of revelation in any other than the Hebrew and Christian scriptures.

But now when we look into these various revelations we find they are always conditioned by the natural and historical circumstances in which they arose. At a primitive level, the image of Deity bore strong resemblance to the peoples and experience which existed in the life of primitive tribes and cultures. It was made in the image of the men and women who created it, and always bore their characteristics.

But as men and women grew in the depth of their humanity, the gods changed their character too, until they became spiritualized. God became the eternal and universal spirit, the creator and father of all mankind.

The same was true of Buddha, a historical figure who gradually took on the features of a divine humanity, and of Jesus of Nazareth, who took on the image of a divine archetypical humanity, the Son of God. There can be no doubt that these images are projections of the human soul, and yet at the same time they are the medium of revelation. In short, projection *is* revelation, a continuing process of revelation; but the revelation does not come from outside – it comes from within.

II

My father saw two very different types of mind attracted to religion. One was the literal mind, which sought to be assured that everything in the Gospels was literally true and wanted to believe that Christianity and the Gospels marked a complete break with the past, a new and completely original religion. The other type rejoiced in the fact that the Gospels and Christianity reveal the fulfilment of many dreams, aspirations, types, images and symbols, whether expressed in writings like the Old Testament or in the legends and traditions of other religions. Inclusiveness, not exclusiveness, Frank argued, was the outstanding character of a great religion.

The literal fact has its place, but its real value is the effect it has on the mind and the imagination. The dry bones of reality are brought to life by the imagination: 'The letter killeth, but the spirit giveth life' (2 Corinthians 3:6). The distinctive mark of the Gospels is just this element of creative imagination.

Here, written in myth and legend, in sayings of simple but profound wisdom, are the ultimate secrets of the spiritual life. Here by the slow growth of spiritual perception and the brooding power of the imagination, concreted around the historical Jesus, here are unfolded the secrets of the way of the soul from spiritual rebirth to union and at-one-ness with the life of God. Here is the gospel of the destiny of the Son of God in every man.

The Old Testament is full of the most striking images and patterns. But the New Testament reaches out much wider than that. It draws upon the ancient religions of Babylon and Persia, the Magi who followed the star and came to the cradle of the new religion; the Mithraic child born in the cave and discovered by shepherds; the Buddhist element in Luke; the revelation to Anna and to Simeon. Here is the call to men of every race and religion, an appeal to the oldest, deepest dreams and images, archetypal patterns in the souls of men and in the Ancient Wisdom. Here in the Gospels, in the outline of an everlasting Gospel, is the resurrection and the life eternal.

Jesus was a prophet and a poet. He spoke all the time in vivid images, never abstract terms, using the story or parable form of speech, which is one-pointed and not, like an allegory, many-pointed. It was the Church which later gathered all these elements into the Gospels and elaborated them to serve its teaching, attaching to them moral and spiritual lessons. There was nothing wrong in this, my father added, as long as we recognize the difference between the original and the elaborated form.

The original message of Jesus had been that the Kingdom of God would come during the lifetime of the first generation of disciples – even, in one version, during his own lifetime. 'Verily I say unto you, There be some standing here, which shall not taste of death, till they see the Son of man coming in his kingdom' (Matthew 16:28). Such fragments of the original message of Jesus, like primeval rocks, stand out in the most unaccommodating way in the Gospels. The failure of the Kingdom to appear must have created a deep problem in Jesus' mind. He responded by presenting his death as the way to the coming of the Kingdom of God, at first to be shared with his disciples but afterwards alone, with God intervening and the Kingdom of God coming in the last desperate moment. 'My God, my God, why hast thou forsaken me?' (Matthew 27:46, Mark 15:34).

One can imagine the desolation and disillusionment of the disciples – but they held fast to Jesus' personality, which re-created faith, and to the conviction that he had spiritually ascended and been raised to the throne of God. From there he would come again to establish the Kingdom – and that immediately.

But the years passed with no Kingdom of God. All things remained as from the beginning of the world. But from within the community (later to be called the *ecclesia* or church) the word was being preached to the pagan world, which accepted it. The centre of attention then passed from the vision of the Kingdom to the vision of the Christ. He was presented as the object of man's faith and hope, as the centre of love and life. 'To be in Christ' was to be in the Kingdom of God.

III

My father saw the historical Jesus as a startling personality, in part hidden and in part superbly presented. The ground for confidence in him is how different Jesus is from conventional people and from what the Church would have liked him to be. It could never have invented or created him. He upsets all the wishful thinking of the idealists. Anonymous in the crowd of John the Baptist's disciples, he comes swiftly on the scene after the Baptist's imprisonment, proclaiming his own original message that the Kingdom of God is at hand.

Unaffected by mass emotion and given to solitary communing, Jesus both attracted and repelled. Impatient of conventional religious observance, he accepts suffering as the will of God for himself. He obeys inner impulses and, like every genius, is unpredictable. Despite the danger, he sets his face steadfastly to go to Jerusalem and challenge the Temple authorities, proclaiming the coming Kingdom and the overthrow of all human tyranny. Having done so, he is swiftly arrested and executed.

If the Gospels presented only historical fact, they would be celebrating a glory that has passed away, leaving us longing for something living, present and immediate. If the glory were only creative imagination and vision, it would leave us hungry for something tangible and concrete. But if reality begins in fact, belonging to some definite time and place, and then that fact grows in the souls of men and women, then surely we have discovered a doorway that opens on to a sea of infinite possibilities.

The Gospels are not merely memorial books – they are abiding witnesses to the reality of a life other than that of the senses and the mind, the spiritual life of the Kingdom of God. Men and women hunger for the life of the spirit, but they perceive this as remote, austere and alien from ordinary human experience. The Gospels reveal the attraction of the spiritual life for ordinary men and women. They were the creation of a proletarian movement, expressing the spiritual life as a creative reality in the market place, on the highways of the Roman Empire, in the very midst of teeming humanity, expressed in tender human stories of birth and love and friendship and in the tragic moments of betrayal, violence and death. This spiritual life is the deepest secret and mystery of our humanity; it finds its focus, its creative power, in the mystery of human personality.

My father saw the Passion as a drama and not a historical happening – the agony in the garden, the betrayal, the trial before the religious authorities, the trial before Pilate, the denials of Peter, the crucifixion between two thieves, the mocking of the crowd, the darkness and the last cry. As we watch these incidents being expanded and multiplied – and some details being omitted and others put in their place – we begin to feel that these elaborations and the whole drama take on the character of a great symbolism. It is in fact a mystery drama whose play of action never ceases and in which Jesus is always being betrayed, always being repudiated by the religious and by governments, always being mocked and spat upon, always being crucified, and yet in the end always being vindicated as the Son of God. We all take part in the drama, day by day, either on his side or against. As disciples, we can do no better than the dying thief who cried, 'Lord, remember me when thou comest into thy kingdom' (Luke 23:42).

No one has illuminated this drama with greater imagination than St Paul in his First Letter to the Corinthians. The facts at first sight are ugly – the horror of the Crucifixion if there is a God, he does not care. You and I would draw from it the conclusion that the universe is a stark and cruel place, indifferent to goodness. If there be a central mind and power which men call God, he has no interest in man and no understandable relation to our human standards of courage and goodness. Jesus died like a dog, in the heart of a great darkness, at the hands of good and respectable people, and there was no one to intervene or save him – a reflection of the fate of thousands of noble human beings through the ages. 'The Jews', Paul wrote, 'require a sign, and the Greeks seek after wisdom: But we preach Christ crucified, unto the Jews a stumblingblock, and unto the Greeks foolishness; But unto them which are called, both Jews and Greeks, Christ the power of God, and the wisdom of God. Because the foolishness of God is wiser than men; and the weakness of God is stronger than men' (1 Corinthians 1:22–5).

How on earth did St Paul transform that sign of despair and darkness into the great word of hope and light? That it is not a hallucination, an escape vision, is shown by the effect of his state-ment upon men and women through the ages. Paul grasped the fundamental spiritual fact that God comes into life by means of the human soul; the power, the life, the illumination are all from within, never from without. Jesus, this young man, dying on the Cross, is the representation of the divine life within the human soul, of the light which is the light of men – and here is the proof that the light shines in the darkness and the darkness never overcomes it. For this is indeed the folly and weakness of God, who 'hath chosen the weak things of the world to confound the things which are mighty; And base things of the world, and things which are despised, hath God chosen . . . and things which are not, to bring to nought things that are' (1 Corinthians 1:27–8).

My father added,

This argument, however, is valid only if we accept Jesus crucified as disclosing the mystery of our own humanity. If he was in any way different from you and me – not just in the degree of his humanity – then for us

273

there is no intelligible word of the Cross. If this was a sham humanity which was really the Godhead and Godhood, then there is no relation between his experience and ours, between the power of his triumph and the promise of ours. But if the divine power is hidden in our common humanity, then indeed the word of the Cross is the word of reconciliation and hope and power and love for us. The great Easter message is the pledge and promise to us – 'Because I live, ye shall live also' (John 14:19).

27

The End of the Pilgrimage

I

It was clear that at some stage my father and mother, who were in their mid-seventies, would have to prepare for retirement. No date was fixed, but a first step was taken by preparing to move out of the house owned by the Church, in which they had lived since 1926, and to acquire one of their own. My wife and I were able to help them buy a new single-storey house on Horton Bank Top, high on the hills surrounding Bradford, and they moved into their new home on 4 July 1963. Frank laughed to discover that his new address, Mandale Road, recalled the Hindu and Buddhist word 'mandala' for a circle enclosing a square as a sacred symbol for the universe.

During this period Frank gave more than 230 sermons, often grouping three or four in a single sequence to give himself more time. The greater number of the sermons – 175 – were delivered before the end of 1963. The range which they cover is shown by two contrasting examples. The first starts with the crisis in the modern world, and Nietzsche's despairing cry that God is dead. The crisis reaches its climax in the rise to power of Hitler and Stalin and expends itself in the most terrible war in history.

Many people thought that this revelation of the abyss of evil would lead to a revival of religion. It has done nothing of the sort, but only intensified the doubts in the minds of thoughtful men and women, while the masses in countries with material resources have handed themselves over to unlimited self-indulgence. The platitudes of conventional religion have little, if any, significance to men and women who feel the desperate condition of a humanity without faith and a world without God.

Nonetheless, my father went on to argue, if we looked deep enough, we would see that the experience of God-forsaken man had occurred several times before, including at the break-up of the Graeco-Roman world which followed the birth of Christianity. Now we were beginning to realize that the healing elements concealed within the wisdom of traditional religion all arose from within the human soul itself. 'Be assured that God is not dead; only the forms under which the divine presence revealed itself in the past. It will reveal itself today under new forms when we have learned to pay attention.'

In the second sermon, Frank examined the state of mind of those who suffered from a hunger of the soul but could not satisfy it by a return to conventional religion.

Man is a spiritual being, and when the horizon of spiritual reality is obscured there arises the sense of abandonment. This suggests that it is not by any revelation from without that man can find reassurance, but that such reassurance must be sought from within. It will not come quickly or easily, but the darkness is the darkness of God and this always ends in a new creative morning.

The third sermon brought those who were searching for the recovery of spiritual confidence face to face with the necessity of faith and its exercise.

The foundation of faith cannot rest upon rational and intellectual grounds. It will not be recognized either by physical signs or by intellectual apprehension. The Apostles' Creed begins, 'I believe in God the Father Almighty, Maker of heaven and earth', and many people regard this as an affirmation of faith. But that is not faith, which is an active attitude of will and emotion, but belief, a static condition of the mind. Faith arises out of the depths of the soul and is in itself a divine energy. It seeks to express itself in words, but in the end recognizes the inadequacy of words and learns to abide in silence. There it can attain a sublime confidence and can make use of an almost infinite range of symbols until at last it can see all nature and history as symbols of the reality which it carries within itself and creates as an instrument of vision and of power. For in the end faith expresses itself in action and in personality; it can never be completely defined, but it is 'the substance of things hoped for, the evidence of things not seen' (Hebrews 11.1).

We have been speaking about faith in relation to religion [Frank concluded], but the field in which faith is necessary and creative is not only within that field. All great art, all great science, all great creative power in society and history arise out of the energy and power of faith. In every great adventure of the mind and of the spirit, and often of the body, the adventure has gone forth not knowing whither it went. And, deep in the depths of life, these same instincts of adventure have been active in the unconscious faith, so that life has progressed from the sea to the land and to the air. If that energy and power ever die, then comes the darkness of despair, the world bereft of hope. But it is in the realm of religion that faith finds its deepest expression, in the vision of God and the hope of immortality.

In the second example my father returned to an earlier interest and in June 1963 devoted four sermons to a collection of mystical writings known as the *Corpus Hermeticum*, roughly contemporary with the period in which Christianity was taking shape in the Gospels and the rest of the New Testament.

While there was no conscious collusion or borrowing between them, the *Hermetica* and the New Testament both drew upon an older wisdom tradition that also came from many sources – Babylonia, Persia, Egypt and Hebrew religious communities. This conception will give great offence to orthodox and dogmatic Christianity. But to you and me it gives great confidence in the tradition of spiritual wisdom, which belongs to the race and not to any exclusive community. The *Hermetica* dramatized the wisdom in an Egyptian form, while the New Testament drew on much of the same wisdom but made use of its own incomparable gift for form to present it.

What fascinates me [Frank continued] is that in both cases we have what is essentially a wisdom religion. It has nothing to do with ritual, priesthood, sacraments or any kind of organized form at all. Communication is solely between a teacher and disciple. These communications in both cases must have been very free in their organization – simply prayer and free discussion in the form of question and answer. The truth shall make you free, and by means of this wisdom you are brought back to the knowledge of your real self.

II

At the time of the move to Horton Bank Top, nothing had been said about my father's date of retirement. In December 1963, however, he suffered two attacks of thrombosis. These made it essential to reach a decision. It was agreed that he should retire at the end of June 1964, fifty years after he had entered the Unitarian ministry. Until then Frank continued to take the services at Chapel Lane and to preach.

This final period shows more and more clearly his commitment to the mystical tradition – for example, in a group of three sermons under the title 'Image of Pilgrimage'. He took his text from Hebrews 11:13: 'These all . . . confessed that they were strangers and pilgrims on the earth.'

We speak of the passing of time, but deeper reflection reminds us that it is we ourselves who are passing through time. While time itself will continue for immeasurable ages in the future as in the past, *we* had a beginning and will have an end in time. The beginning and ending of time is something we can neither grasp nor imagine except in the form of myth and apocalyptic vision. So we come to the conclusion that we are pilgrims through time along with all things physical and material – the sun, moon and stars, all beginning and ending in time. It is these reflections that make us aware of the mystery of existence, strangers as well as pilgrims upon earth and in time.

That we should be in existence in time at all has an element of strangeness in it:

The whole extraordinary coincidence of matter, water, light, temperature, atoms and cells that makes life, growth and existence possible at all is a huge mystery. To consider it as a result of chance appears to many minds an impossible conclusion. Hence the conclusion that somehow, behind and within all this, there is a creative purpose, a mind and invisible cause that we call God. The whole vast process of Creation demands the existence of a creator, and a creative mind.

Frank added that the human spirit was not satisfied with the environment of Creation but for ages had sought to transcend Creation and time in order to find communion and oneness with the eternal spirit, beyond time and Creation.

Man's awareness is expressed in two formats. It is because he is aware of death that he realizes his pilgrimage is of short duration. At the same time he has discovered that all life is involved in another pilgrimage that we call evolution. The human aspect of evolution is recorded in history and the discovery of the soul – the discovery of both the individual and the collective soul.

Here indeed man and woman become a stranger and a pilgrim along the pathway of time and along the pathway of evolving life, yet can see no goal within time, because all Creation is subject to the changes initiated by time. Nothing continues in one state or condition, and all social and historical conditions carry within them the seeds of their own decay.

It was in this deep sense, Frank believed, that thoughtful men and women of all ages – especially in our modern age – confess that each of them is a stranger and pilgrim on earth. Hence the emergence of religion, in which, by means of images and symbols, men and women are made aware of a goal beyond time and death. In religion they seek for another path of pilgrimage, leading to that which is beyond time – a goal where, once reached, all the deepest hunger and thirst of the soul may be satisfied. Can such a path be found?

All creation, history and evolution is a pilgrimage in time, but in the human spirit time leaves a sense of the unfulfilled. We cannot see any goal in time that suggests a complete end and fulfilment of our pilgrimage. We are driven to look for some goal beyond time and to discover – slowly at first – that history and tradition are full of rumours about a hidden way of the spirit leading to such a goal.

Religions of the ancient world were full of the Way – Platonism, Buddhism, Taoism. Christianity itself is described in Acts as the religion of the Way, and Jesus is reported as saying, 'Strait is the gate, and narrow is the way, which leadeth unto life, and few there be that find it' (Matthew 7:14). Those few are the saints and the mystics. The word 'mystic' means in its origin one who sees with closed eyes, who turns from the outer world to the inner world of the soul.

You cannot find the Way [Frank wrote] by any description or discipline, by any book or teacher. As the *Hermetica* says, 'When the soul is ready, God will restore the memory of the Way and the goal.' Too often it has been described as a way of asceticism or of self-discipline. But this too often leads to a turning away from nature and ordinary life. My own favourites among the mystics are Jakob Böhme and William Blake, who lived ordinary lives and rejoiced in the world of nature and humanity. The mystic who appeals to me is the one who finds the hidden Way open everywhere and has nothing to do with self-discipline but awaits the awakening of inner vision.

To me that is the whole secret of the hidden Way: to discover the living water and bread of heaven in all the ordinary ways of life and by continual renewal of the spirit to become a pilgrim towards the goal of the divine life.

For his third sermon Frank chose a double title: 'Hidden Guidance, Guiding Presence'. The two pathways indicated in this title are closely related. Any crisis in the outer life may have deep and subtle effects. Conversely, he pointed out, modern depth psychology, which tries to explore the relationship between the mind and the body, between health and disease, finds that in many cases, if not all, physical illnesses or maladjustments arise from deep and hidden causes in the psyche. We all need to be aware of and respond to the guiding presence which is always there within every human being and has been from the beginning of our humanity. Unfortunately men and women are often insensitive to the presence, and even when aware are indifferent to its guidance.

The central danger of the situation is overconfidence in self. One may become aware of, even fascinated by, the creative capacities of the inner life, seeking to develop them by an effort of the will and the guidance of one's own intelligence. That way is the way of illusion, the inflation of the self, the development of all kinds of discipline of the mind and body. This always ends in resistance and frustration from outside, but – more – it always ends in stagnation within. The pilgrimage is arrested; there is no progress in the inner life; the guiding presence is ignored and progress is judged by outward achievement, not by inner growth.

In all such cases the pilgrim has forgotten and must recover the secret of the still centre, the inaction which is much greater than all action, expressed in words from the ancient scripture:

They that wait upon the Lord shall renew their strength; they shall mount up with wings as eagles; they shall run, and not be weary; they shall walk and not faint. (Isaiah 40:31)

He or she has forgotten that the guiding presence can speak only in the silence:

Trust in the Lord; wait patiently for him and he shall give thee thy heart's desire. (Psalms 37:4)*

III

In one of his 1964 sermons my father underlined the need of religion always to maintain two levels of vision and awareness. One is that of the far horizon, related to the depth of spiritual life, which can be kept alive only by the vision of things before and beyond time; the other is contained in the realization that the contacts, duties and demands of the common way of life, which are so often dull,

* Psalm 37:4: 'Delight thou in the Lord: and he shall give thee thy heart's desire' (Book of Common Prayer).

flat and even exhausting, are the order of reality in which we have
to realize the far-off visions and the depths of our spiritual life.

The hidden treasure of the Kingdom of God must ultimately be discovered
along the common way of life, by making these two levels of vision and
experience one.

What we must ask is whether the common way of life is so common
after all. Is it not rather the quality of mind and emotion we ourselves
develop that makes the common way so flat? Is it not because we have lost
the faculty of wonder? Look back to our own childhood, when everything
– the common fields and streets, the common activities of the body – were
a source of wonder and delight. The summer days seemed to go on and
on, full of sunlight, followed by the excitement of wind and snow and the
thrill of home and firelight. Why should the growth of the mind, becoming
aware of the mystery of life, apparently exhaust the emotion of wonder?

But let us think again. If we had not entered upon the common way of
life we should not have developed the deepest elements in our own humanity,
have found the treasures of friendship and love, and have developed the
capacity for compassion and sympathy, in the company of ordinary men
and women.

It is therefore only along the common way that we can find the integration
of the two great levels of experience and vision, and can realize that only
the experience of the common way can prepare the soul for the experience
of the Kingdom of God.

There is another element of being a stranger that we may notice.
The human spirit is not satisfied with the environment of Creation
but for ages has sought to transcend Creation and find communion
and oneness with the eternal spirit and creative mind beyond time
and Creation.

The awareness of pilgrimage is expressed in two forms. Because
man is aware of death, he realizes that his pilgrimage in time and
on the earth is of short duration. But he has also discovered that
all life is involved in another pilgrimage that is called evolution,
and the human aspect of which is recorded in history. The essence
of man's awareness of this is in the discovery of the soul – both
the collective soul and the individual soul. The collective soul is

related to the soul of nature or the ancient idea of a world-soul; the individual soul has impressed upon it the memory of the whole adventure of life, and this hidden memory provides the energy of consciousness and transformation. It is in this deep sense that thoughtful men and women of all ages – and especially in our modern world – have confessed that they are strangers and pilgrims on the earth. Hence the emergence of religion, in which, by means of images and symbols, man is made aware of a goal beyond time and death. And so he seeks for another path of pilgrimage to that which is beyond time – a goal wherein all the deepest hunger and thirst of the soul may be satisfied.

Can such a path be found?

IV

The agreed date for my father's retirement duly arrived at the end of June 1964 – and with it an unforeseen factor.

After the thirty-seven years Frank had served as minister in Bradford, and bearing in mind the affection with which both he and my mother were regarded, the last morning and evening services were bound to be moving. The unforeseen factor was Frank's announcement that, after 245 years on the existing site, Chapel Lane Chapel and the adjoining Channing Hall would be taken over by the city and demolished as part of a major new development. In the end, thanks to the determination of the chapel committee, everything worked out well. The committee secured compensation and a new site on which a modern purpose-designed church was built. But in June 1964 the future was very uncertain – if there was a future at all.

My father rose to the occasion. He began his evening sermon:

In my last talk with you as your minister I want to consider with you the abiding realities which the experience of change reveals.

To establish and maintain some awareness of these abiding realities and some communion with the spiritual creative power of life is the goal and purpose of all genuine religion. That has been the purpose and aim of the religious community meeting on this site for 245 years; that has been the aim and purpose, however imperfectly achieved, of my own thirty-seven years of ministry; and that is the aim and purpose we must seek to attain and serve in the future that lies before us as a congregation. The forms and the emphasis may change, but the aim and purpose remain the same, and so do the abiding realities of which we have spoken, with their inexhaustible power of grace and beauty.

[At this point my father raised both his hands.] And so into the keeping of their eternal love and life I commit you and myself and all those who still follow after, until at last in the fullness of time we shall attain unto the stature of the Christ spirit and find our fulfilment in fellowship of nature and humanity in the abiding reality of the eternal light.

Epilogue

When I saw my father that summer, I was struck by his frail appearance. He gave the look of a man who had completed a task. He had not long to wait. Early in October 1964 he was taken ill, and before my wife and I could reach him he was gone.

In addition to the sense of loss, there was the mass of lectures and sermons he had left behind from over thirty-five years. With one or two exceptions, these had never been prepared for publication. My wife and I spent much time cataloguing them, but only gradually did we begin to grasp their depth and independence. At one stage I had the idea of writing a 'father and son' account of the twentieth century, only to realize that our interests were too divergent to make such a thing feasible. While many of the lectures were in typescript, the hundreds of sermons were handwritten and often difficult to read. Twice I abandoned work while I concentrated on tasks of my own. But always I came back, moved by two considerations which have gained weight as time has passed.

The first was the fact that, with my father dead and all his papers in my possession, if anyone was to secure him access to a wider audience it would have to be me. The second was my belief that there was much in my father's teaching – especially in his combination of religion and mysticism, on the one hand, and psychology and consciousness, on the other – which marked it as original at the time and has retained its value since.

While my wife, Nibby, and I were preoccupied with making access to my father's lectures and sermons possible, the future of Chapel Lane Chapel and of Channing Hall – where so many of these had first been heard – was uncertain. The local authority was pressing

The demolition of Chapel Lane Chapel (bearing the notice
of the final service, taken by Alan Bullock)

for the demolition of both to make room for new law courts and so complete a much larger scheme already under way. The chapel congregation, however, took a different view. The chapel officers and the management committee (eight men and nine women) had all been appointed during my father's time and were devoted to him. They refused to agree to demolition, or to give up the site, until they had received sufficient compensation to build a new chapel on a new site.

After a long delay on the Corporation side, in 1969 an agreement was reached for compensation of £70,000 (1969 figures). Of that, the new building would cost £40,000 and the land (owned by the Society of Friends) £6,500. The residue was to be invested. The new chapel was finished and dedicated in the summer of 1971.

Long before that, Chapel Lane Chapel itself had been reduced to rubble. In the summer of 1969 (the two-hundred-and-fiftieth anniversary of the original chapel) the congregation arranged to hold a final service, which the Lord Mayor and Lady Mayoress would attend and at which I would deliver the final sermon. On the night before, unknown persons threw a gas cylinder on to an improvised bonfire, causing great damage to the chapel. The next day, efforts to clear it up were set back by a demolition squad whose efforts filled the chapel with clouds of soot as well as noise. Until these could be cleared, I refused to begin, but at least when I did (taking as my text 'Be still, and know that I am God' (Psalms 46:10)) I was moved to speak with power.

As a final gesture, we have called the book *Building Jerusalem*, in the hope that this will recall one of Frank's heroes – William Blake, poet, artist and visionary. Virtually forgotten for over a century after his death in 1827, at the age of seventy, Blake has come to be regarded as an unquestioned man of genius. My father never thought of himself in such terms, but Blake's example has been a constant encouragement to those like my father who are moved to question orthodoxy. Whether preaching, lecturing or introducing his listeners to new experience, Frank found the same satisfaction as a musician in playing an instrument. That was what he had been born for. If I have done no more than restore my father's own voice, I shall be content.

Index

A.B. indicates the author; F.A.B. indicates Frank Bullock. Figures in italics indicate illustrations.

289